ence, social theory
and public knowledge

Science, social theory and public knowledge

Alan Irwin and Mike Michael

Open University Press
Maidenhead · Philadelphia

Open University Press
McGraw-Hill Education
McGraw-Hill House
Shoppenhangers Road
Maidenhead
Berkshire
England
SL6 2QL

email: enquiries@openup.co.uk
world wide web: www.openup.co.uk

and

325 Chestnut Street
Philadelphia, PA 19106, USA

First published 2003

A catalogue record of this book is available from the British Library

ISBN 0 335 20947 5 (pb)   0 335 20948 3 (hb)

Library of Congress Cataloging-in-Publication Data
CIP data has been applied for

Typeset by RefineCatch Limited, Bungay, Suffolk
Printed in the UK by Bell & Bain Ltd, Glasgow

This book is dedicated to the memory of
Christalleni Michael

Contents

Preface

This is an exciting but also an undoubtedly challenging time for science and society. On the one hand, new developments in science and technology – whether the human genome project, medical therapies or advances in computing and information technology – promise a bright and prosperous future. On the other, the emergence of risks, ethical concerns and environmental problems – including mad cow disease (BSE), genetically modified foods and global warming – reminds us of the dangers ahead. Recent scientific and technological innovations have both opened up new social possibilities and drawn public attention to inevitable uncertainties and limitations within our scientific knowledge. At the very core of this book lies contemporary science and the opportunities, challenges, threats and promises it offers both at a grand theoretical level and also in terms of the more mundane operation of everyday life.

Few people want to call a halt to science – even if they did, science could not be 'disinvented'. The social challenge instead is to establish a more productive relationship between science and wider society. This book sets out to explore how concerned citizens, policy makers (both in government and industry), social scientists and campaigning groups have responded to that challenge. We argue specifically that there is substantial scope for social learning and mutual education within the relationship between science, social theory and public knowledge. Along the way, we will make some suggestions of our own about how both sociological thinking and democratic practice can be improved.

If we turn to the relationship between social science and these matters, it seems only reasonable to expect that sociologists would have played a lively part in the debate. Since these questions go to the core of our sense of modernity, citizenship and social change, it can be anticipated that social theory in particular would make its voice heard. Certainly, theorists such as Ulrich Beck and Anthony Giddens have become well known for the argument that we are now living in a 'risk' or 'late modern' society. It is important, too, that we consider the more empirical and case-specific contribution of sociology to these contemporary discussions, including that made by the sociology of scientific knowledge. As we will argue, engagement with science and technology involves more than dusting off established theory. In making this point, we should also observe that the relationship between social theory and modern science represents a challenge and a provocation to both sides of the discussion.

At this stage, the second main strand of our book must be introduced. Whether considered in terms of the changing political climate or more recent empirical studies, the 'publics for science' have become a major focus for attention. As an official report from the UK put it:

> Society's relationship with science is in a critical phase. Science today is exciting, and full of opportunities. Yet public confidence in scientific advice has been rocked by BSE; and many people are uneasy about the rapid advance of areas such as biotechnology and IT – even though for everyday purposes they take science and technology for granted. This crisis of confidence is of great importance both to British society and to British science.
>
> (House of Lords Select Committee 2000: 5)

What is especially striking about this quotation is the central role it gives to public confidence in science. While in previous years public support has simply been taken for granted or else public views ignored as irrational and uninformed, the strength of public reaction to issues such as BSE, stem cell research and genetically modified foods has taken many scientists and policy makers by surprise. Where once we had the 'deficit theory' (whereby public views were either simply dismissed as an irrelevance or else presented as a challenge to science education), we now have 'public dialogue' and talk of wider 'engagement' with science and technology. Very often, arguments from social scientists are drawn upon as support for such ventures – so that the language of 'restoring public trust and confidence' has become the new orthodoxy. However, and as we will again suggest, it is important that we take a critical and informed look at the supposed shift from deficit theory to 'dialogue theory'.

The third relationship to science with which this book will be concerned is that of practical policy and governance. Put succinctly, the notion that government could rely upon 'sound science' as a basis for rational policy has recently given way to a more open and cautious view of the relationship between scientific advice and decision making. Cases such as mad cow disease in the UK – and the current discussion over genetically modified food – have emphasized the uncertainty at the heart of scientific understanding in new and complex fields of study. Rather than viewing scientific advice as self-contained and distinct from ethics, institutional pressures and economic priorities, one important school of thought suggests that scientific advice should now be subject to the maximum level of external transparency to identify areas of doubt and disagreement. At national and international level, the claim is that we can 'democratize science' within policy making and so improve the quality and inclusivity of decisions.

By now, the reader may well have the impression that all is well in the garden of science and its relationship to social theory, public understandings and governance. Scientific progress faces some difficult challenges, but these can be resolved through social theory and increased public engagement. Meanwhile, social theory can both contribute to and learn from contemporary discussions over science and the wider publics – and social scientists experience the mixed pleasure of being granted a more important role than previously in science and public policy. At the same time, for those committed to greater scientific democracy and 'citizen science', the changing climate is a substantial opportunity. The emergence of new forms of theory should assist more practical social experiments in science and democracy. So why do we need a new book? What is there left to say on this subject?

The truth is that *Science, Social Theory and Public Knowledge* has been written as much in frustration as in celebration. In the multidiscipline known as the 'public understanding of science and technology', we would indeed have expected to see innovative social theory brought to bear and, as it were, tested. Instead, we have found, by and large, a commitment to micro-social analysis that has often neglected broader social and cultural processes. Where, in the sometimes overblown world of 'social theory', we wanted more evidence of an engagement with complex empirical studies, we frequently found over-generalization and under-exemplification. When we looked to the practical sphere of 'scientific and public governance', we found understandings and techniques still largely uninformed by the significant insights yielded by 'public understanding of science and technology' and 'social theory'. Of course, not all these relations are negative in character. We have written this book, however, in the conviction that things could be an awful lot better.

More constructively, we will argue that the relationship between science, social theory and public knowledge represents a major opportunity both in terms of academic understanding and practical policy. We are stubborn enough to believe that sociology is capable of grappling with the challenges of science–society relations and coming away considerably wiser (if slightly bloodied). Equally, we see policy making and practical intervention not simply as matters of application, but as important research sites where new ideas and understandings are being forged. Accordingly, social theory should be able to contribute helpfully to these processes.

Just to make ourselves quite clear, we are not suggesting that the social sciences have all the answers – or, for example, that critical public responses to certain areas of science could (or should) be avoided. Instead, this book is written in the belief that all three of the strands considered here can gain from a reassessment of their relationship to science and society. At a time when the practical and intellectual challenges of scientific progress are more pressing than ever, we believe the social sciences have much to offer and indeed much to learn.

What, then, can the reader expect in the following chapters? We certainly promise a varied coverage of theories, empirical projects and policy initiatives. We also promise an approach that is both exploratory and, at times, opinionated in the belief that it is only through conveying a sense of excitement, conflict and debate that this area can be appreciated. We will make use of examples and illustrations to bring the issues home – but also because we believe that the area can only be appreciated through examination of some of the most important cases.

Inevitably, juggling so many concerns has not proved easy. As a way of navigating our way through these various empirical examples, theoretical niceties, and practical and policy challenges, we have been guided by a certain motif which structures the book. The motif is quite simple: two twists of a spiral.

In the first twist, the three strands of *public understanding of science and technology*, *scientific governance* and *social theory* are presented in straightforward terms. So, Chapter 1 considers how each of these three 'approaches' has dealt with a dramatic scientific and public controversy: the case of genetically modified foods. In Chapters 2, 3 and 4, we deepen our appreciation of these three approaches. Chapter 2 provides an overview of the multidiscipline of 'public understanding of science and technology' and details the ways in which it has changed from concerns with quantitative methods, cognition and 'deficit' to qualitative methods, culture and dialogue. In Chapter 3, we turn to 'scientific and public governance' to examine how policy actors have become embroiled in recent scientific controversies. We trace especially how inadequacies in policy actors' responses to scientific controversy are prompting changes in what it means to 'govern' or to be a 'citizen'. Chapter 4 is about those parts of social theory that have most relevance to public knowledge and science. We shall find that while some social theorists are keen to persuade us that 'risk', 'knowledge', 'science and technology' and 'trust' characterize contemporary society, we often do not get much of a concrete sense of how these play themselves out in people's everyday lives. This completes our first twist.

The second twist of our spiral brings these approaches much closer together – indeed, so much so that they begin to re-establish and reshape themselves. This process begins in Chapter 5 where we explicitly draw together the themes of the first four chapters. Each of the chapters (but especially Chapters 2, 3 and 4) will establish key features of the relationship between science and society. We argue that it is important not simply to bring these domains into greater alignment but to extend and reconfigure them. One particular case study is used to make this crucial point. In Chapter 6, we make a radical suggestion for the reinterpretation of science–social relations. Instead of assuming the contrast between science and society, we need new categories and ways of thinking, which, to use our phrase, 'mix things up'. The notion of ethno-epistemic assemblage is one contribution to this analytical and practical process. Chapter 7 begins to address this shift away from the familiar world of science and society in both analytical and practical terms. How can the assemblage be governed and what does this mean for the very notion of governance itself? Finally, in Chapter 8, we draw out some of the implications of the story we have told and make some suggestions for the future.

If that is the shape of the book, for whom was it written? At this point, we have to admit that the book was partly written for ourselves (as most books probably are). Having researched and written about this area for some time, we felt both excited by the changing climate of discussion and disappointed that so much was being neglected (whether in the realm of the changing character of science, social theory, public policy or citizen understandings). More specifically, we wanted to present a more nuanced and critical account of the field than can be captured by the sweeping rhetoric of, for example, 'science and democracy' or 'public dialogue over science and society'. Put differently, we felt that something was missing from the discussion and that this was related to the three-way relationship at the core of *Science, Social Theory and Public Knowledge*.

Certainly we hope that sociologists and social scientists interested in science, technology and everyday life or in social theory will find this book useful. Similarly, we would like the book to serve as a resource for those following courses in such subjects as public understanding of science, science communication or science and technology studies. Hopefully also, this book will appeal to the broader audience of people who wish to increase their understanding of the relationship between science and society. As this book suggests, the relationship between science, social theory and public knowledge cannot be restricted to one narrow field of academic inquiry but instead crosses the social sciences and, indeed, the conventional barrier between the social and natural sciences.

Crossing the barrier between the natural and social sciences is one ambitious aspect of the following account. Crossing the Atlantic is a much more hazardous activity. As we hope to suggest through the force of argument and analysis – and the use of cases and examples – the issues with which we will deal are unavoidably international (or, perhaps, *global*) in character. The specifics can change across contexts (as we will also suggest). Three Mile Island had a greater impact on US public opinion than it had in Europe. The USA has taken a distinctive route on global climate change, while food safety has, at least in recent years, been a significant concern in Europe more than in North America. Countries also vary in terms of their relative levels of public debate over stem cell research and genetically modified food.

These differences are significant and deserve analysis. Nevertheless, we should also keep the larger picture in mind. Inevitably, the following account will reveal our own spatial and cultural location within Western Europe. As some justification for this, we would suggest that the UK and other European countries have been especially important within recent science–society controversies. However, we believe that our argument is applicable outside, as well as within, the UK/European setting. There is not sufficient space in one already crowded book to tie in the examples and illustrations to every national and regional setting (whether North or South America, Australasia, Asia or Africa). Our best hope is to stress the international significance of our analysis and plead the reader's forgiveness for any lapses into Euro-centrism. If nothing else, and as the residents of Jarrow will also suggest, such lapses reinforce our argument for the inextricability of local and global levels of action and understanding. Thankfully, there is no such thing as a disembodied intellectual.

Finally, this book would not have been possible without a myriad of conversations and communications with friends and colleagues. Inevitably, we cannot thank them all, and our apologies to those we fail to mention (you know who you are). Mike Michael would especially like to thank Lynda Birke, Nik Brown, Simon Carter, Rosemary McKechnie, Vicky Singleton, Kath Smart and Jill Turner. Bethan, Aneirin and Yanna Rees were ridiculously forgiving and unfathomably loving. Alan Irwin would like to acknowledge the support of the Leverhulme Trust and the Economic and Social Research Council. He also thanks Peter Healey, Kevin Jones, Anthony Murphy, Tim O'Riordan, Nick Pidgeon, Peter Simmons, Gordon Walker and (especially) Elaine McCarthy. John Ziman deserves thanks for his overall contribution to the field – and the 'public knowledge' in our title is inspired by his classic text.

Both of us would like to express particular gratitude to Brian Wynne, our friend and colleague, without whose pioneering work in the public understanding of science the present volume would barely be conceivable.

1 Introducing theory, context and practice

people have learnt to make up their own minds and take responsibility for their own actions, and people scorn patronising assumptions based on the premise that they don't know what's good for them. On the contrary, people insist that it is their society and their world and they will decide what's acceptable and what is not.

(Peter Melchett, Greenpeace)*

we continue to believe in this technology. We think it can bring important benefits to people around the world and we remain committed to developing good, safe, useful products, but we are no longer going to be engaged in a debate. We are now publicly committed to dialogue with people and groups who have a stake in this issue. We are listening, and will seek common ground whenever it's available and to the extent that it's available, and we'll seek solutions that work for a wide range of people.

(Bob Shapiro, Monsanto)*

How are we to understand the relationship between science and its publics? What would greater public engagement with scientific and technological issues involve? How can social theory help us understand these issues?

This book addresses large and challenging questions concerning the sometimes troubled relationship between new areas of science, the social sciences and the wider publics. In tackling such issues, we will cover a range of abstract theories and scientific questions. We will also consider the diversity of publics and the changing relationship between their knowledges and those of policy makers and 'experts' of various kinds. However, and in the belief that it is important to consider these issues at a specific as well

* Quotations concerning the Melchett–Shapiro debate are all taken from: news2.th1s.bbc. co.uk/hi/english/sci/tech/newsid_468000/468147.stm

as abstract level, we begin with one very important case: contemporary debate (or dialogue) over the safety of genetically modified (GM) foods. Having presented one encounter within this emerging controversy, we will go on to draw out some of the themes and questions at the heart of this book.

In October 1999, the BBC reported on an unusually direct public discussion between one of the world's leading agricultural companies, Monsanto, and the environmental pressure group, Greenpeace. Specifically, it involved Greenpeace's executive director, Peter Melchett, and the Chief Executive Officer of Monsanto, Bob Shapiro. At that time, the subject of the discussion could hardly have been more controversial: the potential benefits and dangers of GM crops. The discussion took place at a conference organized by Greenpeace UK. The following summary is based on the account of that meeting (including a full reproduction of the two main speeches) as represented on the BBC's website. The BBC's environment correspondent described the event in the following terms: 'It was an unusual encounter between two drastically different points of view'. However, the same correspondent continued rather gloomily: 'it covered little new ground and offered slender hope of any meeting of minds'.

Although GM food, and the biotechnology more generally, has been a focus of scientific and regulatory debate since the 1970s, the discussion became decidedly more public – and more heated – with the first imports to Europe of Monsanto's GM soya in November 1996. The US-grown modified soya had been mixed up with conventional soya in such a way as to make meaningful labelling impossible.

Coming in the wake of the 'mad cow' (BSE) crisis, Monsanto's decision provoked a strong public and political reaction. Media references to 'Frankenstein foods' began to appear, with certain governments across Europe clearly irritated that Monsanto had provoked public controversy in this way. Equally, it was not too hard to see amidst the banner headlines and earnest scientific discussions a distinct anti-American sentiment at work. Whether expressed in terms of scientific concerns over human health and the environment, consumer anxieties that free choice had been denied or ethical and political issues over the global power of multinationals, a major row ensued over the future of GM foods.

Against this controversial background, Monsanto put its case to the Fourth Annual Greenpeace Business Conference in, perhaps surprisingly, conciliatory terms. Bob Shapiro began on a personal note:

> I've recently been learning about a distinction that I want to share with you that I'm finding useful as I think about the issues of biotechnology and public reactions. It's a distinction between debate on the one hand and dialogue on the other.

For Shapiro, debate is a 'win–lose process'. The point of debate is to defend one's own position and attack that of the opposition. The aim is to score as many rhetorical points as possible and so gain the upper hand. Political discussion until then had certainly proceeded in that fashion: 'Positions have been fiercely attacked and fiercely defended. There has been no hint of the possibility of common ground or of common interests or of common purposes or of common concerns'. Dialogue, meanwhile, is a 'search for answers . . . for constructive solutions that work for a wide range of people'.

As his contribution to that dialogue, Shapiro considered some of the potential benefits and concerns relating to biotechnology. Very importantly, for him, biotechnology is above all a tool: a rapidly expanding area of *knowledge* and a set of *techniques*. 'Like most tools, like most scientific knowledge itself, biotechnology in itself is neither good nor bad – it can be used well or it can be used badly, and like any important new tool it creates new choices for society'. Accordingly, GM food – just like fire, television or computers – raises questions of how it should be used. Meanwhile, and for Monsanto, there are three main potential benefits. These can be grouped as *agriculture*, the *environment* and *consumers*.

With regard to the first category, Shapiro argued that current agricultural technologies are not inherently sustainable. Biotechnology meanwhile 'can improve productivity while reducing some of the negative effects of current agricultural practises like excessive pesticide usage'. In short, GM food represents a 'sustainable technology'. In environmental terms, biotechnology can reduce the use of insecticides and herbicides, and also decrease water use, soil erosion and carbon emissions. Consumer benefits of the new technology potentially include the incorporation of vitamins and nutrients in grains and oils so as to combat malnutrition, and the creation of novel pharmaceuticals using plants as 'factories' for their production.

Shapiro noted that these potential benefits also raise potential concerns: 'Some are questions of fact, but others are questions of beliefs, of traditions and of values'. Such questions include: Will the food be safe to eat? Is this application of science ethically correct? Will corporations like Monsanto gain too much power over agriculture? Are we playing God and do we have the wisdom to use these technologies well? For Shapiro, these are valid concerns which require careful examination. Monsanto's public commitment was to play a full and open part in their appraisal: to engage 'openly, honestly and non-defensively in the kind of discussion that can produce good answers for all of us'.

> We – and I believe the same is true of other companies who are engaged in developing these technologies – want to participate constructively in the process by which societies around the world try to develop good answers to those questions. To me, that means, among other things, listening carefully and respectfully to all points of view.

How could a group like Greenpeace possibly refuse this generous invitation to join the public dialogue?

In response, Peter Melchett began very bluntly by noting what he saw as the 'massive public rejection' of Monsanto's vision. Referring to Monsanto's decision to mix GM with conventional soya, he observed:

> Monsanto has put itself in the uncomfortable, possibly fatal, position of providing the lightening [*sic*] rod for a quite unprecedented, implacable opposition to GM foods across Europe. The company's in trouble on Wall Street . . . It seems as if every food manufacturer and supermarket in Britain avoids GM like the plague.

Noting Shapiro's call for dialogue, Melchett nevertheless criticized the manner in which 'the public' had been viewed by many influential organizations:

> The economic and political disaster Monsanto contrived has import-ant lessons for the future of every large corporation, and for govern-ments. It's all too easy for the ignorant and short-sighted to blame environmental groups and the media for spreading hysteria using emotional arguments and generally stirring up an otherwise happily acquiescent public. This is an argument we hear from a great many people who should know better. It isn't just a weak excuse, it's palpable and dangerous nonsense.

For Melchett, far from being ignorant in such matters, 'a well-educated and well-informed public have taken a careful look at what Monsanto is offering and have said "no" '. Monsanto's fundamental error was to 'fail to understand' the way in which 'public values are developing in Europe and across much of the rest of the world'. For Melchett, public values are central to the whole GM debate. The public are not 'anti-science'. Indeed, they are enthusiastic for mobile phones, the internet, digital TV and GM medicines. However,

> [t]he people are increasingly aware and mistrustful of the combin-ation of big science and big business. They have a [more] realistic sense of the limits of scientific knowledge and about the genuine unknowns than the scientific and political elite appear to comprehend.

Melchett's presentation centred on this view of the public as informed and resourceful. Thus, the 'coming worldwide rejection of GM food' represents the development of 'civilised values'. On that basis, Bob Shapiro is praised for thinking in a long-term fashion about these issues. However, his particular vision of the future is firmly rejected: 'It promotes false promises of easy alternatives via short-term technical fixes, and it increases the imbalance of power between multinational corporations and farmers in the developing world'. Putting that point even more strongly, Melchett stated: 'Monsanto behaves not as a company offering life and hope but as a bully trying to force its products on us. It sues those that oppose it, suppressing, not encouraging debate. And when it does debate . . . Monsanto gets it wrong'.

Melchett's lecture concluded with a new vision of agriculture based on 'holistic life science' designed to achieve agricultural production while sustaining the diversity of nature. Organic agriculture is directly in tune with public values. It also promises to be a commercial success:

> People know what kind of world they want for themselves and their children. They know how they want companies to behave and they know how they want their food to be produced and Monsanto, I believe, are blocking that progress. The unrealised potential of organic agriculture is immense. It simply needs the application of the sort of technical skills and resources that are being squandered on GM technology and industrial agriculture.

The same BBC website that published the lectures from Bob Shapiro and Peter Melchett also featured a 'have your say' section representing more public comments. Predictably, these encompass a wide range of views. We can only sample a few here:

> The public are being led in a crusade against a scientific advancement that would have been labelled as a 'breakthrough' like any new medicine, had it not been for a decision by the media to make GM their latest target for scare-stories and perpetuation of mis-information.

> Waking up sleeping Americans to the fact that Monsanto is an evil empire determined to control the planet's food supply is no easy task.

> While the world's rich, fat, minority post ignorant comments on a website, precious wildland is gobbled up by subsistence, low-input farming.

> For me the issue is choice. Irrespective of whether GM foods are or are not dangerous in any way, if the majority of the British public want them banned from the country, then they should be banned. This is what democracy means.

> Greenpeace has adopted an anti-technology policy that is archaic . . . Inefficiency in farming through the 'old fashion' [sic] means will

result in substantially higher food costs. As a result the poor, who Greenpeace doesn't give a damn about, will suffer the most.

GM has nothing to do with real problems – it's about greed and profit. There's already enough food to feed the world – it just isn't shared out – and GM isn't going to change that.

Pausing here, many aspects of the GM debate are crucial to this book. Of course, one of the reasons for starting with this particular topic is the *centrality of science and technology* to such a significant public issue. In this case, we can identify in particular the importance of *disputes* over science and technology. Is GM food a sustainable technology of the future or is it, as Melchett suggests, a technology of the past?: 'a past in which over confident technologists, out of touch with the values and aspirations of ordinary people, have tried to impose solutions on society'. The Greenpeace and Monsanto accounts of this technology appear to have very little in common. However, they do suggest different visions of the future which extend beyond technical argument alone to embrace alternative values and patterns of social relations. Both accounts also emphasize just how significant science and technology can be for the future of society.

Looking more generally at the contemporary character of science, for Melchett, '[n]ew scientific concerns surface every week, but are ignored by the biotech industry'. For Shapiro, science is also central, since science has presented us with a tool which in itself is neither good nor bad. While being careful not to downplay the legitimacy of potential concerns, Shapiro is eager to suggest that some questions are those of fact, others are 'questions of beliefs, of traditions and of values'. Meanwhile, some of those who posted comments on the BBC website use much blunter language: 'The Greenpeace people make me believe that "Flat-earth" unscientific society still thrives in backward nations like England'.

Turning to the first main theme of this book, the Greenpeace–Monsanto exchange also reveals the importance of *the public* to these discussions, at least at the level of claims on the public's behalf. Although this is a highly technical area, 'people' feature prominently at every level. Whether in the form of Greenpeace and Monsanto making claims about what 'people' think or need (as in this chapter's opening two quotations), arguments about the importance of public dialogue, accusations of the public being bullied and misunderstood, as objects of persuasion or as quotations on a website, 'people' are being given a significant – and significantly varying – role in these discussions. Linked to this, we can identify different views on the importance of citizen involvement in such debates – although both Monsanto and Greenpeace claim to support a more open and democratic engagement (and thus seem to share a surprising consensus on the importance of dialogue).

At this point, we note our second main theme: the difficult *policy and practical* questions raised by the Greenpeace–Monsanto encounter. If we accept the argument for dialogue, then how in practice should we go about organizing this? How could dialogue be possible over a global issue and one of such apparent complexity? Within public discussion, what status should be given to technical arguments and analyses? We can also consider the role of different institutions in such a public engagement with science and technology. Government, for example, is traditionally the guardian of the public interest, yet it features very little in the statements of Melchett and Shapiro. If this is to be a matter of direct encounter between industry, pressure groups and the wider public, does government have any role at all?

The third main element in our book concerns the character of *social theory*. This may seem an odd theme to draw out at this point, since none of the participants makes explicit reference to any recognized area of theory (if that was social theory, where were Marx, Weber and Durkheim?). While that is obviously the case, it is possible to discern within this discussion a wider debate over the nature of social progress (GM or organic farming?), the character of citizenship (as active participants or representations on a website?), the nature of globalization (good or bad?) and the status of scientific knowledge (a mere tool or the route to truth?). As we will discuss, lurking behind the specifics of this debate are a number of larger questions concerning the structure and experience of life in contemporary society, including such fundamental issues as the relationship between society and nature (and between science and society), the character of democracy and citizenship, and the relationship between knowledge and public dialogue.

In this situation, it becomes important to inquire whether cases such as GM food undermine the traditional agenda of social theory or merely illustrate its main themes and debates. For example, can all this be seen as another demonstration of the risk society at work or, instead, as a challenge for us to create new forms of social theory and analysis? In later chapters, we will advocate fresh theoretical accounts that grasp the significance of science–society relations and suggest innovative possibilities for empirical engagement and practical action.

In the next three sections, we consider some of these issues in greater depth. We also move away from the specific example of GM food towards a broader consideration of the issues at the core of this book. What new questions do these developments raise for academic analysis and public policy? This discussion will, in turn, lead us to the central concerns of *Science, Social Theory and Public Knowledge*.

Science and public understanding

We have already made the point that 'the public' is central to the GM debate. On this, most of the key parties would agree. However, and as this book will discuss, the questions and problems do not end with an acknowledgement of the public's significance. Rather, they only begin.

In the first place, the Shapiro–Melchett exchange suggests a wider debate over the status that should be granted to public opinions and understandings. To put it rhetorically, shouldn't these complex questions best be left to the experts? Melchett, in particular, suggests that industry and government have tended to see the public as 'acquiescent' and vulnerable to emotional appeals. He contrasts that approach with his own defence of the legitimacy of public views and values.

As we will discuss in the next chapter, there has been a long history of the public being presented as operating within a 'deficit' of knowledge and understanding in such matters. Indeed, the assumption that greater public knowledge of scientific and technological developments will lead to greater public acceptance has been the conventional wisdom among government and industry. However, and as the GM exchange illustrates, it may now be timely for us to move beyond the 'deficit' approach and towards new models of the relationship between science and the 'lay' publics. Put bluntly, what might taking public views seriously involve?

Secondly, and very importantly for the treatment of science–public relations, we can identify a discussion taking place concerning the relationship between 'facts' and 'values' in this area – and, more generally, over how terms like 'value' and 'fact' are to be defined. Let us start with the notion of 'value': there is sometimes the suggestion that, on the one hand, these are fixed and unchanging (as when Melchett presents organic agriculture as 'directly in tune with public values') and, on the other, as quite distinct from matters of 'fact' (a distinction Shapiro is keen to emphasize). Social scientific research, as we will see, has questioned both of these assumptions, suggesting that values are not fixed but linked to the contexts of their generation and challenging the idea that 'facts' and 'values' can be kept apart from one another.

This discussion of facts and values leads once again to questions of the status of public values and public knowledge in this area. For many scientific institutions, 'facts' are central with 'values' secondary to these (first we sort out the facts of GM food, then we can talk about values). However, Melchett's presentation suggests almost the opposite: public values must come first with technical debate following. Taking this discussion further, certain sociologists have suggested that the public may not simply embody values about the world but may also have knowledges of its own to offer: forms of lay understanding or citizen science (Irwin 1995).

Thirdly at this stage, we can suggest from what has been said so far that the representation of public views through social scientific analysis is not a straightforward or unproblematic activity. Instead, the public can be presented in different ways. When Monsanto calls for open dialogue, Greenpeace responds that people are constantly bullied and patronized by Monsanto. Each claims to speak for 'people', but who exactly are these people and how are their views to be taken into account?

At a practical level, and as we will also discuss in the next section, these points raise questions of the best form of public engagement: how can these citizens actually join the dialogue in any meaningful fashion? At an empirical level, we are confronted with questions of how to define and 'capture' public opinion. Is it sufficient to post comments on a website or is something more deliberative required? Equally, how can we balance the requirement for representativeness with the apparent need to capture the full depth and complexity of public understandings? It is possible to imagine several ways in which social scientists might gauge public views and assessments of GM food. Specifically, we can identify three common methods that social scientists have used to explore public assessments of science and risk:

- *Questionnaires*: typically these have taken members of the public individually and asked direct questions about their understanding of either science-in-general or particular issues (like biotechnology).
- *Focus groups*: these characteristically allow members of the public to reflect more broadly on areas of concern and to assess the significance of scientific issues compared with other matters within everyday life.
- *Ethnographic analysis*: this approach involves a longer commitment to exploring the particular settings within which 'science' or 'technology' is encountered (often within a specific geographical location).

As the next chapter will discuss, each of these methods contains characteristic assumptions and working principles. Thus, questionnaires are based on the idea that each one of us has individual values and assessments to offer, while ethnographic analysis places great emphasis on the contexts within which values come to be formed and expressed. As the history of the public understanding of science suggests, methods embody assumptions about both society and individuals, even if these are rarely expressed or even acknowledged.

Bringing these points together, we can see that the relationship between science and the wider publics raises many important sociological questions. Looked at in terms of what has become known as the 'public understanding of science and technology', the GM case suggests a number of issues and questions. Among these, we can pick out:

- the different ways in which 'the public' (or 'the people') can be represented within social debate;
- linked to this, the problems for social scientists of defining 'the public' in any particular situation;
- the relationship between public and scientific forms of knowledge and understanding;
- the sometimes disputed character of science–public relations;
- the attention that various policy actors are now paying to public understandings and values.

Beginning in Chapter 2, we will explore some of these questions and consider their implications for better understanding and better public practice.

Science and governance

At a different but related level, the discussion of GM food suggests important issues of public engagement and governance. As noted above, the call for dialogue may be important in itself, but it also raises questions over the form of that dialogue and the manner in which public views are to be incorporated within decision-making processes. How, in short, is the scientific citizen being constructed in this area? More broadly, it is possible to identify within these claims to speak for the 'people' a wider disagreement over who has the right to represent 'the public' and on what terms.

Thus, Monsanto's call for dialogue is premised on the notion that we all have to accept both benefits and concerns over GM technology, otherwise 'there is no room for dialogue'. Meanwhile, Greenpeace speaks in very confident terms about the nature of public values and their opposition to this technology. Either way, we can see both parties as 'spokespeople' for the publics. Equally, while Monsanto presents values as being informed by the facts, Greenpeace's position seems to be that values are solid and that the facts are malleable. When the attempt is made to broaden out the discussion – as in the BBC website's 'read your views and experiences' section – the working assumption appears to be that it is most appropriate to offer a range of views (and typically to emphasize the more extreme positions) in some semblance of fair play. This approach to the management of public concerns operates on an implicit assumption that the truth must be somewhere between these extremes.

Where does the individual citizen stand in all this? Do we even know that members of the public want to take on the responsibilities that are so eagerly being claimed on their behalf? Much is being claimed for 'the people', but this representation is replete with difficulties and apparent contradictions.

As with the previous discussion of research methods, a number of possibilities for the construction of the scientific citizen come to mind:

- *Representative democracy*: one could argue that citizens' views on technical issues are adequately dealt with by the conventional democratic process of parliamentary representation and the associated activities of political parties and lobbyists. Why should scientific and technological concerns be any different from this norm?
- *Referendum*: one way of allowing individual citizens to express their views directly to government is through a national or local vote on the issue. Politicians and civil servants have often been reluctant to use such a measure, since it does not guarantee a sufficiently reflective and informed review of the issues.
- *Citizen's jury*: various social experiments are now being conducted into new forms of deliberative engagement with science and technology. A citizen's jury (and related approaches) allows a group of citizens to meet over a period of time to reflect upon the issues and to review the evidence. Such an approach permits both deliberation and the production of a tangible output.

Our point for now is that each of these approaches carries its own assumptions and implicit definitions of the 'scientific citizen' – and of the wider character of citizenship. While representative democracy suggests that these questions do not differ from the conventional world of politics, it can be argued that issues such as GM food are indeed very distinctive in character. From the link to science and technology to the direct relationship between industry, environmentalist groups and the publics (so that government appears marginalized from the previous discussion), the 'new generation' of scientific and social problems seems to have its own particular characteristics. Thus, it has become a regular feature of publications in this area that they refer to a 'crisis of confidence' in official institutions to deal adequately with such concerns (with the BSE crisis in the UK being a prime example of this). Equally, the governance of scientific and technological innovation raises questions of industrial power and influence – not least, since governments and publics are often responding to previous research and development decisions made in corporate boardrooms.

The Greenpeace–Monsanto exchange also reveals some of the complexities of this debate over who has voice – or the right to voice – in the decision-making process. Monsanto suggests the need for the citizen to be directly involved in a particular form of dialogue: one in which values are clearly informed by facts. Greenpeace, in response, appears to suggest a more confrontational identity for citizens: people's values are clear and explicit but these are being disregarded by industry. As we can see, it is not just a question of which model of citizenship to employ but also of the particular construction of the citizen within this.

This section has raised several questions about the relationship between science, governance and citizenship:

- What is the most appropriate form of decision making in areas of sociotechnical uncertainty?
- What implicit models of citizenship are now emerging?
- What particular identities are being constructed for 'scientific citizens'?
- To what extent are we witnessing the emergence of new forms of governance and politics?

Starting in Chapter 3, these questions will be pursued in the context of modern discussions over science and public policy.

Science and social theory

What, then, can we suggest about the relationship between this apparently non-theoretical case and explicitly theoretical matters? As we discuss in Chapter 4, such a question is made all the more difficult by social theory's traditional disregard for the relationship between science and the publics. Instead, texts on classical social theory have tended to ignore scientific matters altogether – or confine themselves to the old, and sadly misconceived, theoretical favourite of 'is sociology a science?'.

Considering the GM case, a number of theoretical issues come to mind. In the first place, this exchange reveals a series of contested assumptions about the status of scientific institutions in contemporary society. Certainly, both the main protagonists indicate a movement away from the idea that science can produce absolute truths upon which rational policy must be based. However, we can also identify a discussion as to whether science and technology are simply tools – to be used or abused – or whether instead they raise (and reflect) more fundamental matters of value and social choice.

Developing that point further, the discussion here appears to suggest a wider social change in terms of the status of both public groups and social institutions. This change encompasses globalization and the apparent demise of the nation state. In the GM case, national governments were generally reacting to Monsanto's decision rather than controlling the course of events. Given the movement of foodstuffs around the world (the very issue that sparked the UK debate over this question), and the inherent problems of identifying 'GM' and 'GM-free' foods, do national boundaries – or national systems of governance – have any real substance?

The debate considered here also raises important questions of knowledge and epistemology. If we are to take 'lay knowledge' seriously, does this mean that scientific rationality has effectively been downgraded? Alternatively, are we moving away from a singular form of rationality and truth towards a more pluralistic understanding where 'multiple rationalities' co-exist? Does lay knowledge have its own epistemology or is it effectively the same as science?

It is also important to consider the *form* of this debate. Of course, it could be argued that the location of the discussion on an internet site has no significance for the debate itself: the medium is simply a matter of practicality and convenience. However, the representation of democracy in a format which is both international and disembodied does seem a characteristic of contemporary life that cannot be ignored. Given the discussions which we will encounter in the next chapter about 'locality', the widespread use of information technology within such debates raises significant issues for the structure of communication and the character of local/national/global connections. Do local or national boundaries have any meaning in this virtual environment?

In this book, we will argue that the connection between such particular cases and wider theoretical concerns has generally been under-developed – to the neglect of both social theory and practical understanding and action. Rather than using the GM exchange as an illustration of existing theoretical concerns, we will suggest that such instances lead to innovative theoretical possibilities and questions. Rather than simply providing a fresh store of illustrations, they embody new approaches and challenges. In the case of the GM exchange, these include:

- the emergence of new forms of citizenship, governance and institutional process;
- a changing relationship between scientific rationality and more explicitly contextual forms of knowledge and understanding;
- a wider recognition of the significance of public trust, values and identities within the contemporary social world;
- a re-examination of the very ideas of 'progress' and 'rationality' upon which the project of modernity was built (such issues are especially stimulated by the existence of physical and social risks of the kind represented by GM technology);
- an awareness of the global character of these technologies and the public debates over their desirability;
- at a very fundamental level, a contestation over the role of the individual citizen in the face of rapid social and technical change – as a passive consumer/witness or as an active participant and change agent?;
- a recognition of the multi-layered character of interaction in this area; while theory tends to categorize and reify, such cases suggest the more dynamic and multiply constructed nature of social life.

Of course, this section has barely sketched out these possible connections. One important strand in this book will substantiate these areas and develop them in a more adequate fashion. Equally, we will be keen to pick out areas where theoretical debate can assist practical action over such topics.

Setting the scene

If these are the issues with which this book will deal, what can we say about its more detailed structure? As briefly explained in the Preface, we will follow a very simple pattern: two twists of a spiral which encompasses questions of public understanding, scientific and public governance, and social theory.

In Chapter 2, we consider the development of 'public understanding of science and technology'. We trace the ways in which early work in this field – largely quantitative – presupposed a particular model of the public. This entailed citizens that required scientific education, since they were essentially deficient in scientific knowledge and thus disabled from proper involvement in the democratic process that increasingly depended, or so it was claimed, upon a certain level of scientific literacy.

We show how this 'deficit model' has been challenged in a number of ways. In particular, we consider the ethnographic turn within 'public understanding of science and technology' which places emphasis less on cognition and more on culture and context. In this vein, we review two key case studies: the Cumbrian Sheepfarmers in the wake of the Chernobyl disaster as discussed by Wynne, and Epstein's account of AIDS activism in the USA. In the process, we elaborate on how publics' responses to expert knowledge and scientific institutions have been shown to be fundamentally bound up with issues of identity and trust. However, we also draw attention to the ways that these approaches have rather neglected the broader picture – one that has traditionally been provided by social theory.

Chapter 3 explores scientific governance. How in particular do the institutions of government deal with scientific controversies? Where government is directly implicated in the decision making about some scientific fact or other, numerous options are available to it. On the one hand, there can be governmental insistence upon the 'truth of the matter' (government scientists have the facts and there is nothing left to discuss). On the other, there can be an acknowledgement of uncertainty surrounding the facts: the scientists can't decide, the facts no longer speak for themselves, and the truth might be out there but it is, for the moment, beyond reach.

These responses often entail a representation of the public. In the former case of apparent scientific certainty, public anxieties will often be cast as a matter of deficiency: the public is worried because it does not understand the science. A little education and the public will come around to the government's 'objective' point of view. In the latter case of scientific uncertainty, new mechanisms of governance need to be mobilized (or even innovated). Such mechanisms might well involve particular methods of conducting debate over these uncertainties. Some of these will fix upon the scientific uncertainties and be conducted by experts. Others will broaden out to encompass ethical uncertainties where there are conflicting social values and here we might expect to see some measure of public participation. From this perspective, the public is seen as a stakeholder, a citizen, a voice that can contribute to the process of democratic decision making.

For all the over-simplicity of this stark contrast, it does point to the fact that such forms of governance entail models of the public – that is, of the scientific citizen. These models, in part, reflect certain social theoretical presuppositions concerning, for example, the present character of citizenship or the current status of globalization. But further, this contrast also hints at the ways in which such publics are 'made': at the disposal of government is a battery of techniques and resources – many of them social scientific – which serve in the 'construction' of these publics. In what follows, then, we shall look at the shifts in scientific governance, not least as it is given expression in the form and content of official reports. In the process, we pay special attention to the changes in governmental apprehensions of the public, science and the democratic process and the ways in which, under different circumstances, these have all been modelled and remodelled in ways that draw upon, in one way or another, both the public understanding of science and technology and social theory.

In Chapter 4, we consider a number of contributions to social theory that have a more or less direct bearing on both scientific and public governance and the public understanding of science and technology. Social theory has much to say about the ways in which the roles of scientific knowledge and institutions have changed in late modernity. On the one hand, there are various analyses of the problematizations of these institutions. Such problematizations might take the form of commentaries upon the increasingly apparent role of technoscience in the production of risks (Beck), in recent shifts in the character of self-identity (Giddens), in the abandonment of the enlightenment project (Lyotard), or in what has been seen as an increasingly irrational commitment to rationalization (Bauman). On the other hand, partly the medium and partly the result of these problematizations of scientific knowledge and institutions, a range of new social phenomena has arisen and been subjected to social theoretical analysis. These phenomena are multifarious and disparate, but touch upon the following topics: new social movements, citizenship, subpolitics, globalization, self-identity, reflexivity, consumer culture.

In Chapter 4, then, we spend some time explicating the major contributions of Beck (1992), Bauman (1991), Giddens (1991) and Lyotard (1984), clarifying their respective treatments of the nature of the 'public', the character of 'science' and the constitution of the 'political process'. Furthermore, we show how these relate to other recent concerns of social theory, not least citizenship and political agency. As we shall demonstrate, for all the power of these social theoretical analyses, one is often left with a strong sense that there has been a detachment from the messiness of everyday life. That is to say, we show how these theorizations neglect the sort of complexity, ambiguity and multiplicity evidenced by the ethnographic tradition in the public understanding of science and technology.

We are acutely aware that in dealing with various examples of public understanding of science and of related scientific controversy, there is a temptation to reify 'science' in various ways. For example, it might be asked, to what extent are controversies in relation to food, medicine or environment comparable? After all, such controversies will differ in terms of their political dynamics: certain food scares might be more pressing (entail a more compressed time-frame) than certain environmental issues (which might be more long drawn out). Furthermore, how these controversies are played out might differ across national and regional contexts. The analyses we provide in Chapters 2, 3 and 4 admittedly, and inevitably, draw upon limited examples. However, as we make clear below, they serve a broader purpose – one of enabling us to develop the analytic framework which takes up a large part of the second spiral of this volume. It is through this very framework (ethno-epistemic assemblages) that we can explore the differences and similarities, the divergences and convergences, the polarizations and mergers, across scientific controversies, national contexts and expert specialisms.

These chapters are all situated on the first twist of our narrative spiral. They are designed to illustrate, fairly straightforwardly, how our three domains deal with technoscientific debate and controversy. In Chapter 5, we explicitly bring the three elements together and begin to present them in a comparative light. More than that, we start to reconfigure the relationship between science, society and governance. To achieve this, we consider the differential manner in which public understanding of science, scientific governance and social theory has dealt with such common themes as the model of the public, the figure of the citizen and the nature of society. Having considered these linking themes, we are then in a position to make fresh connections. To help with this task, three broader dimensions of science–society relations are distilled at this point: the identification of the social world, the notion of knowing and the character of governance. This allows us to draw out some of the key differences and contrasts between the three core elements of this book.

To test out and explore these elements – and as a prelude to the more speculative analysis of later chapters – we consider in Chapter 5 one case originally developed within the ethnographic PUS tradition. Jarrow can be presented as a classic demonstration of the 'lay local': as a discrete set of contextual relations and the embodiment of a distinct culture. It can also be viewed as a substantial challenge to scientific governance: how can such local voices be drawn into national consultative processes? In reflection of our third element, Jarrow can be presented as a globalized entity complete with an extensive internet presence and its own international tourist attraction. The challenge is to find new ways of grasping these localizing and globalizing conceptualizations and the co-construction of both science and society.

Now, in the first spiral that constitutes this book, the examples of PUS and scientific governance (and, indeed, social theory) are often (but not entirely by any means) drawn from Europe, and within Europe, unsurprisingly, illustrations are taken primarily from the UK. However, the case studies we deploy, while important in their own right, serve a broader purpose – namely, to illustrate the complex interweavings of science and society.

The second spiral comprises our attempt to conceptualize such complex interweavings. This attempt entails the development of what we call *ethno-epistemic assemblages*, a notion that is embedded within a conceptual, methodological and political framework through which we aim, at once, to theorize, study empirically and intervene in science–society relations. The notion of ethno-epistemic assemblage is, we suggest, a heuristic means of addressing science–society relations in *any* context, most obviously that of the USA. Even in those settings where, arguably, the sorts of blurrings between science and society that we describe are less in evidence, the ethno-epistemic assemblages perspective can usefully illuminate how it is that the separations between science and society are reproduced.

Chapter 6 responds to these challenges by examining the manner in which science–society relations increasingly blur and mix previously fixed categories – especially the distinction between the expert and lay. Rather than dealing with the old rigidities, our attention is drawn to the manner in which many natures and many societies are being co-constructed by actors who themselves embody both the lay and the expert. One way of capturing these overlapping relations is through ethno-epistemic assemblages. This slightly ugly term is meant to aid us in examining how new technoscientific and social combinations come together. Having presented and briefly justified the neologism, we address a series of significant issues with specific regard to the construction of the scientific citizen. These issues include the 'tenacious and tenuous dichotomy' between expert and lay, the 'suffering' scientific citizen and emergent forms of scientific accountability and governmentality. Our intention throughout this discussion is to generate much-needed fresh thinking and reappraisal. In this way, ethno-epistemic assemblages take us into a less familiar world than that presented in the first twist of the spiral. Instead, conventional categories become transformed and new possibilities emerge.

Crucial to this analysis will be the figure of the 'scientific citizen'. We aim to show the complexity of models of the scientific citizen as they feature in what has often become a partial coalition between the public understanding of science and technology, and scientific and public governance. For example, versions of the 'local scientific citizen' (e.g. where citizenship is tied to the concerns of local communities) cannot be separated from 'global scientific citizens' (e.g. where citizenship is tied to concerns, partly realized through globalized media, about global changes and to distributed communities such as the environmental 'movement'). Here, obviously enough, social theory will be a major resource. Throughout, we shall be keen to stress how scientific citizenship is itself constituted through the complex discursive and practical processes that make up the public understanding of science and technology, scientific and public governance, and social theory. Our purpose is not to deny the value of these versions of the scientific citizen – they are productive and they enable in particular ways. But, they are also partial. One important feature of the analysis will be to trace some of the limitations of current models of the scientific citizen, and to open up a space for suggesting how things could be otherwise.

In the final two chapters, we draw out the implications of our formalized analytic structure for the study of the public understanding of science, social theorizing and science policy. Thus we ask:

- Where does this leave future qualitative and quantitative investigations? How can these be redesigned, on the one hand, to take into account more global processes and, on the other, better to situate themselves in the policy context out of which they partly emerge?
- Where does this leave conventional social theory? In what ways must this become responsive to the empirical and the political issues that have emerged? Here we suggest a number of potentially fruitful ways of, on the one hand, properly addressing the status of social theory and, on the other, better grounding it in the empirical.
- What are the implications for policy and governance? Here we explore how, in readdressing and reconceptualizing policy and governance, new forms of public engagement and policy responsiveness become possible.

In unravelling some of the 'mutual conditionalities' between social theory, qualitative research and science policy, we at once expand the range of sites where 'science and the public' may be studied, permit a more complex sensibility of the role of social theory in conducting such research, and enhance the possibilities for practical engagement with the publics, science and policy. That, at least, is the challenge we are setting ourselves across the following chapters.

2 The public understanding of science and technology: from cognition to context

A researcher calls at your home. You make her a cup of tea. After taking down some demographic details, she asks a series of questions about science and scientific method. Does the sun go round the earth or the earth go round the sun? Do lasers work by focusing sound waves? How scientific are physics, psychology, history, astrology? How do scientists test a new drug? After the questionnaire (and the cup of tea) has been finished, you are left wondering just how your 'scientific literacy' compares with the rest of the population. A few months later, an article in the newspaper tells you what you had half-expected: many members of the public are revealed as quite ignorant about basic scientific facts.

You have lived in the same area since you were a child. You know nearly all your neighbours. Your town is situated close to a chemical works and many of your friends and relatives work there. Occasionally you hear about things that have gone wrong at the plant: mishaps such as chemical spillages and gas releases. You and your neighbours begin to suspect that the recent increase in local children's asthma may be linked to the plant. The chemical company holds a number of open meetings which you attend. Managers and scientists from the plant reassure you that there is nothing to worry about. At the back of the room are two university lecturers – sociologists – taking notes. You recognize them because they came to your house and interviewed you about the chemical plant, what you knew about it, where you got your information and who you trusted. You ask one of the lecturers after the meeting whether he would choose to live in your neighbourhood. He replies that he is there to listen not to 'bias' local discussions. One of your friends observes afterwards that sociologists probably live in nice houses where there are no smelly factories.

These two simple vignettes take us into the multidiscipline generally known as the 'public understanding of science and technology' (some call it 'PUSET', but we'll refer to it by the more common abbreviation, 'PUS'). That is to say, they are both concerned, in one way or another, with exploring and gauging the relationship between the 'public' and 'science'. Our liberal use of 'scare quotes' should immediately alert the reader to the fact that understanding, science and public are all contestable concepts. That is, they are all interpreted in various, often conflicting ways, among those who work in the field of the public understanding of science and technology.

This point about the contested nature of language in this sub-field is linked to our description of PUS as a *multidiscipline*. As we shall see, PUS incorporates the concerns, assumptions and techniques of several disciplines (especially psychology, sociology and anthropology). However, and as we will later suggest with regard to social theory, PUS has developed at a distance from these disciplines – so that, despite their importance, the issues raised have effectively been dismissed from most social scientific discussion.

Although very simply expressed, our vignettes reflect two prevalent ways of doing research in the public understanding of science and technology. Crudely, these can be labelled 'quantitative' and 'qualitative', but there is more at stake here than a simple question of research technique. Instead, each approach embodies a range of assumptions that are both 'intellectual' and 'practical' in character. Thus, each approach reflects differing tacit models of the nature of the person, the role of knowledge in social understanding, the structure of society and the purpose of politics. On one level, these differences can be seen as typical of academic debates: each vignette reflects separate intellectual traditions that to some extent address different intellectual questions. Within many such controversies, arguments over the 'rigour' of research are paramount. Certainly, these abound in the public understanding of science and technology. As such, the researches being represented in the two vignettes above involve different claims about whether conducting questionnaire studies 'really' does get at people's understandings (ecological validity), and about whether conducting ethnographic studies of local communities 'really' does tell us anything generalizeable (reliability).

In turn, these questions of rigour are bound up with issues concerning what the research is 'for'. If one can show that one's research into the public understanding of science and technology reveals 'something real' about the public, then this 'something real' can serve as the basis for action (e.g. the development of science policy, the production of educational initiatives, innovation in public consultation mechanisms). Practical questions of what to *do* about the sometimes-troubled relationship between science and the public are very much to the fore within PUS research. However, and as we will suggest, the very definition of practical problems (should we be addressing the public understanding of science or the scientific understanding of the public?) has major implications for the form and direction of academic research.

Here, we come to the second level on which one can approach the public understanding of science and technology. It is a multidiscipline that has, in various ways, developed in direct response to the expressed needs of science and scientifically related institutions. Why is the public critical of developments in science and technology? Why can't people take a more careful look at the scientific evidence before getting agitated over nuclear waste disposal, genetically modified foods or the activities of the chemical industry? Questions like these have led to a call for further initiatives in the area of PUS (including social scientific research) from institutions that span central government, local government, research councils and scientific institutions, the commercial sector and charities. We will consider in detail the institutional environment in which the public understanding of science and technology is embedded in Chapter 3. Suffice it to say for now that the institutional context within which funds for public understanding of science and technology research are made available – and within which such studies are received and acted upon – is crucial.

But lest it appear that the public understanding of science and technology is simply shaped by this institutional context, we should make it clear from the outset that these institutions increasingly have come to rely upon the public understanding of science and technology as a multidiscipline. In making this point, we are drawing in particular upon recent European experience. Sceptics would say that this is largely due to the increasing frustration and confusion within industry and government (why can't the public learn to love science and technology?). Certainly, this reliance, as will become apparent in subsequent chapters, reflects a growing number of pressures on scientific institutions. Increasingly, it would seem, institutions must address:

- the requirement to embed research programmes within the concerns of the public;
- the need to assess the economic receptivity of a population to techno-scientific products such as genetically modified foodstuffs;
- the need to map scientific illiteracy to enhance the public's democratic capacities;
- the desire to increase institutional credibility by visibly taking account of the complex and nuanced views of the relevant public.

From this list, it is already possible to see that the different perspectives and approaches that make up the public understanding of science and technology are likely to serve different purposes depending upon the institutional context which, in part, shapes them. However, in this chapter we concentrate on the academic (or internal) development of the public understanding of science and technology. That is to say, we consider what constitutes the multidiscipline of public understanding of science and technology – the range of techniques, models, studies and so on. We trace the ways in which earlier – largely quantitative – work in this field presupposed a particular model of the member of the public. This entailed a citizenry that required scientific education because it was essentially deficient in scientific knowledge. Consequently, the citizen was disabled from proper involvement in the democratic process which increasingly depended, or so it was claimed, upon a certain level of scientific literacy.

We next show how this 'deficit model' has been challenged in a number of ways. In particular, we look at how, within PUS, there has been an 'ethnographic turn' that places emphasis less on cognition and more on cultural context. This turn, we shall argue, involves a more complex conception of the public's relations with science. For this reason, and for the fact that it is beginning to play a greater role in science policy (see Chapter 3), we spend more space explicating and exemplifying it. In particular, we review two key case studies to provide a flavour of this research style. These main case studies will be supplemented by the findings from other selected empirical studies (e.g. Couch and Kroll-Smith 1991; Layton *et al.* 1993; Michael 1996a; Arksey 1998; Barr and Birke 1998). In the process, we elaborate on how publics' responses to expert knowledge and scientific institutions have been shown to be fundamentally bound up with issues of identity and trust. However, we also draw attention to the ways that these approaches have rather neglected the 'broader picture' – one that has traditionally been provided by social theory.

Questionnaire surveys and knowledge

In the context of PUS, the questionnaire survey represents a methodological tool designed, in essence, to determine what it is that members of the public know about science. Perhaps unsurprisingly, what seems to be consistent across many questionnaire studies (notably those by Durant and his various collaborators; also see, for example, Miller 1991) is the finding that there are major shortcomings in the public's understanding of science. In terms of scientific literacy, it would seem that the public is, in general, very seriously lacking. This version of public deficit is something that has been seized upon by the press. As one article put it: 'With more than a third of the population not knowing that the earth goes round the sun, Britain could be in serious trouble' (*Sunday Times*, 19 November 1989).

Attempts at gauging levels of public understanding of science go back at least to the early 1970s with the 'science indicators' programme of the US National Science Foundation (Wynne 1995). Such an approach was given a further boost by the British Royal Society's influential report on the *Public Understanding of Science* (Royal Society of London 1985), which called for further social scientific mapping in this manner. During the 1980s and 1990s, the questionnaire method was very much dominant in PUS research – and it is still highly influential today.

In this section, we will briefly discuss the questionnaire (or quantitative) approach to PUS and consider some of its underlying assumptions concerning the relationship between science, social theory and public knowledge. As we suggest, at the heart of this apparently straightforward and 'rational' (even 'scientific') technique can be found a series of suppositions about 'the public', about 'science' and about the nature of 'understanding' in the contemporary world. Put in very simple terms, questionnaire approaches have generally worked according to a 'deficit' model. Typically, they ask questions about public knowledge of science in a manner that can be contrasted with the 'real' answers (as supplied by science). Accordingly, the key problem is seen to be public ignorance of science. If large-scale surveys characteristically indicate a serious public misunderstanding of science, then what hope can there be for informed social debate? Within this framework, the way forward can only be greater public education about science – or perhaps, and to adopt a more authoritarian approach, the exclusion of members of the public from debate over the future of science. What is also implied by the 'deficit model' is that greater public knowledge of science will lead to a more welcoming public climate for scientific and technological developments.

Certainly, and to take one of the key assumptions within the 'deficit' approach, several commentators have noted that it is often assumed by policy makers and researchers alike that increased public knowledge of science will lead to a more positive attitude towards it (e.g. Yearley 1993; Wynne 1995). Indeed, there is some evidence that those who are more informed about science are also more supportive (Evans and Durant 1995). However, this correlation does not necessarily suggest a causal relation – it might be the case that support for science has led to the pursuit of scientific knowledge. Furthermore, possessing more knowledge can also mean an increased awareness of the contingencies and uncertainties associated with specific scientific knowledges, and thus, potentially, less support for (or confidence in) science. And, of course, 'support' can take many forms, ranging from vehement advocacy of specific scientific research programmes through to pragmatic willingness to acknowledge the value of science to society. Regarding these points, Aldhous *et al.* (1999) observe that providing information about the use of animal experimentation in medical testing led to greater (though still contingent) support for animal experimentation. Meanwhile, Beveridge and Rudell (1988), in reviewing the 1985 *Science Indicators Report*, note that while expressions of interest in science are great, science informedness is considerably lower (irrespective of whether such informedness was self-reported or externally measured). What emerges then, even within the survey literature, is a complex picture where knowledgeability is related to 'support' in rather diffuse ways (cf. Wynne 1995).

While we have questioned the meaning of 'support' for science, we also need to look at how 'understanding' (and related terms like knowledgeability and scientific literacy; cf. Durant 1993) is operationalized in questionnaires.

Questionnaire studies that aim to measure the public understanding of science do so by asking questions about specific aspects of scientific knowledge. These questionnaire studies take many forms and we cannot hope to do justice to their variety here. For example, questionnaire studies have been used to measure understandings of specific topics such as biotechnology (e.g. Marlier 1992; Durant *et al.* 1997) and of science-in-general (Durant *et al.* 1989). Equally, they have been conducted for the purpose of serious policy development (e.g. Durant *et al.* 1997) and for popular entertainment (e.g. Durant 1992). However, the key feature shared by all these approaches to questionnaire design is a 'quizzing' of the lay respondent over a range of 'scientific facts' (such facts can be about an accredited finding or 'standard' scientific procedure). These standardized questions lead to answers that can be reliably coded by researchers. However, and we return to this issue below, the relation between the answers that are possible in the context of these questionnaires and the role knowledge plays in people's everyday lives (that is, the questionnaires' 'ecological validity') is far from clear in these studies.

Let us examine this last point in further detail by looking more closely at the characteristics of 'quizzing' within questionnaire surveys. In particular, we will consider an item from an important survey into the public understanding of science funded by the UK's Economic and Social Research Council (e.g. Durant *et al.* 1989). Question 7 asks respondents to rate on a scale of 1 ('not at all scientific') to 5 ('very scientific') a number of subjects such as biology, economics, astronomy, chemistry and astrology. This question aims to assess whether people can identify some of the basic characteristics of science and evaluate the named subjects in terms of the extent to which they share such characteristics. The underpinning assumption is that science has a core set of, let us say, universal or absolute procedural values, against which these subjects are measured.

One of us (Michael 1992), on the basis of lay people's commentaries on Question 7, has suggested that respondents are able to operate with a variety of criteria as to what is to count as 'scientific'. Thus, a subject might be regarded as scientific because of its 'intrinsic interestingness', or the obsessiveness of its practitioners, or the utility of the knowledge it produced. Each of these lay criteria could at least potentially be articulated in the context of answering Question 7. However, the format of the questionnaire does not allow the expression of such diverse assessments of what it means to be 'scientific'. Rather than drawing upon lay people's more complex and ambivalent relations with science, scientific institutions and expert knowledge, the questionnaire format imposes a one-dimensional framework. Of course, the selection of this framework means that members of the public who consider astrology to be scientific according to some of the above criteria (surely astrologists are rigorous and serious-minded in their approach?) can readily be labelled as 'ignorant'.

Another example of the problematic validity of such question formats can be drawn from 1991's Eurobarometer 35.1 that studied the opinions of Europeans on biotechnology (Marlier 1992). The question upon which we focus asks: 'I have here a list of some areas where new technologies are actually being developed. In your opinion, which are linked to biotechnology and genetic engineering and which are not?' The following technologies are then listed:

1 Research on early detection and treatment of cancer.
2 Changing hereditary information within an organism to alter that organism's characteristics.
3 Producing new kinds of organisms using hereditary information from other species.
4 Improving traditional methods of cross-breeding plants or animals.
5 Making use of living micro-organisms, for example, for plant protection (bio-pesticides).
6 Food processing such as using yeast for the production of bread or beer.
7 Treating hereditary human diseases by modifying the tissue involved.

The 'scientifically correct' answers are 'yes' for both biotechnology and genetic engineering for all seven examples. However, Hill and Michael (1998) draw attention to the fact that this question allows only for a 'yes' or 'no' answer. The various listed activities can be more or less 'linked to' biotechnology or genetic engineering. This suggests a homogeneous, unitary entity called biotechnology or genetic engineering with definitive biotechnological principles, procedures, knowledges – a domain within which any listed topic can be defined as either 'in' or 'out'.

The further implication is that what is being measured here is not understanding but some sort of 'product recognition'. In so far as these technologies can be 'linked to' the label 'biotechnology and genetic engineering', they become products of a quasi-commercial enterprise. Biotechnology or genetic engineering is the enterprise (corporation, company or producer) '[p]roducing new kinds of organisms using hereditary information from other species', '[i]mproving traditional methods of cross-breeding plants or animals' and '[m]aking use of living micro-organisms, for example, for plant protection (bio-pesticides)'.

The critical point regarding this question is that it assumes the intellectual unity of technologies that are culturally and socially disparate. That is to say, even if the listed technologies could persuasively be attached to some invariant principles of biotechnology, they are also very likely to be perceived as being associated with different more or less credible institutions, legislative regimes and potential risks. Our discussion of the GM crop debate in the preceding chapter demonstrates very clearly the range of assumptions that can be linked by the public to even a single technology. In sum, the restricted answers allowed by this question compromise any 'validity' they might have. Furthermore, techniques such as the Eurobarometer can be seen as treating the public not as citizens but as individualized consumers (cf. Hill and Michael 1998).

Now, behind this quantitative approach there often appears to be the common-sensical assumption that having 'scientific literacy' is a good thing. This is perhaps most clearly articulated in the Royal Society of London's (1985) report on *The Public Understanding of Science*. Here, we find the following advantages claimed for greater scientific literacy: enhanced practical competence in everyday life; greater capacity to make informed decisions; enhanced employability; increased ability to get involved in Western civilization and culture; an enhanced capacity to contribute to the democratic decision-making process (which nowadays entails a much greater element of scientific knowledge).

It is upon this last 'function' of scientific literacy that we shall focus here, not least because it deeply informs the rationale behind survey questionnaires. Scientific literacy (or scientific ignorance) is equated with the capacity to act as a citizen in a democracy. In sum, to have improved scientific literacy is to be intellectually better equipped to contribute to the processes of a liberal democracy within which scientific knowledge has become fundamental. But this already presupposes that it is mainly *scientifically accredited* knowledge that is relevant to the policy-making process. As we shall document in detail below, this is not necessarily the case. Lay publics also possess local or situated knowledges, experiences and skills that can play a major part in the crafting of policy. The implication also is that methodologies such as survey questionnaires (with their privileging of accredited scientific knowledge and procedures) form part of a battery of communications that flow from elite expert institutions to lay public groupings in which the public's knowledges are systematically derogated. Again, as we shall illustrate below when we consider the ethnographic approach to the public understanding of science and technology, this 'body language' (Wynne 1991) towards publics can lead to deep suspicions among the public, and catastrophic loss of legitimation for scientific institutions.

The 'discovery' by quantitative research of the public's lack of scientific knowledge is not, therefore, innocent. As Brian Wynne (1995) has noted, this perspective entails several normative assumptions – assumptions that partly reflect the roots of the questionnaire method in psychology. First, there seems to be a view of the *person as a repository of knowledge*. That is, we are cognitive containers in which one can rummage around (with the aid of such tools as the questionnaire) and extract golden nuggets of correct knowledge and putrid clumps of incorrect knowledge, or detect the absence of any knowledge altogether. This model clearly removes the person from their social context – a criticism often levelled at cognitive psychology (of many examples, see Harre and Secord 1972; Shotter 1975; Sampson 1981, 1983; Gergen 1982; Wexler 1983). Secondly, and relatedly, informing this approach is what has been labelled (e.g. Wynne 1995) the *deficit model*. These questionnaires are structured for the purpose of measuring the extent to which lay people's knowledge falls short of accredited scientific knowledge (e.g. Wynne 1991, 1992, 1995; also Gregory and Miller 1998). As many analysts from the 'ethnographic' tradition in PUS have argued, people possess all sorts of highly relevant and useful knowledge, even if such knowledge doesn't meet the exacting standards of scientific inquiry. This point is increasingly being conceded by those who conduct survey questionnaires (for a good example of the circumspect and nuanced use of questionnaire surveys, see Durant *et al.* 1997). Thirdly, this approach does not take into account the fact that people are *reflexive, moral beings* who are perfectly able to monitor the status of their understanding and warrant both the knowledges they possess and the knowledges they lack (their so-called 'ignorance'). In other words, this approach neglects the fact that people, even in the microsocial encounter of a question-and-answer session, have the capacity to elaborate their responses, accounting for them in relation to a variety of moral, ethical and political concerns (see, most obviously, Garfinkel 1967; Heritage 1984). This crucial dimension of all social interaction is, one might say, systematically screened out of questionnaire studies (cf. Michael 1996b).

In summary, then, the questionnaire approach to PUS might appear to be a neutral tool. However, in this section we have suggested that certain intellectual assumptions are inevitably embedded within this 'scientific' framework. We have pointed to the constrained and one-dimensional format within which public responses to complex technical and cultural questions must be expressed. We have indicated in particular that the 'quizzing' of members of the public in this fashion leads to their construction as ignorant and uninformed. Such a formulation is, in turn, related to the prevalent views and assessments of many scientific institutions for whom the only logical explanation for public scepticism is that the public must be uninformed about what is really going on in science and technology.

One general criticism of the questionnaire approach has been that it removes scientific questions from their social and cultural *context*. Rather than addressing issues of health risk, ethics and consumer choice in the more mundane manner in which they are generally presented within everyday life, such issues are presented in an abstract and de-contextualized fashion. In the next section, we turn to an approach that has sought to consider scientific and technical issues in full context. On the one hand, this suggests the need for a very different methodology – typically built upon a qualitative and ethnographic approach. On the other, it presents a very different social and political perspective – so that the operating assumptions of scientific institutions are opened up to the same scrutiny as has been previously applied to members of the public.

The questionnaire approach has tended to ignore the possibility that people are engaged in a process of 'lay epistemology'. That is to say, lay people may not only possess knowledge, but have knowledge of how they know: they are able to reflect upon why they take on board some 'scientific facts' but not others; they are competent in accounting for why they prefer some sources of knowledge (e.g. personal experience) over others; and they can justify why they trust some expert authorities and are suspicious of others. Put differently, people are able to reflect on the fact that their knowledge is derived from the media (or some other source), are able to assess the credibility of that source and to evaluate their knowledge in terms of its contingency (for example, whether it is the best currently available or is broadly appropriate for present requirements). As should be clear, 'lay epistemology' is not concerned with exercising formal criteria by which to determine what is true and what is false. Rather, it is concerned with the way that people are engaged in a complex of judgements about trustworthiness, credibility, usefulness, power – judgements which reflect, for example, social identity, practical circumstance, personal responsibility and community autonomy. It is this nexus of issues that the ethnographic tradition in public understanding of science has sought to address.

The 'ethnographic turn' in public understanding of science

One significant difference between the preceding approach and ethnographic public understanding of science can be sketched by considering how each would deal with the following simple and, for some, lamentably common response by a member of the public to a question about one scientific fact or other: 'I don't know'. Within the dominant tradition of questionnaire analysis, the 'don't know' category is typically represented as a void, a marker of absence or, worse still, of 'ignorance'. It offers a cognitive space which remains unfilled. By contrast, for ethnographic public understanding of science, this statement may be of considerable significance, especially when respondents are allowed to elaborate.

As Michael (1996a,b; Turner and Michael 1996) has shown, 'don't know' responses can be analysed in terms of at least three categories (or what he called 'discourses of ignorance'). Grounded in interview data with volunteers in a radon survey of Lancaster (a small city in the North West of England), a panel of residents from Lancaster and environs, and twenty time-served electricians working at the Sellafield reprocessing plant, Michael traced how laypeople warranted – justified or excused – their ostensible 'ignorance'. In particular, he pointed out that in the process of such warranting, people not only attempted to manage the impression they gave (Goffman 1959; Potter and Wetherell 1987) to the interviewer, but also were engaged in drawing on certain cultural resources to forge, or at least to represent, particular sorts of relations with science and scientific expertise. In brief, the three 'discourses of ignorance' were: mental constitution, division of labour and deliberate choice.

Mental constitution is a discourse that presents manifest lack of scientific knowledge as a result of a 'not-knowing', sometimes due to a lack of education but mostly grounded in a constitutional incapacity. That is to say, people presented themselves as being mentally incapable of grasping the science: they did not have a 'scientific mind'. The ubiquity of this response (even among those who were evidently 'knowledgeable') suggests that this was culturally a highly available discourse. Ironically, and importantly, the process of reflection upon one's unscientific mind is a social demonstration of one's ability to be self-critical (a capacity which is often regarded as highly 'scientific'). But this self-criticism also reflects a tacit relation to science – one in which self is subordinate, at least in the relevant scientific matters, to the experts. Here an identity is played out that encapsulates a particular cognitive state, a self-critical member of society and a layperson dependent upon science.

The *division of labour* discourse warrants 'ignorance' rather differently. In this case, 'ignorance' is embedded in an account within which difference between science and other spheres of action or expertise is functional. That is to say, absence is here represented as a more or less necessary constituent of the division of labour. The layperson does one job, the scientist does another. Together they complement one another to fulfil the overarching goals to which they are both committed. The layperson might, within this relationship to science, be active and skilled (e.g. electricians) or might be passive and unskilled (volunteers in a radon survey). The overarching goal might be that of an organization like Sellafield (the plant works efficiently and safely) or of society as a whole (ensuring safety from radon poisoning) (cf. Michael 1991, 1992). The warrant of ignorance here can be encapsulated in the phrase: 'it's not my job'. This stresses that the layperson has a role to play, one that complements or supports the work of scientists, and one in which particular skills or particular motives are crucial. The tacit relation to science is thus one of complementarity.

Finally, there is a discourse which accounts for 'ignorance' as a *deliberate choice* ('I don't know, and I don't want to know'). Here, scientific knowledge is consciously bracketed, ignored, jettisoned or avoided because it is perceived as essentially peripheral to, or a distraction from, the primary issues at stake. For example, knowledge about ionizing radiation does not necessarily help when one wishes to argue that nuclear power is economically and politically calamitous. In this way, scientific experts are seen as opposed to the views of the layperson, introducing knowledges that are irrelevant to what are seen as the primary issues at stake. The point here is that people can warrant 'ignorance' in terms that diminish the role of scientific knowledge and that assert the right to re-define both the respective character of, and balance between, ignorance and knowledge (it is now scientists who are 'ignorant').

This brief (and far from definitive) review of the 'I don't know' response has already thrown up a raft of issues. We have touched upon a number of different identities, a range of culturally available resources, and a variety of relations of power between publics and sciences. Moreover, we should not expect these to remain separate or distinct. It is not difficult to envisage instances where people move across these identities, resources and relations as day-to-day they engage in different scientific issues, knowledges and institutions (for examples drawn from anthropology, see Hobart 1993). Already, it is possible to see how, for ethnographic public understanding of science, even the 'absence of scientific knowledge' must be analysed in relation to multiple and complex contexts.

As might be expected within this multidisciplinary domain, 'ethnographic public understanding of science' has a disparate, complex and overlapping intellectual lineage that takes in traditions such as the sociology of scientific knowledge (SSK; e.g. Irwin 1995; Irwin and Wynne 1996; Wynne 1996), social anthropology (e.g. Franklin 1998; Martin 1998), feminism (e.g. Barr and Birke 1998) and cultural studies (e.g. Haraway 1991, 1997; Ross 1991). Although we will touch upon all of these, we focus primarily upon the links to sociology of scientific knowledge. This is because sociology of scientific knowledge has played a major role in interrogating the social role of science as the arbiter of 'truth', has increasingly entered into the social domain – both as the object of public scientific derision (in the so-called 'science wars'; cf. Kleinman 2000) – and, latterly, has made a contribution to policy deliberations (House of Lords Select Committee 2000).

Now, in what is to follow, our move from the traditional questionnaire approach to PUS to the 'ethnographic perspective' raises a number of issues. As we shall see, the distinction between the questionnaire approach (with its emphasis on cognition and objective knowledge) to the ethnographic approach rests upon *a priori* differences in the two perspectives' respective models of the person, science, understanding, society, politics and so on. We shall illustrate these differences with a select number of key case studies. Although it would be possible to exemplify the ethnographic approach with many more such fieldwork case studies, these would not necessarily add to our key point regarding the different conceptual frameworks that characterize the traditional and ethnographic approaches. Furthermore, we have chosen to treat our examples of ethnographic material 'lightly'. That is to say, we could have given much thicker descriptions that would provide the depth of detail that would be typically regarded as 'ethnographic'. However, again, in our view, this would not have added very much to our analytic point that the ethnographic approach deploys a particular set of assumptions about the 'public understanding of science', and these assumptions enable it to ask different sorts of questions about the nature of the public's engagement with scientific knowledge (and, indeed, science policy). Of course, such detail is important, not least rhetorically in so far as it makes an account of the substantive issues more persuasive. On this score, we can only recommend to readers that they read the originals.

In the present context, we will exemplify the SSK version of 'ethnographic public understanding of science' with the aid of two short case studies. The case studies have been chosen to reflect a series of dimensions: whether the lay public is part of an existing local community or a collective or movement that is distributed; whether laypeople draw upon their own folk or situated knowledges, or whether they have recourse to expert knowledge; whether that recourse to expert knowledge involves the 'education' of lay people or dependency upon other existing experts. In addition, we wanted to consider two different substantive fields in which public understanding of science was expressed, the environmental and the medical. As we shall see, Wynne's now classic study of the Cumbrian sheepfarmers examines a local community which draws on its own local knowledges in challenging the expert pronouncements of environmental scientists. Following this, Epstein's account of AIDS activism in the USA explores how a distributed community – that is to say, a movement – came together so as to intervene in the production of medical and clinical knowledge, in the course of which many activists had to educate themselves in the 'relevant' science.

Before going on to look at these studies in detail, it is important to lay out their common SSK assumptions. For sociology of scientific knowledge, nature does not speak directly to scientists, yielding her 'truths'. What is to count as 'fact' (or a datum, or an artefact) depends upon processes of argumentation and negotiation in which are deployed rhetoric, discourse, representation. We find these resources mobilized at the putative heart of science – in the laboratory. We find them operating in controversies that range across research groups, institutions, disciplines and countries. Very often, these controversies are conducted through scholarly journals and in conferences and seminars. In addition, other resources may be mobilized in such struggles – monetary, reputational, political. The upshot is that, in the course of a controversy, one faction is discredited while another emerges triumphant. It is at this point that what counts as 'a fact of nature' is settled, and that science proper is differentiated from marginal science or pseudo-science (e.g. Bloor 1976; Barnes 1977; Latour and Woolgar 1979; Mulkay 1979; Wallis 1979; Knorr-Cetina 1981; Gilbert and Mulkay 1984; Collins 1985; Latour 1987; Collins and Pinch 1993).

One of the observations that SSK researchers have routinely made is that science itself is intrinsically uncertain, always renegotiable. Scientific knowledge rests on practices grounded in assumptions and presuppositions (about theory, about technique) that cannot solely be justified by recourse to nature, because what is to count as nature depends on these assumptions and presuppositions. This also implies that scientific knowledges are local (cf. Turnbull 2000) – that is, the product of assumptions and presuppositions that are part of *particular* laboratories, institutions or disciplines. Other *particular* laboratories, institutions or disciplines (and, indeed, lay constituencies) can always, in principle, and often do, interrogate and problematize these scientific knowledges.

Rather than continuing to discuss such matters in general terms, we now turn to two major examples from the ethnographic literature, starting with Wynne's study of a group of farmers in the North West of England.

The fallout from the fallout

In a series of publications on the Cumbrian sheepfarmers, Brian Wynne (1991, 1992, 1996) has developed perhaps the most famous case study of the problematic character of science–public relations. Rather than assuming that the key problem is the public ignorance of science (as in the conventional deficit theory), in Wynne's account it is the representatives of science who emerge as both ignorant and unreflexive in the face of public understandings. Equally, and rather than drawing upon questionnaire studies, this research builds upon a series of interviews, observations and 'thick descriptions' of local life during one social and environmental crisis.

Wynne provides an account of the social ramifications for scientific institutions and local communities alike when heavy rain deposited fallout from the Chernobyl nuclear power station explosion on the Cumbrian fells. Soon after the rainfall, during May and early June in 1986, confident ministerial and scientific statements were issued reassuring farmers that the problem would clear up within a few weeks. However, by 20 June restrictions on movement and slaughter of sheep were implemented, although it was also announced that these would be temporary. Most worryingly, on 24 July the ban was extended indefinitely. A key observation for Wynne is that one consequence of these abrupt and unexplained changes in policy was for the credibility of the scientists of the Ministry of Agriculture, Fisheries and Food (MAFF) to become severely compromised among affected farmers.

The sheepfarmers' scepticism regarding MAFF expertise was triggered and exacerbated in several other ways. For instance, the solutions offered by MAFF scientists tended to neglect the constraints on farmers' practices (e.g. regarding the movement of sheep) and seemed to be alarmingly uninformed about very basic farming methods (e.g. what could be fed to the sheep). Over and above this, scientists issued pronouncements that were routinely couched in terms of certainties that contradicted the farmers' own experiences of the contingencies and incertitudes of hill farming. More generally, Wynne has observed that, while MAFF scientists drew confidently on laboratory studies of radio-active materials, the terrain on which they were operating was very different in character. In this way, scientific expertise was over-extended across very different contexts – but the self-confidence (or perhaps intellectual arrogance) of the scientists insulated them from these local factors and obstructed their learning from the 'local experts'.

This problem of over-extension applied, for example, to MAFF's attempts to measure radioactive levels on the fells by standardizing and randomizing the areas to be monitored. This 'scientific' approach took no account of the peculiarities of the fell terrain, peculiarities with which the farmers were intimately familiar. This familiarity meant that the farmers knew the location of the sheep's favourite drinking places. For them, it seemed logical to concentrate monitoring on these likely exposure sources. The point is that standardized, highly scientific measures, which were presented by MAFF as the 'right' way to gauge radiation levels bore, in the eyes of the farmers, little relevance to the realities and uncertainties of the fells and the sheep.

The outcome of these disparate perceptions was that the farmers, in problematizing the certainty entailed in the scientists' assessments, began to see them as part of either a conspiracy or cover-up. Denied access to the underlying uncertainties involved in the scientific evaluations of the longevity of radioactivity on the Cumbrian hills, farmers tended to view the changes of policy made by MAFF and its scientists as responses to other political factors (such as the imagined need to cover up the levels of radioactivity released from the nearby nuclear reprocessing plant at Sellafield).

Wynne argues that the scientists' expertise encroached upon and often derogated the farmers' own local knowledge. Proclaimed as being in the farmers' best interests, the work and techniques of the scientists failed to take into account, let alone complement fittingly, the comparable skills of the farmers. While the farmers generally recognized that such monitoring was the proper domain of scientists, they were disillusioned by the ways in which this, and other, scientific techniques and the knowledge they generated were applied without entertaining, let alone recognizing, the relevance of their local non-scientific craft knowledge. This wholesale, unreflexive transplantation of scientific knowledge into the Cumbrian fells devalued the farmers' hard-earned, less formally organized knowledge (see also Croll and Parkin 1992). The Cumbrian sheepfarmers came to view what Wynne terms the 'body language' of MAFF as posing a threat to their local craft knowledge, their collective way of life and, in sum, their social identity.

We can now abstract some of the key features of Wynne's highly influential analysis. What is noticeable here is the assumption, following the sociology of scientific knowledge, that all knowledge is derived from its particular cultural and social context. Wynne's analysis charts the clash of cultures between the expert and the lay, both conceptualized as local 'actors' (institutions or communities). The farmers' 'lay local' knowledge is viewed as qualitatively different from that of the scientific experts in so far as it does not share in certain key assumptions and practices that undergird the scientific enterprise. Crucially, the farmers' knowledge is based on collective, culturally mediated experience of the fell terrain and upon a keen sensibility for the uncertainties and contingencies found within a harsh and unpredictable environment. The association of local knowledges to community and experience means that such local knowledges are intertwined with, and are partly constitutive of, local cultural identities. These local cultural identities are placed at risk by virtue of the expert knowledges imported into the lay local context.

Expert knowledges are thus threatening because, by virtue of the unequivocal ways in which they are presented, they undermine the status of local knowledges that are intimately tied to lay local identities. The result is that scientists and scientific institutions endanger their credibility and trustworthiness. As Wynne (1996) puts it when summarizing the critical PUS approach (and counterposing it to the standard analysis of the 'risk society'): 'the fundamental sense of risk in the "risk society", is risk to identity engendered by dependency upon expert systems which typically operate with such unreflexive blindness to their own culturally problematic and inadequate models of the human' (p. 68). That is to say, expert scientific knowledge which 'neglects and thus denigrates specialist lay knowledge' (p. 68) poses a threat to lay local identities and, indeed, to our sense of personhood.

In Wynne's version of ethnographic public understanding, lay local and expert knowledges are examined, at least in part, in terms of whether they sustain or jeopardize local social identities. Indeed, one might say that, contrary to the generally positive view of the value of science promulgated by survey questionnaire approaches, Wynne tends to point to the cultural dis-utility of scientific knowledge. Rather than acting as agents of the enlightenment, the mediators of scientific knowledge undermine, or attempt to colonize, the lay local and its related social identities – with negative consequences for the local publics.

From community to movement

The previous case study attempted to embed PUS in its social and cultural context. In particular, that case emphasized the importance of community dynamics and a geographical sense of locality. Thus, community played a crucial role in the lay public's use of 'situated knowledge'. This knowledge, in turn, intertwined with social identity within a very loaded social situation.

In this second case, we consider an example in which the 'community' is expanded beyond geographical borders (though, of course, 'community' is an entity that always has to be culturally reconstructed; cf. Cohen 1985). While 'community' is sometimes used as a way of identifying the relation of certain publics to scientific institutions, we will focus in this section upon public groups as constituted within a social movement. That is, the discussion will concern how particular publics have emerged, partly through their inter-actions with science, in relation to more or less specified issues, controversies, apprehensions and problems (cf. Melucci 1989a,b; Eyerman and Jamison 1991; Della Porta and Diani 1998). However, we must stress that the distinc-tion between community (which suggests a social collectivity prior to a per-ceived problem) and a movement (which evokes a collectivity drawn together around some 'problem' – though the problem might also be constituted in the process of being drawn together) is not hard and fast. The 'gay community' in the USA pre-existed the AIDS movement but was nevertheless crucial to it. Furthermore, in the same way as 'identity' has been seen to be a key compon-ent of community, so it has too for social movements. While the identities of communities might have greater 'longevity' (in the sense of being more rou-tinely 'practised'), and those of social movement be more 'opportunistic', they still play an important role in shaping the relations that emerge – the percep-tions of trust and credibility – between these lay publics and scientific institutions.

In this section, drawing in particular on the work of Epstein (1996, 2000), we focus on medical social movements and specifically that movement which had such a profound impact upon research into AIDS in the USA from the mid-1980s. As Epstein shows, this movement was partly enabled by a series of pre-existing ones, most obviously the lesbian and gay movement. But the AIDS epidemic also lent itself to social movement activity. As Epstein (1996) puts it: 'An epidemic whose social definition lies at the intersection of cultural dis-courses about sexuality, the body, and identity is, arguably, the ideal staging ground for the emergence of a new social movement' (p. 20).

Epstein explores the complex interactions between activists and scientists, not least in the efforts of the former to influence the development of AIDS treatments and drug trials. However, this puts the contrast between activists and scientists rather too baldly. The gay communities, from which the move-ment in part derived, included 'white, middle-class men with a degree of polit-ical clout and fundraising capacity unusual for an oppressed group . . . [and included] doctors, scientists, educators, nurses, professionals, or other varieties of intellectuals' (Epstein 2000: 18). This meant that the AIDS movement had considerable resources with which to challenge 'mainstream experts on their own ground' (p. 18) and through which to facilitate communication between 'scientific' and 'public constituencies'. The AIDS movement engaged in mul-tiple forms of activism, not least in raising the profile of AIDS as an epidemic through various forms of direct action. But for present purposes, we focus on the main contribution of the AIDS movement to the various and manifold scientific arguments that were associated with the epidemic. These contributions concerned not so much the expert analyses of the aetiology of AIDS, which, as might be expected, tended to be conducted within the scientific community, but the possible ways in which treatments should be developed and tested.

Epstein traces in rich detail the way that the AIDS movement impacted upon the scientific perspective on treatment issues. In particular, he notes how the traditional model of testing of drugs through clinical trials was fundamentally revised by the AIDS movement. AIDS activists succeeded in influencing such dimensions of clinical trial design as the entry criteria (who was eligible), the types of controls and the point at which a trial could be deemed to have ended (demonstrating 'success' or 'failure' of the specific treatment regime under test). Partly, this foothold was gained by virtue of the fact that the communication networks within the movement meant that excluded AIDS patients would soon find out – the resulting clamour and criticism severely dented the medical establishment's credibility. This was because clinical trials were concerned with painstakingly establishing 'pure, objective' scientific knowledge, while patients were looking for possible treatments in the here-and-now. Moreover, patients would subvert the trials in various ways, for example by not sticking to their allotted treatment regimes and by using additional treatments.

In the face of these 'disruptions', the medical establishment had to retain its credibility if it was to conduct viable clinical trials. One way in which this was managed was by accepting that members of the movement could make legitimate contributions to the debates around treatment. However, this proved challenging for AIDS activists, since they now had to *learn the science*. Only by taking on, and becoming highly proficient in, the technical details of, for instance, trial design, could they gain credibility within the medical establishment. Epstein (2000: 20–1) summarizes the tactics by which the activists managed to gain influence:

- acquiring 'cultural competence by learning the language and culture of medical science';
- presenting 'themselves as the legitimate, organized voice of people with AIDS or HIV infection';
- yoking methodological and moral arguments to 'multiply their "currencies" of credibility';
- taking advantage of divisions 'within the scientific establishment to form strategic alliances'.

Now, there were downsides to this hard-won voice. In particular, those activists who had become schooled in the science also risked being seen as having, to some degree, left the movement, or as being less responsive to the issues current in the movement and more attuned to dealing with the technicalities of clinical trials.

This case study, very superficially covered here, illustrates a number of important points about the ethnographic study of public understanding of science. First, it shows that publics can mobilize around particular issues to force major inroads into scientific institutions. Secondly, it suggests that this is partly dependent on some activists from the movement becoming adept in the relevant scientific knowledge. In this, it credits the public with a greater capacity for taking on scientific knowledge than is often acknowledged by scientific institutions (as demonstrated by the sheepfarmer case). This is a point to which we shall return when we consider the attempt to increase public participation in science policy. Thirdly, a stress is placed upon the disjunction between the sorts of knowledge that are 'needed' by science and the public, respectively. For the former, pure objective knowledge is the desired goal. For the latter, it is knowledge that can inform immediate, situated practice that is the goal. In the case of repetitive strain injury (RSI), for orthopaedic surgeons this was evidence of organic damage to the muscles, for patients this was techniques of relieving the pain (cf. Arksey 1998). Fourthly, for certain forms of science to be done, the social world must be accommodating: patients must offer themselves up as obedient clinical trial subjects. Science is thus, under certain circumstances, dependent upon the appropriate conduct of publics. Fifthly, science is not treated as a unitary body: it is internally fractured and certain factions within it can be 'recruited' by movements – in the case of RSI, this was physiotherapists and osteopaths. Note that these are likely to be more 'practice-oriented' professionals not so interested in abstract scientific knowledge. Finally, those of the movement who do become 'lay experts' can come to be seen as divorced from the movement – as being more involved in the concerns of scientific institutions than in those of the movement.

These six observations can be recast in terms of Wynne's analysis of public–science interactions, especially in relation to his focus upon issues of trust and social identity. What we see are shifting identities and alignments of trust. Movements trust some parts of science, science trusts some parts of the movements. The identity of both science and movement is thus not uniform but multiple. Those scientists who 'go over' to the movement risk being seen as no longer trustworthy, as abandoning their identities as 'proper scientists'. Those activists who 'go over' to scientific institutions risk being seen as no longer trustworthy, as abandoning their identities as 'proper members of the movement'. Where publics are the 'object' of scientific study, they must be trusted to retain their identity as 'obedient subjects'; but to do this they must trust scientific institutions to be working in their best interests. That this is the case can depend on the hybrid identities of 'lay scientists' (activists who become schooled in science, and scientists who become schooled in the social exigencies of a particular medical condition). These mediate between scientific and lay constituencies and, to do this successfully, they must be trusted.

In summary, here we see the complex, shifting patterns of trust and identity through which science–public relations are played out. More generally, we see that we are no longer dealing in the 'public understanding of science' *per se*. Rather, the focus of attention has shifted from the cognitive (what is known) to the contextual (the cultural conditions in which trust and identity shape the relations between science and public).

Conclusion

This chapter has taken us rapidly from the notion that the general public operates within an absence of knowledge and understanding to the suggestion of more complex social and cultural interactions between *communities, knowledge and context*. Whereas the questionnaire method suggests that it is possible to gain useful insights from the study of individual members of the public, the ethnographic perspective characteristically emphasizes the more contextual (and contextually shared) dimensions at work. While the questionnaire approach has been open to criticism for its over-abstracted and 'science-led' perspective on issues, the 'contextual' perspective has attempted to capture the wider dynamics of science–public interaction, especially the importance of cultural identity. The ethnographic turn has also broadened considerably our definition of what counts as 'legitimate knowledge' and, indeed, as a 'legitimate knowledge broker'. In both of the case studies, forms of local knowledge, citizen science (Irwin 1995) and lay epistemology have come to the fore. As in the sheepfarmer case study, lay people become experts in areas of everyday experience. As in that case also, experts have potentially much to learn from 'citizen scientists'.

As has already been emphasized, we have only been able to present two case studies in this chapter as a means of establishing our general point. However, other cases could certainly be used to supplement and extend this analysis. Thus, Françoise Zonabend has conducted an ethnographic analysis of those who live and work at a nuclear facility in Normandy, France (Zonabend 1993). Zonabend explores the relationship between a 'nuclear community' and the varying construction of both the technology and its risks. While local residents might view the nuclear plant as an alien presence, workers typically see the plant in very different terms: as under their personal control, as the focus of a whole repertoire of strategies and everyday practices. Once again, our attention is drawn to the specific cultural conditions within which different 'publics' make sense of science and technology. Rather than being presented as a series of isolated individuals responding uniquely to science, Zonabend reminds us of the significance of cultural identity and of the resourcefulness of different social groups in reconstructing social and technical systems.

As a second brief illustration of this wider international literature, Phil Brown and Edwin J. Mikkelsen's study of a community near Boston, Massachusetts, facing up to toxic waste contamination deserves particular mention (Brown and Mikkelsen 1990/1997). Brown and Mikkelsen place the town of Woburn in its unique context but also link this study to other US cases of toxic waste contamination and community activism. Especially prominent in Brown's work is the notion of 'popular epidemiology'. Originally developed to describe residents' efforts at another waste site – Love Canal – popular epidemiology is 'the process by which laypersons gather scientific data and other information and direct and marshal the knowledge and resources of experts to understand the epidemiology of disease' (Brown and Mikkelsen 1990/1997: 125–6). In the case of Woburn, Massachusetts, this has involved a long fight by local people to have community health problems taken seriously. As in the earlier case by Epstein, communities can both initiate research and inquiries of their own – often in the face of official scepticism and antagonism – and form new alliances with 'experts'. As Brown and Mikkelsen present this, such knowledge-making is built around the concerns and perceptions of local people themselves: so that the prime motivation is 'public health significance' (i.e. what could this mean for our families?) rather than (for them) the abstract notion of 'statistical significance' (which can serve to protect industry until an overwhelming body of evidence has been accumulated).

Throughout this community study, attention is drawn to the dual process of building a local social movement and a popular epidemiology. Once again, this account of local people's perseverance and determination, set in the context of a childhood leukaemia cluster and strained relations between different agencies, presents a very different picture to that offered by traditional PUS survey research. In particular, and rather than being presented as a neutral activity, science becomes both an obstacle *and* a potential source of local support (a theme also developed by Beck 1992). However, for this beneficial effect to occur, 'publics' must battle against the essentially conservative and 'pro-establishment' tendencies of scientific institutions. In this way, as often in the ethnographic literature, we are presented with an inversion of the conventional PUS model. Public groups become the key agent confronting scientific institutions reluctant to take meaningful action. Rather than problematizing the 'public understanding of science', the 'scientific understanding of the public' becomes the real barrier to change.

Taking these cases together, none of this suggests that the 'ethnographic turn' is unproblematic. Thus, the general emphasis on 'context and community' can risk a romanticization of lay people and their relationship to expertise. There can also be something rather too crude in the occasional suggestion that 'science' and 'the public' inevitably work in opposition to one another. As the AIDS case implied, more subtle relations are in operation between sometimes knowledgeable publics and experts who are themselves also members of the public. As the medical domain illustrates so regularly, at a time when access to the internet can quickly turn an uninformed citizen into a 'citizen scientist', it makes little sense to maintain a rigid expert/public dichotomy. Equally, and at a time of rapid technical change, it is reasonable to suggest that scientific knowledge (concepts of health and disease, energy and ecology) and technological artefacts (whether television, mobile telephones or computers) have become a major constituent of our self-identity. Rather than something being imposed 'from outside' our apparently ringfenced communities, science and technology have become an essential element in the very constitution of society.

Meanwhile, and though the stories of Cumbrian sheepfarmers and AIDS activists represent a powerful counterblast to the deficit theory, they can reasonably be presented as by definition atypical. What happens when members of the public do not constitute a shared community or when they are confronted with issues outside their previous experience? The very notion of 'community' may also conceal divisions and disagreements among members of the public in their response to technical concerns (and especially to risks). In Wynne's research, a rather unitary portrayal of the 'farming community' is presented. However, British experience of the 2001 foot and mouth crisis suggests a much more divergent pattern of response.

At this point, we must consider where these ethnographic studies fit within wider, more social-theoretical discussions of such claimed phenomena as globalization, risk and self-identity. As mentioned briefly at the start of this chapter, PUS research has developed at some distance from social theory. Typically, PUS has adopted a very empirical and grounded perspective, rather than seeking to make larger claims about the character of modernity, the changing political economy of science and the nature of contemporary citizenship. In Chapter 4, we turn to a discussion of social theory to assess its implications for the relationship between science and the publics.

Before considering theoretical matters, however, it is important that we consider the relationship between PUS issues and questions of governance. As we have emphasized at several points, this multidiscipline has been heavily influenced by the perceived need to engage politically and socially with problems of public response to science and technology. To what extent has the research reviewed in this chapter changed practical policy making? How, in turn, has the development of policy changed this field of research? In Chapter 3, we turn to the relationship between PUS research and scientific governance.

3 Science and public policy: from government to governance

The previous chapter traced the development of public understanding of science research from the deficit approach through to the 'ethnographic turn'. Along the way, we suggested that the 'multidiscipline of PUS' (to employ a rather ugly phrase) has been driven as much by practical concerns as by academic curiosity. Faced with apparent resistance to technical change in areas such as biotechnology, nuclear power and food safety, institutions have consulted and sponsored PUS research in the hope that it can generate new practical possibilities in dealing with the wider publics.

It is not too difficult to see the questionnaire approach as fitting comfortably with the worldview of scientific institutions inclined to believe that public mistrust must be generated by public ignorance (and, equally, that 'to know science is to love it'). The 'solutions' to public ignorance and misinformation – typically in the form of more energetic dissemination of scientific information – do not threaten scientific institutions' self-perceptions or operating assumptions. It is for this reason that the very label 'PUS' is for many (including, as we will see, those at a senior governmental level) synonymous with the deficit notion of the public as a target for active scientific dissemination. At a cognitive level, such a perspective implies that, while science needs to be 'communicated' to public groups, the rational basis for science policy should remain 'best science'. Accordingly, and while it is essential for scientific thinking to be explained to uninformed members of the public, the decision-making process itself is effectively insulated from public concerns and demands.

Certainly, much of the qualitative research referenced in the previous chapter was developed with the intention of challenging *both* the intellectual framework of the deficit theory *and* the policy/political assumptions which followed from this (see, for example, Irwin 1995). Thus, it has been axiomatic for qualitative research in this area that it should engage 'symmetrically' with both scientific and public constructions of issues rather than simply assuming that science was rational (and public views correspondingly irrational). The immediate practical consequence of this academic perspective is to open up the assumptions and working practices of government and industry to the same scrutiny that has previously been applied to public groups. This, in turn, raises key questions for the relationship between science and the publics – all of which point to the need for more open and two-way communications rather than the traditional 'top-down' (or expert-driven) approach. Certainly, such a conclusion follows quite explicitly from Wynne's sheepfarmer case study in the previous chapter.

The qualitative approach, therefore, suggests a series of important concepts for scientific policy – even if their application is less straightforward. Expressed in summary form, these policy implications from the 'ethnographic turn' include the need to recognize:

- the multiplicity and diversity of the publics;
- the knowledgeability and 'local expertise' of lay groups;
- the limitations of technical knowledge when applied to new settings;
- the legitimacy of public concerns and questions;
- the importance of values, ethics and prior experience;
- the requirement for more open and two-way communication, including the communication of scientific uncertainty;
- the fundamental importance of self-critical and reflexive institutional processes.

However, and far from representing an end point to policy debate, such recommendations raise an important set of questions concerning *how* existing policy processes are to alter and *whether* such an approach might actually improve science–public relations. It is this set of issues that will be considered here. As we will suggest, at the heart of current scientific policy discussions is a debate over, on the one hand, the status and applicability of scientific knowledge and, on the other, the changing definition and character of citizenship (especially of what we can term 'scientific citizenship'). As has been suggested, the discussion of these issues draws strongly upon social scientific research into the public understanding of science and technology (even if it often does so in a partial and under-acknowledged fashion). By the end of this chapter, we will be able to take initial stock of the emerging challenges to scientific governance as new issues come onto the social and institutional agenda.

Now, it needs to be quickly stated that these questions are by no means new. There has been a literature since at least the 1970s exploring the relationship between science and democracy (e.g. Nelkin 1975) and (going back even further) between scientific advice and public policy (e.g. Price 1967). However, the experience of public and scientific controversies during the 1990s – and particularly an awareness of problems of science–public relations – has helped create a new climate for questions of scientific governance and public engagement with science policy. In this chapter, we will map some of these changes and consider their implications. We start with a brief review of recent science–policy relations.

Science and the policy process: democracy or technocracy?

Put very simply, the relationship between science and the policy process can be seen as offering a fundamental choice. The *technocratic perspective* suggests that decisions should be made on the basis of 'best science'. Faced with highly complex technical questions, the only rational way forward is to let the experts decide. How can members of the general public reach suitably informed decisions about the safety of genetically modified organisms or the rate of decay for nuclear wastes? Of course, this technocratic perspective fits well with the conventional deficit model of an ignorant and uninformed public.

The alternative approach, the *democratic perspective*, argues very differently. Given that technical decisions such as those over GM foods or nuclear waste management are likely to have a substantial effect on people, surely it is only right that the public should have a powerful say in decision making? Certainly, it is a taken-for-granted principle in many societies that people have a right to influence decisions which might directly affect their safety and well-being. At the same time, the democratic perspective suggests the need to keep technical experts in check lest human liberty and choice are eroded.

In practice, national decision-making systems have tended not to fall so simply into either the 'technocracy' or 'democracy' camps. Instead, a mixture of both elements has generally been present. However, and as we will suggest in this section, at the core of both these policy styles has been a heavy emphasis on technical expertise and a reluctance to take lay knowledge seriously within institutional processes. Even more pluralistic and 'open' policy styles (as identified in the USA during the 1980s; Brickman *et al.* 1985) have tended to build upon a rather restricted definition of expertise. Meanwhile, more closed systems (such as the traditional UK approach) have operated at a very considerable distance from the lay locals discussed in the previous chapter. As we argue more generally in this book, both 'democratic' and 'technocratic' approaches need revision in the light of changing developments in this field.

If we start by considering the recent history of UK science policy, commentators during the 1980s tended to characterize the UK 'regulatory style' as being distinctive in a number of ways – especially in comparison to the US approach to regulatory and environmental decision making. As Vogel, for example, presented this in 1986, the UK approach to environmental regulation was seen to be flexible and informal, based on cooperative links to industry and relatively free of controls set by central government. Commentators have also emphasized the importance of expert advisory committees for scientific policy making and, at the same time, the closedness of such bodies to external scrutiny. As one study of the British control of chemical carcinogens (cancer-causing chemicals) noted in the early 1980s (Irwin and Green 1983), none of the relevant advisory bodies published transcripts of their deliberations, nor did they produce minutes nor even agenda, although some did publish a proportion of their reviews. Overall, the regulatory system was characterized as operating on a highly confidential basis, with important consequences for viable public participation.

This regulatory style was typically defended by insiders on the grounds that the closedness of the system permitted a flexible approach that could be highly responsive to new scientific evidence and findings. Increased public scrutiny and engagement would lead to a cumbersome process and might also undermine the 'expert' character of decision making. As one spokesperson for British pesticide manufacturers put it in 1981 (quoted in Irwin and Green 1983), wider participation in decision making must be opposed since such questions should be settled by 'objective and impartial experts looking at scientific facts and scientific facts alone'. In this context, collective bargaining 'could spell the end of our superb safety record'. The perceived strength of the UK regulatory and decision-making style was that it could engage rapidly and open-mindedly with scientific facts without the burden of public scrutiny and the rigidities imposed by external justification. Of course, this policy style fitted well with the 'deficit' approach to public understanding of science. Equally, an important premise for the whole regulatory system was that scientific facts could be straightforwardly separated from cultural and contextual factors of the kind discussed in the previous chapter.

Now, it would be wrong to suggest that every developed country has followed the same pattern of science–public relations. Vogel's 1986 study, for example, suggested important differences between British and US 'national styles' of regulation. Thus, Vogel observed the more pluralistic and open tradition of scientific government in the USA. Aided by the Freedom of Information Act, a plethora of environmentalist and consumer groups was able to challenge government policy at every stage:

> Over the last fifteen years American environmental organizations have acquired extensive rights to information about various public policies, the right to challenge a wide variety of administrative decisions in the courts, and the right to be heard in various administrative proceedings. British environmental organizations, by contrast, possess remarkably few rights. The information they receive from government officials . . . remains extremely limited.
>
> (Vogel 1986: 175)

In a study of road traffic safety published in the mid-1980s (Irwin 1985), a strong contrast was drawn between the 'closed but consensual' style of decision making in Britain (where a restricted group of experts, civil servants, established pressure groups and industrialists could heavily influence policy) and the 'open but adversarial' style of US decision making (where much greater freedom of information was linked to very protracted disputes over rule-making). Within this situation, there was a tendency for British critics to look to the US as a more open and participatory system (as exemplified by, for instance, the US Freedom of Information Act; Millstone 1986). Meanwhile, US academics such as Vogel appeared to admire the efficiency and effectiveness of the less public and entrenched British policy style.

In making this important contrast, however, the similarities as well as differences between the two national styles must be noted. In this case, the power of the automobile industry was roughly equivalent across the two nations and this proved at least as significant as the policy differences. Thus, road traffic safety measures in both countries were typically built around the motor vehicle rather than suggesting more radical transport alternatives. What must also be emphasized is that scientific advice was still highly important even within more adversarial and open policy processes. In particular, public hearings tended to become a battle between competing technical assessments rather than an opportunity for more diverse voices to be heard. Although the US process might be more 'public', the underlying model of 'scientific citizenship' remained very restrictive. In both nations, the wider citizenry played an essentially passive role within the policy process.

In her 1990 study of 'science advisers as policymakers', Sheila Jasanoff acknowledges the pluralistic character of the US process. At the same time, she emphasizes the importance of scientific advice to policy. By the late 1980s, scientific advisory committees had become an indispensable feature of the US political landscape. However, and while the conventional technocratic perspective suggests that science simply 'speaks truth to power', Jasanoff traces the more complex processes of negotiation, reconstruction and boundary work which allow scientific advisory committees to conduct their business:

> The notion that scientific advisers can or do limit themselves to addressing purely scientific issues ... seems fundamentally misconceived ... Rather, the advisory process seems increasingly important as a locus for negotiating scientific differences that carry political weight.
>
> (Jasanoff 1990: 249)

Jasanoff paid special attention to the phenomenon of 'regulatory science': forms of knowledge and understanding developed in response to the requirements of government and industry in the context of the regulatory process.

She also drew a particular contrast between research science and regulatory science. While research science seeks 'truths' of originality and significance, regulatory science has as its goal the development of truths relevant to policy. While the former is conducted by universities, the latter is driven by industry and government. The time-frame for the former is characteristically open-ended, whereas that for the latter is generally set by political pressures and the regulatory agenda. In this way, Jasanoff reinforces the significance of scientific advice for the policy process but also emphasizes that, far from meeting the technocratic ideal, more subtle processes of social negotiation and knowledge development are at work:

> in regulatory science, more even than in research science, there can be no perfect, objectively verifiable truth. The most one can hope for is a serviceable truth: a state of knowledge that satisfies tests of scientific acceptability and supports reasoned decisionmaking, but also assures those exposed to risk that their interests have not been sacrificed on the altar of an impossible scientific certainty.
>
> (Jasanoff 1990: 250)

However, and as a subsequent European study of regulatory science has suggested (Rothstein *et al.* 1999), one consequence of the restricted world of regulatory science is that wider public groups are effectively excluded from discussion. On the one hand, most regulatory science is conducted in the private sector. On the other, the limited peer review and the intricacies of the regulatory process mean that even external scrutiny becomes very restricted. Calls for greater 'democracy', therefore, need at the very least to take account of this technical and institutional nexus. In particular, 'participation' in this complex domain has very restricted significance without appropriate skills and expertise.

The study of regulatory science also suggests that both innovation and regulatory demands are increasingly *global* in character (Irwin and Rothstein 2003). This means that, for example, in Europe, national governments must harmonize their regulatory requirements and recognize that regulatory frameworks can no longer be simply national. This is partly a response to the global character of many of the operating companies – so that in areas such as pesticides development, the larger corporations are transnational in character and sell their products across many different countries. In turn, national governments must recognize that they are part of a larger pattern of international trade and exchange. This, then, has major consequences for the notion of 'national regulatory systems', since countries cannot operate in an entirely independent manner. Meanwhile, globalization places new demands on scientific evidence and on the relationship between science and public knowledge.

This section has given a brief background to the contemporary debate over science, the publics and policy making. Based on discussions in the 1980s and early 1990s, we have seen something of the alternative 'policy styles' that have been identified. We have also suggested the restricted definition of scientific citizenship within most policy debates – even those which can claim to be 'open' in character. At the same time, Jasanoff's work reinforces the point that science is not removed from the institutional setting in which it operates. The phenomenon of regulatory science indicates (as we also saw in the previous chapter) that knowledge claims operate within particular *contexts* of sponsorship and enactment. In this way also, scientific advice can never function according to the technocratic ideal, since it is inextricably bound up with social and institutional commitments. Equally, conventional calls for greater democracy (while potentially important and helpful) appear naive unless they take full account of the new conditions of scientific and policy development. We have also noted some of the global challenges to regulatory science now being generated. In a world where both science and industry are international in character, what hope is there for the 'lay locals' to make an impact?

In this situation, the policy challenge has been to find new forms of governance which can move us beyond the simple technocratic/democratic division while also, based partly on the PUS research discussed so far, drawing upon more heterogeneous and active understandings of the public. In the next section, we will consider some recent policy discussions that point in this direction. Given recent developments in the UK which have explicitly attempted to address some of these issues while also drawing upon PUS research, we will pay particular attention to that country.

The new agenda for science, the publics and policy making

> Those directly affected by an environmental matter should always have an accepted right to make their views known before a decision is taken about it. Giving them that opportunity is also likely to improve the quality of decisions; drawing on a wider pool of knowledge and understanding (lay as well as professional) can give warning of obstacles which, unless removed or avoided, would impede effective implementation of a particular decision.
>
> (RCEP 1998: 102)

The 1990s witnessed a series of challenges to the characteristic UK regulatory style. The case of mad cow disease (BSE) led to a widespread perception (as expressed, for example, in the 2000 Phillips Report) that not only did a government department provide inappropriate technical advice but also that relations with 'the public' were badly managed. The continuing controversy over genetically modified foods has also led to suggestions that it is no longer appropriate to assume that these matters are simply 'technical' problems but rather that ethical, cultural and economic questions are central to their definition and handling. Meanwhile, a steady stream of social scientific reports has called for a revised approach to scientific decision making under conditions of social and technical uncertainty (for example, within the ESRC Global Environmental Change programme: ESRC 2000). This research has built upon the qualitative perspective on science and the publics so as to develop a critique of conventional technocratic modes of decision making. In this situation, the intellectual and policy climate has moved away from the old orthodoxy based on 'letting the facts decide' and towards at least the recognition of a more open and fluid set of relations between science, policy making and the wider publics.

The focus of this section is on a series of official publications and initiatives which have appeared in the UK since the late 1990s. Taken together, these suggest a substantial shift in governmental thinking about the relationship between science, the wider publics and policy making. Accordingly, several key reports and policy initiatives will be discussed. The intention is not to summarize these – or to give a full chronology – but instead to draw out the main issues and areas of debate. In particular, we will explore the relationship between these policy discussions and PUS research. We will also identify critical issues as we move from traditional notions of national government to a broader sense of *governance*.

One of the more significant UK official publications in this area during the late 1990s was the Royal Commission on Environmental Pollution's 21st report on *Setting Environmental Standards* (RCEP 1998). Since environmental standards are a key, and sometimes highly controversial, focus for issues of science and governance, the Royal Commission's objective of identifying a 'more consistent and robust basis for setting standards for environmental protection' (p. 1) is highly relevant to our discussion. As the report observed: 'There are various tensions within the present system of environmental regulation. Doubts have been voiced about the objectivity and adequacy of its scientific basis' (pp. 1–2). The Royal Commission noted, among other things, the increased influence of non-governmental organizations (NGOs) within environmental standard setting and the fact that most UK environmental legislation now has its origin in European institutions. The report's main concern, however, was with the relationship between scientific appraisal, the assessment of risk and uncertainty, and the articulation of public values.

In terms of scientific understanding, the report argued that science must be the 'essential basis' for environmental standards. However, and in line with the conclusions from various social scientific investigations, it was noted that relevant data are often absent and such data as exist are often very uncertain. As the Royal Commission observes, there are numerous sources of error in assessing environmental pathways and exposures. For example, behaviour of a pollutant in one location does not necessarily guarantee the same behaviour in another (as suggested also by Wynne's study in the previous chapter) and the form in which a substance is released is not necessarily that in which it remains. Such issues have certainly been to the fore in the scientific assessment of the environmental implications of GM crops. For the Commission, the implication is that hard questions need to be asked about particular forms of scientific evidence: Are uncertainties and limitations in the data being properly recognized? Does the science provide a firm basis for decision making?

> Scientific assessments should indicate where the boundaries of knowledge lie. To be helpful to policy-makers they should indicate clearly both what is known or considered to be indisputable and what is considered to be speculative . . . Transparency should be the watchword in presenting assessments.
>
> (RCEP 1998: 29)

While this commitment to the transparent and critical review of scientific evidence may seem unexceptional, the open discussion of such matters by the Royal Commission represented at least the attempt to engage with non-expert groups concerning the scientific basis of environmental standards. However, we can also see that the Commission was clinging firmly to the notion that certain areas of scientific understanding are 'indisputable' even if others are 'speculative'.

More radical in terms of the Royal Commission's thinking was its treatment of the wider publics. Echoing our review of PUS research in the previous chapter, the report notes: 'Traditionally, communication of information to the public about risks was seen in terms of the technocratic, or top-down model, in which an expert transmits a message to a non-expert audience' (RCEP 1998: 57). The report argues instead – in direct reflection of the research discussed in Chapter 2 – that risk communication should be seen as a much more complex and two-way process. In particular, 'People's reactions to information about risks are considerably influenced by the circumstances in which it is presented to them' (p. 58). The report also emphasized that scientific uncertainties should be openly acknowledged rather than glossed over, and that trust can only be built up through 'open and honest communication over a continuous period'.

The most noteworthy aspect of the Royal Commission Report was its treatment of 'articulating values'. In a sharp move away from the previous conventional wisdom of 'sticking to the facts', the report suggests that values are 'an essential element in decisions about environmental policies and standards'. These values represent 'beliefs, either individual or social, about what is important in life, and thus about the objectives which should govern and shape public policies' (p. 101). Such environmental and social values are not necessarily 'preformed or fixed' but for many people 'emerge out of debate, discussion and challenge, as they encounter new facts, insights and judgements contributed by others'. The report distinguishes also between 'people's values' and 'the interests of stakeholders'. This formulation of values as being contextually generated owes a major debt to qualitative work on PUS.

At this point, the report presents four familiar methods of capturing people's values with regard to environmental issues: public opinion surveys, consultation exercises, public inquiries, parliamentary procedures. *Public opinion surveys* are dismissed as being incapable of providing useful information about values. *Consultation exercises* are seen as operating within the stakeholder model (i.e. they typically include only those who have already expressed a direct interest in an issue) but could be used to draw in wider audiences. However, the report makes the crucial point here that the 'contribution a consultation exercise makes to opening up decision making depends on prior decisions about its scope . . . Exclusion from the initial framing of the problem disempowers people' (p. 103). *Public inquiries* are useful in settling differences between interests but do not necessarily elicit deeper values and concerns. *Parliaments* are seen as having a significant influence on environmental standard setting but it is concluded that 'governments should use more direct methods to ensure that people's values, along with lay knowledge and understanding, are articulated and taken into account alongside technical and scientific considerations' (p. 104).

In discussion of more effective procedures for articulating values, the report argues that values should indeed be seen as an 'essential' aspect of the standard-setting process but that 'traditional' forms of consultation are not adequate for this task. Suggested methods for articulating values include focus groups, citizens' juries, consensus conferences and deliberative polls. Lay membership of expert bodies is also discussed, although it is noted that: 'Appointment of lay members is certainly not a substitute for making expert bodies more transparent and open in their working methods. The real requirement is that expert bodies themselves should develop a sensitivity to questions of values' (p. 109).

Finally, the report looks ahead to a more robust basis for environmental standards. At this point, the 'apparent erosion of public trust in environmental regulation' is highlighted. Among various points made by the Royal Commission, the following are especially significant:

- the need to indicate clearly the 'boundaries of knowledge' so as to avoid 'spurious accuracy';
- the recognition of 'human factors' within the assessment process;

- linked to this, risk communication should 'begin at the outset and inform the framing of the assessment' (p. 114);
- underlying assumptions and limitations of analysis should be clearly presented to decision makers;
- the need for 'openness and transparency' in all aspects of environmental management.

> A basic requirement for public trust which is not in general met at present is that the bodies setting environmental standards must operate in an open and transparent way. By 'transparent' we mean that there must be full publicity for their existence, their terms of reference, the decisions they take and the reasons for them. By 'open' we mean that there must be adequate opportunities for those outside an institution, especially those with a particular interest in a given decision, to contribute fully to the decision-making procedure.
>
> (RCEP 1998: 124)

Towards the end of the Royal Commission Report, an explicit link is made to the field of public understanding of science, but in a manner which suggests the lingering influence of the deficit approach:

> In the last decade, great efforts have been made to increase public understanding of science both through the media and through mechanisms such as public meetings and science fairs. Initiatives of this kind should be continued and extended, with the aim of reducing or eliminating distortions which enter into the environmental debate, especially about what science has to offer. There should be a long-term programme of public education, extending across all ages, about the true nature of our understanding of the environment and its management.
>
> (RCEP 1998: 127)

While undoubtedly representing a significant change from the previous UK orthodoxy of 'leaving it to the experts', a tension can be identified in the Royal Commission Report between the call for public engagement and the emphasis given to scientific evidence. Thus, and although the importance of public knowledge and understanding is acknowledged, the challenge is to find ways of reconciling public and scientific views within the policy process. The clear implication is that, while public values are highly important, these will only be expressed within the frameworks devised through scientific understanding – suggesting at best a secondary role for public assessments and evaluations within policy making.

The RCEP Report certainly drew upon a critical reading of the PUS literature – even if the document also attempts to incorporate both a deficit and a more ethnographic approach. A second report which provides further evidence of the changing social climate for science–public relations (and of the growing influence of PUS research) was produced by the House of Lords Select Committee on Science and Technology in February 2000. This report had a much wider scope than the Royal Commission on Environmental Pollution, as its title *Science and Society* implies. However, similar themes can be immediately identified, especially with regard to public trust and confidence in scientific developments. More generally, this report suggests an even greater acceptance of the ethnographic and qualitative approach.

Similar to the Royal Commission Report is the significance accorded to values by the Lords Select Committee: 'Policy makers will find it hard to win public support on any issue with a science component, unless the public's attitudes and values are recognised, respected and weighed along with the scientific and other factors' (p. 6). In parallel with this, the Lords report stresses the 'new mood for dialogue' over science and technology. On the one hand, a whole range of practical activities is reviewed, including focus groups, internet dialogues and local consultations. On the other, these are presented as 'isolated events, and no substitute for genuine changes in the cultures and constitutions of key decision-making institutions' (p. 7). Overall, the Lords report views science's relationship with British society as being 'under strain'. The only constructive response is greater dialogue. This can be achieved through:

- public understanding of science activities;
- improved communication of uncertainty and risk;
- changing the culture of policy making 'so that it becomes normal to bring science and the public into dialogue about new developments at an early stage' (p. 13).

With specific regard to the language of 'public understanding of science', the report expressed its concerns that such terminology might express (to quote the government's Chief Scientific Adviser) a 'rather backward-looking vision' (p. 25) or be what the British Council termed 'outmoded and potentially disastrous' (p. 25). The report noted the argument that 'PUS' seemed to blame the ignorance and misunderstanding of the public for any problems now being encountered. For that reason, the report preferred to adopt the phrase 'science and society' 'because it implies dialogue, in a way that "public understanding of science" does not' (p. 27).

The Lords Report on *Science and Society* was followed by the Department of Trade and Industry (2000) White Paper on *Excellence and Opportunity: A Science and Innovation Policy for the 21st Century*. As the Secretary of State's foreword emphasized, this report was very much about the possibilities for science-led economic growth. However, 'confident consumers' were presented as an essential part of this process: 'as the debate on GM food has shown, consumers will only buy new products which they trust. People rightly expect proper safeguards against potential public risks and full information on the implications of scientific developments' (p. ii).

Once again, the new agenda of transparency and openness, public dialogue and active communication is very apparent. Consumers are presented as 'agents in the process of innovation'. The government's role is to spread the benefits of innovation as widely as possible while also 'assuring consumers that the highest possible standards of safety are being adhered to' (p. 49). Although expert scientific advisory committees are 'absolutely essential to our society', it is also stated that 'science is too important to be left only to the scientists. Their knowledge, and their assessment of risks, is only one dimension of the challenge for society. When science raises profound ethical and social issues, the whole of society needs to take part in the debate' (p. 54).

On that basis, the British Government has established new strategic bodies with representatives from a range of interested parties and a remit to facilitate public debate (for example, the Human Genetics Commission and the Agriculture and Environment Biotechnology Commission). At the same time, a code of practice has been developed which scientific advisory committees are expected to follow. As subsequently revised for the second round of consultation in Spring 2001, this code of practice once again emphasized transparency and openness (Office of Science and Technology 2001).

Published alongside the 2000 White Paper were the Chief Scientific Adviser's guidelines on scientific advice and policy making, which advocated three key messages to government departments:

- think ahead and identify early the issues on which they need scientific advice;
- get a wide range of advice from the best sources, particularly when there is scientific uncertainty; and
- publish the scientific advice and all relevant papers.
(Office of Science and Technology 2000: 1)

The more negative case for such an approach was provided at the end of 2000 by the Phillips Report on mad cow disease (BSE) in the UK. Among the various, diplomatically worded criticisms made by this official inquiry, one major identified problem concerned the relationship between governmental reassurances of safety and the declining public trust in such statements. As the report concluded, the government did not actually lie to the public about the risks of beef consumption. However, it was so preoccupied with preventing an alarmist over-reaction that it undertook a major campaign of reassurance. As a direct consequence, '[w]hen on 20 March 1996 the Government announced that BSE had probably been transmitted to humans, the public felt that they

rayed. Confidence in public pronouncements about risk was a
ty of BSE' (Phillips Report 2000: xviii). It would appear that at the
mment activity in this area – and especially of the communication of risk – was a 'consuming fear of provoking an irrational public scare' (p.
264). In the case of BSE, this fear of public response led to a characteristic
denial of risk and a very British concern among officials not to 'rock the boat'
when presenting public information.

As the Chief Scientific Adviser, Sir Robert May, is quoted in the Phillips
Report: 'My view is strongly that . . . the full messy process whereby scientific
understanding is arrived at with all its problems has to be spilled out into the
open' (p. 265). Certainly, the Phillips Report served as a timely reminder of the
problems faced by the traditional British approach to scientific governance
and, especially when taken together with 2000's other main reports in this
area (the Lords Select Committee and the science and innovation White
Paper), provided further evidence of the changing climate for governmental
activities in this field.

Meanwhile, it is not just UK policy making that has been taking this new
line on scientific advice and policy making. Similar discussions are taking
place across Western Europe, with Denmark, The Netherlands and Sweden
especially prominent examples. The European Commission, long criticized for
its technocratic approach to policy making, has started to address matters of
scientific governance in very similar terms. At the end of 2000, and as part of
the White Paper on European Governance, a Commission Working Group was
established on 'democratising expertise and establishing European scientific
references'. Main issues for consideration by this group included the management of a plurality of expertise, ensuring its independence, increasing its
accountability and examining how the greater transparency of expertise can
'improve the legitimacy of decisions and, eventually, their social acceptance'.
As the working group described its remit – and in terms very similar to those of
the House of Lords:

> Be it genetically modified food, nuclear waste management or medical
> advances, science and technology are shaping our lives. However,
> such developments appear to evade political control. Science and tech-
> nology are playing an ever more important role in public policies . . .
> While Europeans are demanding more involvement in decisions that
> concern them, the answers on scientific issues are given by a scientific
> elite. So how can we make scientific expertise more democratic and
> enable citizens to participate in public decision-making process
> touching on scientific issues? This working group will propose pro-
> cedures for a meaningful dialogue between experts and citizens in
> areas where scientific evidence is a key component of policy decisions.
>
> (European Commission 2000)

In 2002, the European Commission produced its Action Plan on Science and Society (European Commission 2002). In many ways, the chapter headings within this document tell us all we need to know about the new policy paradigm: 'Science and society: towards a new partnership'; 'Promoting scientific education and culture in Europe'; 'A science policy closer to citizens'; 'Responsible science at the heart of policy making'; 'Maintaining the momentum'. Specific actions proposed by the Commission include the establishment of an 'open dialogue' over the new technologies, the creation of guidelines for the use of expertise at Community level, the development of an information 'observatory' to track ethical debates and best practice across Europe. As the Commission document concludes: 'The proposed action plan marks the beginning of a long process, the objective of which is to change the relationship between science and society' (p. 27).

All of the reports reviewed here trace a link back to PUS research. This is especially explicit with the House of Lords Select Committee, where the two main advisors were researchers in this field (both quoted in the previous chapter: John Durant and Brian Wynne) and several cross-references are made within the report. This represents a major change from the general climate of discussion even as recently as the mid-1990s. For qualitative researchers who began their work in opposition to the then conventional wisdom of deficit models and quantitative surveys, this represents a dramatic shift.

However, and very importantly, it is also possible to see a tension running through these documents concerning the relationship between science and its publics. On the one hand, there is a general emphasis on inclusion, openness and public values. On the other, there is a tendency to retreat to more technocratic and 'top-down' models. While there is indeed an expressed willingness (indeed enthusiasm), especially at UK and European Commission levels, to adopt many of the recommendations from recent qualitative research, this does not mean that the previous emphasis on 'sound science' has been abandoned. It is especially noticeable in the Royal Commission Report that there are two separate voices being expressed. While one voice argues for greater inclusion and a sophisticated treatment of the publics, the other retains more traditional notions of 'best expertise' and 'public education'. In this, the Royal Commission – like many other official publications – reflects the fact that the deficit notion of the public is still a lingering element within institutional practice. Equally, it must be remembered that cases such as GM food and BSE represent decidedly atypical examples of official practice – in many ways, far removed from more routine (and less publicly challenged) areas of policy activity.

From deficit to dialogue: new themes and issues

What underlying messages for the relationship between science and its publics emerge from these reports? The UK Government response to the House of Lords Report on *Science and Society* summarized the key issues as follows:

- 'the need to create a new culture of dialogue between scientists and the public;
- the need to heed public values and attitudes;
- a perceived crisis of public trust in scientific advice to Government;
- the need for all advisory and decision making bodies in areas involving science to adopt an open and transparent approach to their work; and
- the need for scientists and the media to work constructively with each other.'

(Department of Trade and Industry, undated, p. 1)

In terms of the two key issues raised at the beginning of this chapter, concerning scientific knowledge on the one hand and citizenship on the other, we can identify several points. With regard to the status and applicability of scientific knowledge, these documents suggest an acknowledgement of both the significance and limitations of science in areas of social and technical uncertainty, but also the need for scientific governance to be informed by the values of the wider publics. Put differently, science is seen to be necessary but not in itself sufficient. Sound science remains essential – but not sound science alone.

In terms of citizenship, there appears to be a broad acceptance of the wider importance of citizens within decision making – and especially of the significance of public values. 'Dialogue' is preferred over one-way communication. Without public support, innovation cannot take place. Trust in scientific institutions becomes a central dimension of governance. Trust can only be developed through greater transparency, openness and two-way communication. The public has in some way become an essential ingredient within scientific governance.

This emerging approach clearly draws substantially (if also partially) upon previous social scientific research of the kind discussed in the latter part of Chapter 2. Engagement, dialogue and the multiple publics have become watchwords of this new approach, while the deficit model is widely dismissed (at least in principle if not in practice). In that way, it is difficult for social scientists to criticize an approach which builds so heavily upon their own earlier criticisms of the closed and expert-dominated system. However, the new agenda raises many issues and questions:

- How can these general objectives and broad rhetoric translate into specific forms of practice? To focus on the House of Lords and European Commission Reports, the language of 'science and society' may represent a step forward from the deficit-based assumptions embedded in 'public understanding of science'. However, such terminology is also very abstract and non-specific. What does (or should) 'open dialogue' involve? How widely will this be practised?
- More particularly, in what specific ways can science and public values be reconciled? While it may be true that these elements are not necessarily contradictory to one another, the possibilities for disagreement cannot be ignored (as, for example, in the GM food debate). Certainly, the promotion of public assessments to the same status as science raises further questions about the compatibility and practical relationship between such terms.
- Linked to that point, it is implicit in these official statements that a boundary (or 'firewall') can be maintained between scientific analysis and public evaluation. These are routinely presented as essential but *separate* processes. Meanwhile, the sociology of scientific knowledge has suggested that cultural assumptions and professional judgements form an integral part of scientific assessments. This strongly suggests that no firewall between 'science' and 'society' can be established.
- One important influence which such documents generally downplay is that of global capitalism. Closely linked to this, the abiding governmental commitment to scientific innovation should not be ignored (at least for the majority of nations). As we have previously suggested, national governments – or even international bodies such as the European Union – cannot isolate themselves from global pressures towards economic competitiveness and industrial development. Public dialogue over science and technology must therefore be seen in a wider context of international corporate strategy and governmental commitment to economic growth.
- Finally for now, we suggest that, while social scientific studies of the public understanding of science have served an important role in highlighting issues of trust and public values, the reception of this research by policy audiences remains partial. Thus, and despite talk of 'public values', notions of popular epidemiology and citizen science are typically downplayed – and are seen as secondary to scientific forms of understanding. Equally, the tendency remains to view 'science' and 'society' as being in dialogue, rather than acknowledging the polycentric, shifting and mutifaceted character of both science and society. Trust likewise is regularly presented as a fixed entity rather than a more fluid set of social relations.

In this chapter so far, we have both offered an introduction to science and public policy and seen something of the partial incorporation of PUS research within the policy process. One obvious question is *why* this research has gained such an audience, especially when qualitative researchers were very much excluded from these processes through the 1980s and most of the 1990s. One immediate answer is that this 'success' can be attributed to a mixture of public controversy (for example, over BSE and GM foods), frustration on the part of key institutions (especially government and industry), a wider change in government styles (towards a general emphasis on the language of inclusion) and (of course) the novelty and persuasiveness of the emerging research perspective. However, it is also important that we take a quick look at some of the practical consequences of this new agenda before reaching any easy conclusions about the impact of social science on policy.

At this point, our review of scientific governance can turn away from broad discussion and general principles towards one particular case of the new agenda in action. To explore some of these issues in practice, we will briefly consider one important UK initiative in 'science and democracy': the Public Consultation on Developments in the Biosciences. Conducted between 1997 and 1999, this government-led exercise aimed to engage with the public about the 'biosciences' (including xenotransplantation, animal and human cloning, GM food and genetic testing). The consultation broke new ground in governmental engagement with the public over scientific issues. However, and as we will discuss, it was also marked by a series of assumptions about scientific democracy that restricted its openness to public concerns and questions (for a fuller account of this case, see Irwin 2001a).

Putting scientific citizenship into practice

In November 1997, the Science Minister announced his intention to hold a public consultation exercise on bioscience issues. The main purpose of the exercise was to identify and explore public hopes and concerns but also to feed these into the policy process. In June 1998, an advisory group to the consultation was appointed with membership from a range of bodies, including the Green Alliance, Wellcome Trust, a key industrial company, a research council and a supermarket chain.

Right from the start, this body was confronted with challenging questions concerning the form and focus of the consultation. At least one member of the group queried the feasibility of maintaining a broad coverage across the biosciences as a whole. Shouldn't issues like GM food be kept apart from medical applications? Could anything useful be concluded about public assessments across such a range of different issues and contexts? Certainly, previous exercises like the *Citizen Foresight* consultation (London Centre for Governance,

Innovation and Science 1998) and Lancaster University's *Uncertain World* report (Grove-White *et al.* 1997) had kept a much narrower focus. For the new exercise, government officials were keen to focus on generic issues and to consider in particular the operation of advisory and regulatory bodies.

Immediately, we can identify the institutional framing of this exercise and its significance. The consultation was designed to feed into the policy process in a very direct fashion. As later became apparent, it was essential for the civil servants involved that the exercise should inform a major policy review of biotechnology regulation which was being simultaneously conducted. On the one hand, this imposed a very tight time-scale on the project, since final results would be needed by April/May 1999. On the other, it gave the consultation an enhanced status, especially when one of the familiar criticisms of public consultation exercises is that they often have limited practical relevance. However, it soon became apparent that government was providing more than a broad framework for the exercise and a time-scale. In October 1998, the minister established several specific aims for the initiative:

- What is the level and nature of people's awareness of technological advances in the biosciences?
- What issues do people see arising from these developments in the biosciences and how important are these compared to other major scientific issues?
- What is the extent of people's knowledge of the oversight and regulatory process in the United Kingdom and Europe?
- What issues do people believe should be taken into account in any oversight of developments in the biosciences?
- What information should be made available to the general public from the regulatory system and about advances in the biosciences?

There are a number of aspects of these questions that deserve our attention. First, it is important to note that they were set by government rather than by those being consulted – and as such they closely mirror the concerns of officials rather than (necessarily) public groups. Secondly, they assume that 'scientific' issues are separable in the public mind from other, perhaps larger, issues (e.g. the social necessity for rapid technological change or the quality of existing food and healthcare provision). Thirdly, they emphasize knowledge and information as if they can be discussed apart from wider questions of institutional legitimacy and public trust. Fourthly, they seem to assume that there is indeed a general awareness of the biosciences as a distinct category – actually, most members of the public initially expressed themselves as quite unfamiliar with such topics. Overall, the minister's questions emphasize the point that the agenda for this consultation was being set by government (and, to a limited degree, the steering group) rather than by the wider publics.

Two further characteristics of the biosciences exercise must be considered. There was great concern within the initiative that the scientific content of briefing materials should be beyond reproach. While this emphasis on 'getting the facts straight' seems very laudable, it does assume that 'scientific facts' can and should be removed from public debate and questioning. Rather than adopting the consensus conference approach of experts undergoing direct cross-examination (so that the public set the agenda), such matters were centrally predetermined. While the Phillips Report (2000) emphasizes the 'messiness' of science–policy relations, the biosciences consultation sought to separate the 'hard facts' from 'public opinion'.

Finally, and perhaps most significantly, it was considered essential that the exercise should generate qualitative *and* quantitative data. In this way, the exercise neatly mirrored both the approaches to PUS discussed in Chapter 2, suggesting also an attempt by government to reach a 'compromise' rather than backing either perspective. Accordingly, the consultation consisted of both a series of generally lively focus groups and over a thousand statistically coded individual interviews. Importantly, the focus groups did not serve merely as a means of deriving questions for the statistically coded individual interviews, but were also taken seriously in their own right. However, the very use of the latter approach raises questions as to whether the public could be consulted on such a complex and unfamiliar range of topics in what was essentially a questionnaire format. Certainly, the quantitative phase allowed little opportunity for personal reflection or for informal discussion. The major justification offered was that quantitative data were essential if the study was to be taken seriously by ministers and other observers. The government-led nature of this exercise was again very apparent. By this stage, and despite its billing as a 'public consultation', the initiative had become a sophisticated social research project designed to tell government what the public think.

In taking this approach, the exercise was also reflecting a common interpretation of the qualitative–quantitative relationship: that the former provides depth and 'colour' but that the latter is more representative and 'black and white'. Of course, this common-sensical account ignores the more profound issues of context, community and knowledge identified in Chapter 2. It also operates on the crude realist notion that public opinion is 'out there' to be mined and collected rather than being actively *created* within particular cultural and discursive settings.

The results of the consultation were published in May 1999 alongside the government's announcement of a new regulatory structure for biotechnology (MORI 1999). Among the key findings were:

- 'that the public believe advances in human health represent the biggest benefit to arise from scientific developments';
- 'the vast majority of people (97%) believe it is important that there

are rules and regulations to control biological developments and scientific research';

- 'The main issues people say should be taken into account when determining whether a biological development is right or wrong are whether people will benefit from it and whether it is safe to use';
- 'The thing that people most want in relation to the biosciences is more information on the rules and regulations'.

The professional quality of the exercise was undoubtedly high (especially given the time constraints). However, and as the Lords noted in their report, the framework was 'closer to market research than public consultation' (House of Lords Select Committee 2000: 37). While the initiative was a significant step forward from previous institutional practice, its democratic limitations are clear. Thus, the research ethos of the exercise meant that civil servants and members of the advisory group did not meet directly with any members of the public since this would contaminate the data. Although the avoidance of contact might be justifiable in professional research terms, it did prevent any real dialogue between scientists, policy makers and the wider publics. Rather than being able to speak for themselves, public voices were channelled according to the needs and constraints of the policy process. It is, meanwhile, very hard to say whether public groups would have reached similar or different conclusions had the exercise been conducted in a 'citizen-led' and more democratic manner.

In contrast, then, to the more general talk of dialogue and engagement, this exercise represented a self-conscious attempt to incorporate findings from PUS research within a very practical form. As such, it revealed many of the difficulties of establishing scientific citizenship in policy terms. More particularly, it suggests some of the inherent problems of moving from PUS research to the business of government. Certainly, a number of immediately practical implications emerge from this specific example of the 'new agenda' for scientific governance:

- That it is not sufficient simply to call for 'scientific democracy'. Instead, it is necessary to consider carefully the *form* of any initiative and its *operating principles*.
- That there may be, as the House of Lords Report suggested, a significant difference between *public consultation and engagement* and (as here) exercises designed to improve *policy makers' understanding of the public* – even if their rhetorical presentation blurs this distinction.
- That there may be particular advantages to forms of dialogue that allow members of the public to *set their own agenda* and also to *reflect* upon their own and others' views, especially when issues are both unfamiliar and complex.

- That public groups are capable of treating *scientific information* in a considered and responsible fashion. However, consultation should be allowed to open up and challenge areas of science rather than simply treating them as sacrosanct.
- That, based on the qualitative phase of the biosciences consultation in particular, it is clear that members of the public can bring a range of relevant and useful *observations, questions and opinions* to policy debate once proper deliberation has been allowed.
- That while this initiative was undoubtedly valuable and important, it only represents a *first step* towards citizen engagement and dialogue in the UK.

In the wake of BSE, openness, democracy and the maintenance of public confidence have become standard terms within UK science and technology policy. This case suggests that the practical *application* of such terminology is at least as important as the general rhetoric. Meanwhile, the question must at least be asked whether the difficulties identified here are simply practical matters of implementation or whether they suggest more fundamental limitations on the possibilities for dialogue within modern capitalist societies. Certainly, an acceptance of the principle that members of the public are active citizens who have the democratic right to refuse global technologies such as GM food would have far-reaching implications. It may be that exercises in dialogue represent a difficult balancing act between, in this case, a broad political commitment to biotechnology and the need to take wider public opinion seriously (or at least to be seen to be doing so). In this situation, it is possible to represent social experiments in this area as both a substantial step forward from traditional expert-led approaches *and* as being inherently restricted in character.

Conclusion

Considering issues of scientific governance more generally, this chapter has suggested a number of conclusions. Certainly, it seems appropriate to view the new agenda of scientific governance as a continuing debate rather than as an irretrievable policy shift. In particular, and as demonstrated by the House of Lords Select Committee Report, although the case for 'public dialogue' has been convincingly made, there is a substantial gulf between such discussion and particular examples of practical engagement. As the public consultation discussed in the previous section indicates, it may be easier to criticize the deficit model than it is to devise new mechanisms and methods of procedure.

As this chapter has also suggested, at the heart of the current discussion of scientific governance lies an unacknowledged tension between the intellectual authority of science (and indeed government) and the perceived need to incorporate public views, values and assessments. The importance of greater transparency and openness is widely acknowledged and 'dialogue' has become a central concept within policy initiatives. However, the precise form of this dialogue and its implications for both scientific authority and scientific citizenship have not as yet been fully established. In this situation, the attempt to build a 'firewall' between these two 'essential' components of scientific governance may not offer a meaningful basis for future action, not least because of the unavoidable cross-connections between science and the wider public culture.

Turning explicitly to the 'citizenship' dimension of this relationship, the biosciences consultation suggests an understanding of contemporary citizenship almost entirely removed from the social theoretical debates to be considered in the next chapter. The attempt to gather individual responses through a standardized and quantified methodology indicates an atomized and fixed view of citizen understandings which is contradicted by the notion of more fluid and shifting social and cognitive relations. While the public is invited to join the dialogue, it does so within the rather rigid frameworks and established cultural understandings of policy makers and politicians.

One other immediate point appears very significant. The debate over scientific governance as described here has largely been conducted at a national level and between the publics and government. Such an account takes little note of the wider phenomenon of globalization and the power of industry to create scientific and technological futures. Arguably, the locus of scientific governance is shifting away from the nation state to corporate boardrooms where national boundaries are of little significance. As was suggested in the introductory chapter, companies such as Monsanto exert enormous influence and in many ways set the pace for governments to follow. The question then arises of how scientific citizens are to make themselves heard when the processes of governance are not under the direct control of their elected governments. Equally, we are made aware of the possibility that wider theoretical reflection on scientific governance might suggest new possibilities for citizen engagement and scientific citizenship. It is to this task that we turn in Chapter 4.

Pulling these points together, this chapter suggests the importance of a move from *government* – where it was possible for individual governments to keep issues of scientific policy under central, rationalized control – to *governance* – where systems of control are inherently more complex, participants are more diverse and nation states cannot act with complete independence. In a context where multiple publics are expressing divergent views and the role of science has become open to question, these challenges may be even greater than the policy shifts reviewed here acknowledge. To consider some of these larger shifts in the global context for science and public knowledges, we now address wider social theoretical discussions. How does the previous social scientific PUS research and the current debate over scientific policy making appear when viewed from the perspective of contemporary theoretical debates?

Although most theoretical discussion has developed apart from the empirical research considered in Chapter 2 and the policy debates reviewed here, we will argue that this does not undermine its potential relevance. Certainly, and as we will suggest, there is a particular danger that policy discussion in this area accepts some of the more specific findings of PUS research (for example, the need for 'dialogue' or the significance of 'trust') but fails to recognize larger changes in the climate of global governance and contemporary culture. Equally, there is a potential tension between qualitative PUS research (with its strong emphasis on specific cultural contexts) and the wider picture presented by contemporary social theory. At this point, we turn to the third main element of this book.

4 Social theory and science

In Chapter 2, the multidiscipline of public understanding of science was reviewed. In the process, we traced the movement from an emphasis upon cognition to a concern with the cultural context in which 'understanding' is embedded. It became apparent that understanding is a highly complex concept, which, from the perspective of ethnographic public understanding of science, incorporates: the use of ignorance; local or situated knowledges; the appropriation and production of expert knowledge; relations of trust with experts and expert bodies; the mutual embedding of knowledge and social identity.

The discussion of ethnographic PUS was specifically structured around the gradual expansion of the social context of understanding – from a local community whose identity was crucially bound up with situated, practical knowledges through to a social movement where the relations to expertise were much more variegated, and where scientific knowledges were a major, if contingent, resource in the forging of social identities. But these 'contexts' – comprised of relations within public constituencies, and between the lay and scientific actors – cannot be assumed *a priori*. They reflect and mediate what might be thought of as much broader social processes that characterize the contemporary Western world. These contexts at once *emerge* out of these broader processes and serve in their *making*. For example, the AIDS movement has contributed to a restructuring of conditions which has, in turn, facilitated the rise of subsequent new social movements. At this point, we must turn to social theory and its analysis of the modern social world.

In the preceding chapter, we considered the trajectory from 'government' to 'governance' in the context of science policy, and the changing relationship between expertise, the state and the public. From the top-down perspective in which it was assumed that the public must have cognitive deficits corrected through information and education, we traced the emergence of more participatory, dialogic relations. Now, as various government reports and statements have made clear, the public's views and knowledges need to be incorporated within the process of science policy making. However, we also documented that this was a compromised vision. There were still powerful residues of the old deficit model concerning the relationship between laypeople and experts. These 'residues' are not simply historical but reflect wider tensions between democratic engagement and international economic competitiveness, and between the commitment to technological innovation and open dialogue.

We noted, too, that these developing concerns with dialogue and participation were neither uniform nor coherent. Differences between various sectors of government mean that there is currently an uneven engagement with the public. As we write, there is a new social experiment being conducted in the UK over GM food, which, yet again, raises questions about the relationship between public consultation, scientific investigation and economic assessment. It is likely that this Agriculture and Environment Biotechnology Commission consultation will reveal once again the difficulties of conducting a democratic engagement within such loaded, and inevitably fraught, settings and where there is little social consensus over the operating assumptions or indeed status of such exercises.

These differences of approach and perspective become even more evident when we consider the international character of contemporary science–public relations. We pointed to the ways in which the issues and concerns that characterize governance have transcended the boundaries of the nation state. The relations between public and scientific experts now span the globe as multinational corporations and international social movements directly engage in debate, simultaneously bypassing and embroiling the institutions of national governments.

This last point echoes the debate between Monsanto and Greenpeace considered in our introductory chapter. Here, we saw a series of complex interactions between 'global' actors that were effectively beyond the reach of nation states. Furthermore, as we drew out in that chapter, the *content* of that debate had major implications for the status of scientific knowledge within public controversies.

There are additional things to say about this exchange between Greenpeace and Monsanto, not least when we turn our attention to its general *form*. For example, it was presented on the web (in fact, on the website of a state-sponsored broadcasting corporation, the BBC). Thus, this debate was, potentially at least, globally accessible. To access it, however, a number of conditions have to be met, including the ready availability of the hardware and software, and the sorts of capacity and self-identity that enables one to 'surf the web' and to assimilate the debate. At this point, wider questions of culture and technology begin to emerge. To put all this in the terms of social theory: what is the nature of the social, cultural and technological processes through which such interactions are facilitated and 'make sense'?

Of course, social theory does not (and probably cannot) offer a coherent picture of these processes – after all, it is an intellectual activity that spans many contrasting traditions. Therefore, we do not intend to provide a comprehensive review of the various writings that can be said to be a part of recent social theory. In being necessarily selective, we have been guided by a concern to detail the work of those influential social theorists which has a bearing on our fields of interest, namely 'scientific governance' and 'public understanding of science and technology'.

Social theory certainly has much to say about the ways in which scientific knowledge and institutions have changed in late modernity. On the one hand, there are various problematizations of existing institutions. Such problematizations take the form of commentaries upon the increasingly apparent role of technoscience in the production of risks, or in the recent shifts in the character of self-identity, or the evident abandonment of the enlightenment project, or our increasingly irrational commitment to rationalization. On the other hand, partly the medium and partly the result of these problematizations of scientific knowledge and institutions, a range of new social phenomena has arisen and been subjected to social theoretical analysis. These phenomena are multifarious and disparate, but they touch upon some of the topics introduced in previous chapters: new social movements and forms of citizenship, subpolitics, globalization, reflexivity, consumer culture.

In sum, social theory is important to this book because it:

- engages with the 'broader' empirical dynamics of Western and globalized societies in which science–public relations are embroiled and to which they contribute;
- provides a range of theoretical characterizations and conceptualizations of recent and contemporary Western society which, at least potentially, can help in better understanding the current and potential state of science–public relations;
- broadens the horizons of science–public relations beyond the nation state and the lay local to encompass global or transnational actors or groupings;
- refashions the notion of cultural identity such that it can be seen to be constituted through a range of resources, both local and distant, and be directed towards expressive as well as instrumental ends;
- articulates the emergence of hybrid actors that, in so far as they embody elements of the public, expert institutions, regulatory bodies, communications specialists, commercial players and so on, blur the science–public divide.

In this chapter, then, we spend some time explicating major themes that are said to characterize the 'Western modern'. In the process, we draw upon the work of such theorists as Beck (1992), Giddens (1991) and Lyotard

(1984). More particularly, we engage with these theorists' treatments of the nature of the 'public', the character of 'science' and the constitution of the 'political process'. Furthermore, we show how these topics relate to other recent concerns of social theory, not least issues of citizenship and political agency. As we will suggest, for all the power of these social theoretical analyses, one is often left with a sense that there has been a detachment from the messiness of everyday life. That is to say, these theorizations neglect the complexity, ambiguity and multiplicity so well documented in ethnographic PUS studies and evidenced in the convoluted and contradictory practices of governance.

This chapter is organized as follows. We consider several of the most prominent themes in recent social theory which appear relevant to our present concern with the public understanding of science and the processes of governance. The themes we have derived are not at all distinct, let alone mutually exclusive – there are overlaps and mergings – and their ordering does not imply any hierarchy or ranking. Partly for explanatory reasons and partly to ground these very abstract themes, we will draw upon the GM case study introduced in Chapter 1. This serves not only to render each theme somewhat more concrete, but also to illustrate its value for a more nuanced understanding of public–science relations. On that basis, we will consider in turn recent social theoretical treatments of:

- rationality, progress and differentiation;
- trust and ambivalence;
- risk and globalization;
- consumption and citizenship;
- self-identity and 'fluidity'.

To reiterate, the items on this list fold into one another in various ways, not all of which we will be able to explicate. As such, they form a nexus of issues that is addressed, in one way or another, by various prominent social theorists. In exploring the ways that the relation between scientific knowledge, policy and lay actors are theorized, it is certainly possible to pay close attention to the differences between various theorists. However, important though these differences certainly are, for present purposes we will stress *common* themes. In summarizing these common themes, we emphasize especially the de-differentiation of both science and the public, and the global and the local. As such, we provide an initial outline of how we might go about reformulating the simultaneous blurring and interaction between expert and lay constituencies. Furthermore, given our concern to show how ethnographic PUS can inform and enrich social theory, we end, ironically, with a brief illustration of how the complex processes described by social theory become even more complex when one looks closely at empirical examples of 'public understanding of science'. All this serves as a basis for subsequent chapters that will draw the domains of social theory, public understanding of science and governance together (Chapter 5) and elaborate a framework for better analysing the relations between science and public (Chapter 6).

Finally, we should acknowledge that we are about to embark on a very rapid tour of what for many will be a rather unfamiliar world of social theory. Let us emphasize before embarking that the detail of what follows is less important than the general sense of activity and debate over the meaning of contemporary social change. Equally, we do not claim to offer an authoritative account. Our aim is the more modest one of opening up a productive exchange between PUS, scientific governance and social theory.

Rationality, progress and differentiation

In the GM food debate presented in Chapter 1, what is the status of the science under discussion? It is obvious enough that both sides of the controversy draw on a picture of science that is somewhat blurred. Both Monsanto and Greenpeace (as well as the various lay contributors) deploy a version of science that is thoroughly embroiled in society. Thus, the public features both as a contributor and as a representation in that the ostensible views, needs and interests of the public are mobilized in the argument to warrant and justify particular scientific and technological strategies. This blurring touches on several aspects of the relation between science and society: the 'rational' status of science; the position of science *vis-à-vis* other institutions in society; the role of science in Western 'progress'. All of these topics have been subject to sustained exploration by social theory. It is to several of these treatments that this section is devoted.

Many social theorists, going back at least to Max Weber, have identified *rationalization* as a key characteristic of modernity. Three aspects of this rationalization can be drawn out (cf. Crook *et al.* 1992):

- the requirement for rational action to be informed by *factual knowledge*;
- the growth of *impersonal systems* (e.g. bureaucracies, the market) that structure moderns' lives;
- the extension of *control over social and natural worlds* not least through making these worlds calculable.

Various theorists have gone on to critique this process of rationalization (notably critical theorists such as Horkheimer, Adorno and Habermas), not least because it has meant that substantive values have been overtaken by instrumental ones. That is to say, instead of an orientation towards the 'good life' (in political, economic, social and cultural terms), modern rationalization has been concerned with determining the most efficient *means* (in terms of, for example, organization and distribution of resources). This drive, it has been argued, lies at the heart of such modern travesties as the Holocaust (Bauman 1989, 1991; Beilharz 2000).

Associated with rationalization is the process of *differentiation* – the increasingly refined separation of various spheres of human activity from one another. This process of differentiation has been thoroughgoing, ranging from such structural changes as the separation of economic and political 'systems' from the 'lifeworld' (the everyday world of lived experience) to differentiation between different aspects of culture (high and low art). Most relevant in the present case is the differentiation between *science* (and more generally expertise) and *society* (cf. Nowotny *et al.* 2001). Separate, distinct, expert institutions and scientific disciplines have proliferated as more and more aspects of the social and natural world have been rendered calculable and controllable. Importantly, such expert systems have been woven into states and corporations. However, as Crook *et al.* note, this differentiation and rationalization is not simply and uniformly driven by some 'logic' of modernity, but is a messy and contested process.

This last point evokes the issue of progress. Modernity, as an albeit complex and contradictory reaction against the constraints of feudal society, entailed a social commitment to such substantive goals as increased political enfranchisement and economic equality. In relation to science, this notion of progress has been manifested in a number of ways, most obviously in terms of the accumulation of knowledge and the incremental movement towards the 'truth'. Less obviously, science has been both an *icon* of modernity (in so far as it has been presented as an embodiment of all the best aspects of modernity, e.g. freedom, truth and equality) and a central part of the *master narrative* of modernity (cf. Lyotard 1984).

Now, a number of contemporary social theorists suggest that, in various ways, this picture has changed fundamentally. A confusing array of labels has been attached to these changes – late modern, high modern, postmodern to name but three. But what seems common among them is the idea that there is increasing 'fluidity' in society. The seeming rigidities of modern structures, institutions, forms of life appear to have 'loosened up'. The old categories used to describe the modern world have become inadequate. For example, Lyotard (1984) has argued that the grand narrative of science is no longer valid or recognizable. That is to say, the once entrenched stories that were associated with science have stopped structuring the way we think about the nature of social life and the possibilities of progress. This is because, according to Lyotard, (postmodern) science is no longer at the core of the modernist project: it has failed to deliver its Enlightenment promise. Science is now just the technician-servant of industry, uninterested in political and economic progress towards greater equality and freedom. Indeed, as we shall see, science is better thought of as 'technoscience'.

Furthermore, as Nowotny *et al.* (2001) note, the erosion of the status of science in the postmodern world is allied to the *de-differentiation of science* from other spheres. The differentiation (or professionalization) of science from other sectors of society was hard won – a major accomplishment (e.g. Whitley 1984; Shapin 1991; Gieryn 1999) by scientific institutions. But latterly, science seems to have diffused into a variety of fora and settings. Nowotny *et al.* point to several factors that have led to the increasing 'alignment' – that is, the co-evolution – of science and society:

> it has become increasingly difficult to establish a clear demarcation and differentiation between science and society. The fundamental categories of the modern world – state, society, economy, culture [and science] – have become porous and even problematical . . . [Further-more] both science and society . . . are subject to the same, or similar, driving forces.
>
> (Nowotny *et al.* 2001: 47)

These driving forces are listed as:

- The overall *growth of uncertainty* – 'both science and society have opted for the production of the New in an open-ended process of moving toward a plurality of unknown futures' (p. 35).
- The pervasiveness of *new forms of economic rationality* that centre in particular upon speculation and which are echoed in science as the production of 'insubstantial promises, which are based upon a poten-tial that is difficult to assess properly and which will take time to develop fully but which are amplified through the media, excite the imagination of industry and the public and influence decisions about which parts of basic research are to be funded and which lines of inquiry are to be pursued' (p. 38).
- The *transformation of time* into an 'extended present' wherein future prospects are experienced as closer to the present: in both science and society, there is an enhanced sense of mastery of the future world (in biological terms, for example).
- The *flexibilization of space*: while there has been a compression of space, time and distance, not least through new information and communication technologies, distance has also become ambiguous. On the one hand, certain local sites appear closer together (more 'stitchable together'). On the other, as knowledge or technology or cultural images speed across these sites, differences as well as similar-ities become apparent.

- The *self-organizing capacity of science and society*: both sectors are now, partly in response to the potentially disruptive 'closeness' of other local sites, engaged in processes of reflexivity, self-scrutiny and definition, aiming to derive a 'main reference framework in which a sense of stability and orientation can be constructed' (p. 44). However, part of this reflexivity is also an attempt to accommodate the demands of other actors – say, of the demands for accountability placed by society on science.

To reiterate, these abstractions (and highly abstract dynamics these are indeed) are not supposed to describe causal relations between science and society. Nowotny *et al.* (2001) are rather more interested in the processes of *co-evolution* in which one finds the clustering and interdependent influence of science and society. At the very least, these authors point to the ways in which science has, if not divested itself of, certainly supplemented its modernist character. As the preceding list suggests, the relation of both science and society to rationalization and progress has become altogether more complex and contingent.

Rationalization is as much about reflexivity and accountability as efficiency and instrumentality, and progress has been redefined in the context of space–time compression and the open-endedness and uncertainty of the future. Already, then, we can see a view of social and scientific change which offers a challenging contrast to the discussion in the previous two chapters.

Trust and ambivalence

Within the GM debate, the statements put forward by the key protagonists are not only addressed to one another, but also (and primarily) directed towards a broader audience – the public. Indeed, this particular instance of the debate (in public, on the web) might be seen as an exercise in garnering support from lay constituencies. The arguments made by each side are not simply a means of presenting the 'facts', because as the debate amply demonstrates, those 'facts' are always liable to problematization and contestation by the other side. Rather, and as we saw in Chapter 2, such arguments are about engendering trust: they are directed at lay constituencies partly as a way of persuading them of the trustworthiness of the speaker (Monsanto or Greenpeace) and thus the truth of each spokesperson's 'facts'. That this is one of the functions of these arguments (indeed, that there is a public debate at all) suggests that both protagonists are aware of the ambivalence of the public in relation to expertise.

The public no longer believes (if it ever did) automatically and unreservedly in scientific experts, and any trust it invests in such experts is likely to be contingent. Furthermore, the public messages to the website make it clear that there is no singular public – rather, there are many different publics. And, of course, individual members of these publics can themselves be ambivalent. For example, while general disagreement with GM food might be expressed, this can co-exist with support for the genetic modification of animals for xenotransplantation (Lundin 1999). In this section, we consider how social theorists have treated these relations of trust and ambivalence and, in particular, address the ways in which social theory has attempted to embed the ambiguous status of science and scientific institutions in the context of broader social and cultural changes.

In his now classic analysis of the postmodern condition, Lyotard (1984) has pointed to a generalized disillusionment with science. However, other authors present a much more subtle picture of the relation between publics and science. One of the key characteristics of contemporary social life for Giddens (1991; see also Giddens 1990) is what he calls 'disembedding'. By this he means that where once we drew on local communities for our understandings of the social and physical world, now we are dependent upon expert systems. Without reflecting upon it consciously, we automatically invest trust in a range of scientific institutions which ensure that things, by and large, run smoothly and are predictable. The range of activities in which such institutions engage in order that we don't have to think about things (literally) is huge, from standardizing such units as the volt and the metre, through ensuring that materials used in everyday items do what they are supposed to do (i.e. do not fall apart, poison us or explode in our faces), to monitoring the environment for signs of all manner of dangers (natural ones such as seismic activity, artificial ones such as global warming and ozone depletion). Nowadays we are deeply dependent on these institutions (or 'abstract systems' as Giddens calls them).

Of course, while this sort of trust in expert systems is tacit and often unremarked, it is also, under various, often complicated circumstances (cf. Sztompka 2000), very much liable to becoming questioned, circumscribed and sometimes even withdrawn. Science, mediated as it is within and by these institutions, is often identified with those moments when things do not run smoothly and life becomes anything but predictable. The spate of problems and outright disasters that have entered popular culture recently (see Chapter 1) has led to the public becoming deeply suspicious of the expert pronouncements made over, for example, the safety of the MMR vaccine, the appropriate measures to be taken for foot-and-mouth disease, and the release of genetically modified crops.

At a wider level, Rampton and Stauber's (2002) popular book, *Trust Us, We're Experts!*, illustrates well how, especially in the US context, the language of science and expertise can be used to support corporate activities and, specifically, public relations initiatives. As Rampton and Stauber argue, the notion that the public is emotional and 'incapable of rational discourse' can be used as justification for a range of public relations exercises employing the discourse of expertise and making claims to 'sound science'. Meanwhile, pro-industry groups use the term 'junk science' to undermine the arguments of their opponents – as, for example, in the public controversy over the chemical *alar*. The implication of junk science is that corporate America is the victim of irrational health scares which can only be contained by the 'sound science' of industry-supported experts.

As Rampton and Stauber suggest, and as we have already discussed, not just industry representatives but also many scientists share this view of an irrational public which needs careful handling (and even deliberate manipulation). It is not hard to see how this climate of mutual distrust can lead to further questions about the public role of technical experts – as also in the UK official inquiry into BSE (Phillips Report 2000). While, for example, the Western European and North American debates over science and governance have at times taken different forms, similar questions are certainly being asked about the role of expertise within public policy and how we are to interpret competing claims to know best about such matters as health, environmental pollution and the direction of technical change. Thus, Hilgartner (2000) has provided a lively account of US science advice over diet and health as a form of public performance aimed at maintaining credibility under social and technical challenge, a framework that could be applied to many other national settings. Nevertheless, and as Beck (1992) points out, without scientific institutions going about their routine expert business, we would almost certainly remain unaware of very many problems that have come to public attention. Indeed, such environmental conditions as ozone depletion, global warming and increasing ionizing radiation levels are undetectable without technical investigations and scientific studies.

As both Giddens (1991) and Beck (1992) note, laypeople are caught in a relationship that is variable, shifting and unstable with regard to scientific institutions. We can sketch out the following cross-cutting and sometimes contradictory patterns of trust. There is a chronic, systemic and unreflected-upon dependence upon such institutions (routine standardization and safety testing). There is a virulent distrust of, and disillusion with, them (when things go wrong). And there is a pervasive but provisional trust in them (as problems are identified and solutions are offered and implemented). In other words, laypeople in late modernity display an 'integrated ambivalence' towards expert systems. As Beck (1992) phrases it: 'the risk consciousness of the afflicted, which is frequently expressed in the environmental movement, and in criticism of industry, experts and culture, is usually both critical and credulous of science' (p. 72).

Importantly, our dependence on expert systems also increasingly extends to the social and individual or personal world. Thus, risks about how we should behave as parents, as lovers, as members of a couple, as emotionally balanced people, have all become the object of increasing expert scrutiny and advice. In fact, because we have become disembedded – because we are 'made' (cf. Hacking 1986) or constituted through very many interactions with other sources of knowledge such as experts (e.g. general practitioners), the media, friends and relatives – the roles we take on are no longer unproblematic or transparent. We don't simply become a worker, a sexual partner or a layperson – an ordinary member of the public or citizen – as we used to. Rather, our self, instead of being largely shaped by our community, locality, class, gender or ethnic position, is becoming, it is argued, much more *fluid.* We are now in a position to make choices about our identities rather than those identities being fixed through the social context into which we are born. We are engaged in what Giddens calls the *self-as-project.*

As Giddens (1992) puts it in *The Transformation of Intimacy*: 'The self today is a reflexive project – a more or less continuous interrogation of the past, present and future. It is a project carried on amid a profusion of reflexive resources: therapy and self-help manuals of all kinds, television programmes and magazine articles' (p. 50; cf. Beck and Beck-Gersheim 1995). Crucially, this self-as-project also encompasses the complex figure of the 'scientific citizen' (to whom we will return in later chapters).

Risk and globalization

If we consider once again the GM debate, it is apparent that the arguments put forward by Monsanto, Greenpeace and several of the lay correspondents draw upon interpretations of global processes. Thus, there is reference to the need to 'feed the world', emphasizing either the global lack of food (to be solved by GM crops) or the inequities of food distribution (of which there is already enough worldwide and thus no need for GM crops). The key point for this section is that the debate is partly structured by concerns with global risks: either there is not enough food and this necessitates the global solution of GM food production, or GM foods, by virtue of their supposed properties, engender risks that can be globalized (e.g. pesticide-resistant weeds). Social theorists have recently become very concerned with the dynamics of globalization and risk. However, and as the GM debate itself suggests, these globalized risks are also the topic of reflection by scientific and lay actors – it is not only social scientists who are attuned to these processes. Indeed, for some social scientists, these very reflections upon the globalization of risks are a crucial part of the phenomenon itself. In this section, we review some of the ways in which the dynamics of risk globalization have been analysed and consider the implications for the divide between science and society.

Globalization has become a term with considerable currency in academic and political parlance. It refers to the fact that different parts of the modern world have become much more closely interconnected. Or, to put it another way, it refers to the ways that 'stuff' flows more readily and freely between the far-flung corners of the planet. Information, food, people, money, consumables of all sorts flow and circulate with an ease unimaginable just a few decades ago (e.g. Harvey 1989; Lash and Urry 1994; Walters 1995; Urry 2000). As we have already seen, this means that people are constantly exposed to knowledges whose sources are 'at a distance' – not a part of the locality or community, but derived from, or through, abstract systems. Furthermore, this exposure to other ways of life means that laypeople increasingly have the opportunity to identify with a multiplicity of others, thus rendering their own identities, as we have just discussed, more 'fluid'. In this section, however, we will consider in particular how globalization entails the *generalization of risks*.

Beck (1992) has argued that recent developments in modernity mean that society has increasingly come to be characterized by the 'bads' (as opposed to 'goods') that circulate within it: accordingly, we live in a *risk society*. Many of these risks – notably ionizing radiation, global warming, ozone depletion and, most recently, biological and biotechnological dangers (e.g. BSE, foot and mouth disease, GM food) – now move across national borders with almost complete freedom. However, these risks are not unproblematically real: they are constructed, not least by expert systems which must recognize cases, collate statistics, develop accounts of causal mechanisms and, finally, 'identify' the risk. Recently, Beck (2000) in gathering together his various arguments on the risk society, has listed what he sees as the core features of this globalization of risk. We can abstract and summarize some of the most relevant arguments as follows:

- Risk does not refer to some simple reality, but rather is a type of *'virtuality'* – risk society is concerned to calculate, and 'deal with', potentialities and probabilities. This means that present-day society is oriented to the future (where such risks might be realized as actual disasters) rather than being 'caused' by the past. Furthermore, the process of calculating the risks faced by risk society is not objective but entails values. Risk calculations are, as Beck puts it, 'mathematicised morality' (p. 215).
- Risk society partly emerges out of the 'logic of control' of modernity, but the promise that instrumental rationality necessarily leads to control of the natural and social world has backfired: there is a *disassociation of rationality and control*. Thus, as we 'rationally' attempt to 'confine and control risks' so there is a 'broadening of the uncertainties and dangers'. This is a 'peculiar synthesis of knowledge and unawareness' (p. 216) where, on the one hand, risk calculations based

on empirical knowledge are increasingly refined and, on the other, decisions have to be made in a context of chronic uncertainty.

- Risk blurs the *apparent contrast between the local and the global* as the 'new types of risks are simultaneously local and global, or "glocal" ' (p. 218). Given the perception that environmental dangers know no boundaries, we are now living in a 'world (or global) risk society'. The contradictions between various expert pronouncements (sometimes across sectors such as insurance and industrial, sometimes across national divides) also means that the constructedness of risks becomes increasingly apparent (they are 'man-made hybrids', p. 221), just as they are also understood as very real. The awareness of the conflict over, and thus constructedness of, risks makes risk society potentially much more 'self-critical'. This self-criticalness crucially pertains to the fact that nation states are no longer the structures most favourably placed to manage these risks.

One consequence of these preceding points is that publics can no longer simply trust experts because each calculation of risk brings into view all sorts of uncertainties and values concerned with, for example, what is to count as tolerable risk, or what is to count as a suitable response (that is, what type of politics should be engaged in). Once again, the perspective that emerges from social theory is deeply challenging both to PUS research and to practical interventions in scientific governance.

Consumption and citizenship

The GM debate on the BBC website is interesting because, as mentioned above, it is a political debate in which the nation state is at once prominently absent and tacitly present. Regarding its absence, this is most obvious in that neither of the protagonists represent a part of the state: we have instead a spokesperson from a biotechnology multinational corporation and a spokesperson for an international environmental non-government organization. However, the UK nation state is present in so far as it 'sponsors' the BBC and thus, indirectly, the website. More importantly, it is one of the undefined audiences to which the protagonists direct their statements. Meanwhile, it is doubtful whether those members of the public who contributed to the debate were addressing the UK Government (or, indeed, any government in particular). Rather, it is more likely that they were addressing other surfers like themselves, and the main protagonists. Moreover, we must not assume that these lay contributors were themselves of any particular nationality.

All this suggests that, in so far as a contribution to this debate comprises a civic or citizenly intervention, it is not necessarily citizenly either in relation to any national government or one's own national government. In other words, the doing of politics, the performance of 'civic duty', takes on a much more global and variegated complexion. This reshaping of citizenship has other dimensions to it. If, for example, a contributor to the debate were to be antagonistic towards the position of Monsanto, one form of action would be to boycott Monsanto's products. Here, citizenship is primarily conducted through economic activity – that is, through consumption.

To complicate matters still further, we can return to the issue of trust. If our antagonist to Monsanto is actively pro-Greenpeace, we might ask why this is so. We have already suggested that trust is key in such a situation. But trust can also be regarded in terms of identification. With regard to trust in Greenpeace, this can be recast in terms of an identification with either Greenpeace or the social movements of which it is putatively a part. This form of identification is expressed, as we have noted, in acts of consumption (and non-consumption) as well as other forms of political action. However, what is being consumed (or not consumed) is not just the product but what the product 'means' – the product as a sign, as it were. In consuming, say, the signs of Greenpeace (its media representations, its paraphernalia, its arguments), one simultaneously contributes to its cause and signals one's identity – who one is. There is, in other words, a *conflation of identity, politics and consumption*. This sort of argument has been key to recent social theory in its attempts to grapple with shifts in political process and the rise of consumer culture. In this section, we consider some of the social theorists who have examined this complex of issues.

Consumption has increasingly been seen to characterize the contemporary Western world. Thus, Lash and Urry (1994) suggest that one of the prominent characteristics of contemporary society is what they call 'specialized consumption', where individuals are constituted in 'disembedded lifestyle enclaves' which are subject to niche marketing. People no longer identify themselves in terms of class or community, but in relation to such enclaves and the patterns of consumption associated with them. However, what is being consumed here are not just material objects but, as the term 'lifestyle' implies, what these objects can signify or express. As Featherstone (1991) argues, everyday life has become aestheticized (or stylized); that is to say, for some commentators everyday life is typified by 'the rapid flow of signs and images . . . consumer society . . . confronts people with dream-images which speak to desires, and aestheticize and de-realize reality' (pp. 67–8). The upshot of this is that consumption is as much concerned with attaining images as material things. Goods are now used as if, as Lury (1996) frames it, 'they were works of art, images or signs, to be engaged with via processes of fantasy, play, daydreaming and image-making' (pp. 77–8).

Now, this process can also be linked to how particular forms of consumption are modelled and 'sold'. Bourdieu (1984) calls attention to a recent class faction – the new petite bourgeoisie engaged in the 'cultural' professions: 'occupations involving presentation and representation (sales, marketing and advertising, PR, fashion, decoration . . .) and in all institutions providing symbolic goods and services . . . medical and social assistance (marriage guidance, sex therapy) and cultural production and organization (youth leaders, radio and television producers)' (p. 359; also see Lash and Urry 1987). Members of this faction have taken up lifestyles that involve a form of consumption that is eclectic, rapidly changing and conspicuous, enabling members to differentiate themselves symbolically and culturally. By virtue of its visibility, this class faction serves as a model group which fosters a similar lifestyle among other groupings.

Of course, and as Lury comments, the flow of influence is not one way (note the impact of street fashion on high culture). Moreover, individuals' background (local culture, economic resources, political affiliation) will still shape whether this mode of consumption is attainable, let alone desirable. And it is unwise to over-generalize this particular mode of consumption over others, or to generalize across different contexts (cf. Miller 1995). Nevertheless, it has certainly been argued that *modern culture is a consumer culture*, and a central dimension of this is that identity has come to be mediated through acts of consumption, even if such acts of consumption are oppositional or subcultural.

In sum, we now live in a culture of consumption where acts of consumption are predominantly the means by which we realize identity. As Michael (1998) has noted in relation to the public understanding of science, this means that we have to see the relation between publics and science as also one of consumption. Science is thus 'consumed' by publics in a number of ways. For example, science – notably in its popularized forms of books and documentaries – is a consumable good that confers particular identities. Within certain subcultures, to have not read (or at least commenced) Stephen Hawking's *A Brief History of Time* would have mildly endangered one's social standing (or cultural capital; cf. Bourdieu 1984). More worryingly, science can be used as a means to aestheticized consumption, for example, redesigning oneself or one's offspring through biotechnologies of various sorts.

In the context of this discussion of consumer culture, another nexus of issues arises: the possibility that *citizenship is partly mediated through consumption*. Recently, the division between the 'citizen' and the 'consumer' has been subject to close scrutiny. One important account points to the pre-eminence of the 'New Right' and the attendant advocacy of the rights, choices and decisions of 'the customer'. The enhanced standing of the 'customer' is manifested in the way that several domains that were hitherto regarded as lying outside the market (for example, the public services) are now judged in terms of how they cater for the 'consumer' (Keat *et al.* 1994). This has been partly responsible for the blurring of the boundaries between 'citizen' and 'consumer'. Saunders (1993), for example, argues that possession of the financial resources to consume, in what he refers to as a privatized mode, leads to the 'experience of controlling one's immediate life and environment [which] fosters a degree of confidence and self-esteem . . . which appears crucial as the foundation for a lively and cooperative civil society' (p. 86).

Now, it could be argued that this version of the relation between consumption and citizenship does not properly address how such rights and choices are themselves socially constituted. For instance, can the fulfilment of 'needs' or 'wants' that are in some sense 'inauthentic' – say, partly driven by commercial interests – really comprise an exercise of citizenship? Of course, what counts as 'authentic' is always a matter of great contention, and there are innumerable criteria by which to judge this (cf. Slater 1997). The main point meanwhile is that Saunders offers but one version of the interweavings of consumer and citizen. As Gabriel and Lang (1995) document, there are very many different ways in which the relation between consumer and citizen can be articulated, from consumers/citizens 'voting' with their purchasing choices to making concerted efforts to influence policy making with regard to the production of certain consumables (such as GM foodstuffs).

One of the key sites where these processes of consumption, expression of identity and citizenship cohere is, at least according to some (see Melucci 1989a,b), the 'new social movement'. The new social movement is not simply concerned with instrumental action and intervention in the political process, it is also constituted through the production of certain identities. What one wears, eats, drinks and smokes serves in the expression of identification with a particular social movement (and in some cases might even stand as a partial exemplification or prefiguration of the form of life that is advocated by that movement). But this identity, partly wrought through acts of consumption, also enables political action: these two moments are not separate.

In summary, then, it seems to be becoming increasingly problematic to keep apart the practices of citizenship from those of consumption. Of course, this in turn raises further questions concerning the nature and definition of the 'scientific citizen' when the conventional modes of democratic expression (voting, lobbying, campaigning) can no longer represent the full character of 'politics' in the modern age.

Self-identity and 'fluidity'

The preceding discussions of the culture of consumption, ambivalence in expert systems and new social movements all suggest what might be called a *fluidity of self-identity*. As we have mentioned before, with the rise of late modernity or postmodernity, there has been a range of developments which have disembedded people from their previous social networks and communities. In relation to the GM debate documented in Chapter 1, such disembedding is partly evoked by the sorts of laypeople who contributed to the debate. The social and cultural attachments which motivate such interventions are not simply the old ones of class or gender or ethnicity or nation. They are much more variegated, hybrid even.

However, this is a rather simplistic view of people's social and cultural attachments, for the *sociotechnical form* of the debate also mediates such attachments. By sociotechnical form, we are referring to the medium through which the debate is conducted: the computer, the net, the web. We say 'socio-technical' because we do not want to see these as 'pure' technologies – they are thorough-goingly social (e.g. Latour 1987; Bijker and Law 1992; Bijker 1995; Michael 2000). Our main point is that the web is a means by which identity might be rendered more 'fluid'. Coming across the GM debate as one surfs does not necessarily reflect one's pre-existing attachments, it can also serve in the production of new social and cultural connections. This is only one of various contemporary technologies which enable such new connections and attachments to be enacted. Social theorists have been especially interested in the processes by which identities might be becoming more 'fluid' in the context of these various technologies. Let us consider these processes in a little more detail.

Gergen (1991) contrasts the more fluid or, what he calls, saturated self to the romantic and modern selves. The romantic self of the nineteenth century hinged on a vocabulary of 'passion, purpose, depth and personal significance' (p. 27) and the 'romantic individual was forever a mystery – the vital essence quixotic and out of reach' (p. 47). By comparison, the modernist self is infused with reason – it is 'reliable, self-contained and machine-produced' (pp. 44–5) and, as such, is fundamentally knowable and measurable. However, in the wake of what Gergen calls the 'Technologies of Social Saturation' (p. 49) – that is, the variety of high technologies such as air travel, video and television and new information technologies such as electronic mail, faxes, satellites, computers – there is a population of the self which opens 'relationships to new ranges of possibility' and renders 'subjective life . . . more fully laminated' (p. 71). Indeed:

> we find a profound sea change taking place in the character of social life during the twentieth century . . . We engage in greater numbers of relationships, in a greater variety of forms, and with greater intensities than ever before. With the multiplication of relationships also comes a transformation in the social capacities of the individual – both in knowing how and knowing that [*sic*] . . . A multiphrenic condition emerges in which one swims in ever-shifting, concatenating and contentious currents of being.
>
> (Gergen 1991: 79–80)

Lash and Urry (1987) have also analysed the postmodern world's impact upon identity. A key dynamic is what they call the 'decentring of the subject'. In the past, subjects were historically furnished with the cultural resources (e.g. narratives, images, icons) through which to socially construct more or less coherent identities. However, in the postmodern era, such texts have become unstable – they have no singular meaning, being subject to transgression (by other narratives and images) and accelerated turnover (substitution by other narratives and texts). They can no longer sustain the integrity of the individual. According to Lash and Urry, this decentring has come about because of such factors as the fragmentation of working-class communities and the occupationally structured experience of sections of the middle class, the influence of electronic mass media, and disruptions in our perception of space and time in everyday life. The role of television in the decentring of identity is also highlighted: by exposing individuals of all groupings to a general information system, there is a negative effect on our collective identity.

In contrast, David Harvey (1989) lays special emphasis upon the speeding up of production processes, exchange and consumption patterns with an attendant acceleration in information flows and communications. With respect to consumption, Harvey focuses on the mobilization of fashion in mass markets and the increased consumption of services whose relatively short life-span (in contrast to durables) facilitates accelerated consumption. All this interweaves with a heightening in the volatility and ephemerality of products, ideas, ideologies, images and values. As Harvey would have it, there is an increase in the values and virtues of instantaneity and disposability. This, in turn, is associated with what Harvey identifies as 'space–time compression'. This term attempts to capture the processes by which time and space become much more 'proximal': with the advent of ultra-fast transport and communication systems, space shrinks to a 'global village' or a 'spaceship earth'. The result of these systems is that images tend to congregate locally and become interchangeable – 'spaces of very different worlds seem to collapse upon each other, much as the world's commodities are assembled in supermarkets and all manner of sub-cultures get juxtaposed in the contemporary city' (pp. 301–2). In consequence, a strong sense of the 'Other' is overtaken by a weak sense of plural 'others'. To summarize: *contemporary structural change is associated with characteristic postmodern experiences: fragmentation, ephemerality, dispersal in philosophical and social thought, radical discontinuity, decentring.*

Subject to a constant bombardment of disparate images, caught up in a multiplicity of flows of information, knowledge, representations, people in the late modern world are, according to this general argument, furnished with a range of cultural resources through which to fashion and re-fashion themselves. This fluidity in self-identity is not confined simply to laypeople, or rather, in this context, the term 'laypeople' applies to scientists as well: these professionals too are no less subject to such fluidities. Where once scientists were deeply suspicious of those colleagues who deigned to 'communicate with the public', and were cautious about popularizing their own work (cf. Gregory and Miller 1998), now we see scientists emerging as financial or media stars. Not only do scientists 'popularize', they also distribute press releases as a means of establishing their priority claims as the 'discoverer' of fact X or inventor of artefact Y, and thus announce their right to patent. The identity of the scientist thus increasingly blurs into that of the entrepreneur, not least when such announcements are designed to serve in the protection or raising of investment. Similarly, such pronouncements are timed to respond to developments in relevant policy making or legislation. Here, scientists are seen to be political actors, attached to pressure groups or economic or political interests. Seen in that way, the phenomenon of regulatory science discussed in the previous chapter emerges as one part of a larger pattern of cultural and intellectual change.

Now, as various sociologists of science have noted, this heterogeneity has always been characteristic of the activities of scientists (e.g. Latour 1987). However, it seems to be much more in evidence nowadays as the differences between science and society erode and the range of possible identities expands. What is perhaps new is the way that scientists have become more prominent in the entertainment (or infotainment) industry. Not only can they advertise products, but they appear 'as themselves' in popular programmes (for example, Hawking's appearances in *Star Trek: The New Generation* and *The Simpsons*). Obviously such appearances reinforce as much as undermine the mystique of the scientist, but they also act, it might be argued, in rendering the representation of scientist, media star, entrepreneur, layperson as altogether more interchangeable.

A brief summary

As we indicated in this chapter's introduction, our account of social theory has been both general and un-nuanced. We have not dwelt on the differences between the various authors on whose work we have so superficially drawn. For example, no mention has been made of the disputes over whether there is a definitive break between contemporary society and modernist society, or whether the former is a 'natural' development of the latter. We are certainly (but unashamedly) aware that we can be accused of 'analysing to the lowest common denominator', emphasizing only those points that are common across (influential parts of) contemporary social theory. However, the overwhelming point here is to show that, at least according to one account, there are certain broad changes under way and that these need (in some way) to be incorporated into our thinking about the public understanding of science.

The changes we have summarized above under the headings of Rationality, Progress and differentiation, Trust and ambivalence, Risk and globalization, Consumption and citizenship, Self-identity and 'fluidity', present a series of interconnections. There are multiple linkages across the various processes we have described, and it would be well beyond our scope to draw these out in detail. Nevertheless, we can give an indication of these connections as a means of summarizing the characterization of the contemporary social world that has been sketched here. To put our theoretical narrative in minimalistic terms:

- Globalization leads to fluidity in identities through the increased flows of images, representations and knowledges.
- Such fluidity is part and parcel of disembedding from local communities – increasingly we laypeople look to sources beyond our immediate environs to fashion (by no means consciously) 'who we are'.
- Such sources include experts but, because we are exposed to many of these experts, we also see that their accounts (not least of the risks we face) are partial.
- As such, the trust we invest in experts is contingent – we are ambivalent towards sources of expertise.
- We can also choose not to invest trust in these experts, especially when particular dangers are becoming prominent.
- While the identification of these problems is often dependent upon experts, account should also be taken of our identifications with particular distributed (as opposed to local) cultural and political groupings (identifications which often enable us to attribute trustworthiness in the first place), such as new social movements or pressure groups (with which experts are also sometimes associated).
- Our attachment to these groups is not simply a matter of practical activity, it is also concerned with consumption of those artefacts that signify belonging to such groupings.
- Consumption can also act as a mode of political – that is, citizenly – intervention (e.g. boycotting of multinationals' products or services) now that, in face of the globalization of risks, nation states can only intervene in highly partial ways.

Conclusion

From this nexus of connections portrayed by social theory, we can bring into focus some of the points most relevant to ethnographic public understanding of science. As Michael (1998) has noted, the role of social identity in shaping relations of trust between lay publics and experts needs to be refashioned. This is because lay publics, as this chapter indicates, can no longer be thought of solely in terms of 'embedded' local communities: as if they were separable from larger social forces and changing cultural patterns of the kind identified above by social theorists. As we have seen, the publics are now thoroughly traversed by global flows of risk, knowledge, material and cultural goods. Indeed, in the context of this account (where society and science have de-differentiated), it becomes exceedingly difficult to talk of the 'public' at all. In ethnographic public understanding of science, the public as a political actor has been very much emergent from its locality and the contextual knowledges derived in that locality [or 'taskscape' as Ingold (1993) would call it – crudely, the social-material world in which people are both enabled and constrained]. However, knowledges nowadays are also global: as Macnaghten and Urry (1998) note, science is a fundamental part of laypeople's contemporary taskscape.

Speculatively, we might say that rather than talk of the public, as juxtaposed to expertise, we should be developing new configurations of lay and expert, especially in light of the supposed de-differentiation of various groups and institutions in late (or post) modern Western societies. Instead of the contrast between 'expert' and 'lay', what might be emerging are coalitions or assemblages or nexûs. Sometimes these are new social movements, sometimes they are pressure groups bringing together both the lay and the expert (and also 'intermediaries' – experts in communications or publicity skills of various kinds). Such hybrid groups entail scientific, political, experiential and communicational knowledges and resources (of course, there might also be other resources involved, importantly those provided by fund-raisers). It is such coalitions or nexûs or *assemblages* which are in conflict (rather than science and public): it is these which battle with one another for legitimacy in the eyes of both the wider public and also prime political (e.g. regulatory authorities) and commercial (e.g. pharmaceutical companies) institutions.

In this landscape, the relationship between public and science is far from fixed or dichotomized. Indeed, we might call these alliances or assemblages 'ethno-epistemic' in character. By this term, we mean that they are locally situated, have more or less well-delineated identities (though drawing on global flows of knowledge and culture) and are, crucially, involved in the 'establishment' of knowledge and the production of knowledge claims. The latter half of this book will include further discussion of these ethno-epistemic assemblages and their implications for both PUS and scientific governance.

So far we have stressed how social theory can contribute to ethnographic public understanding of science. However, we suggested above that we are also keen to show what ethnographic public understanding of science has to offer social theory. In the Introduction to this book, we expressed a concern that social theoretical accounts rarely engage with the complexity of empirical material, not least the data that comes out of studies in the public understanding of science.

On this score, we can suggest that it is certainly necessary to take a more grounded look at the relationship between 'local' and 'global' identities. It may well be that the specific and situated circumstances of a science policy debate or scientific controversy will influence what sorts of identities and what sorts of connections are mobilized. Kerr and Cunningham-Burley (2000) have noted in relation to the public's responses to the new human genetics that not only late-modernist (or reflexive modernist) relations are evidenced in people's assessment of these innovations (that is to say, they are critical or ambivalent towards them), but so too are modernist ones (they are highly trusting of experts). Moreover, in this particular context of human genetics, there is also recourse to pre-modern identities concerned with kinship and blood. This is important because it hints at, and this is something that Kerr and Cunningham Burley neglect, the fact that such reflexive modernist, modernist and pre-modern 'repertoires' or 'discourses' might be resources that can be deployed in the appropriate circumstance.

This point is elaborated by Michael and Carter (2001). In considering the efficacy of schools teaching materials (research updates on cystic fibrosis, for example) produced by the Medical Research Council, Michael and Carter held focus groups with school students. What emerged was that the students (as well as the teachers and scientists who contributed to the updates) assessed sources of knowledge (over and above the updates, sources such as the web, GPs, medical journals, family, soap operas, science fiction were mentioned) in terms of *product*. How did the knowledges available from these sources measure up against objective scientific knowledge, and in what ways did they contribute to coverage of the curriculum? Obviously enough, this is a deficit model of understanding: in the context of examination and curricular requirements, judgement of these disparate sources was in terms of whether they would enable students to assimilate the correct knowledge.

However, running concurrently with this valuation of sources, students also engaged in a process whereby they subsequently problematized their valuations. Thus, as soon as one person suggested that source X was good, the next speaker would say that she doesn't trust X and quite trusts Y, which another speaker would immediately derogate in order to express a preference for source Z, and so on. Here, we might say that we are witnessing public understanding of science as a cultural practice wherein everything is rendered contingent, including scientific materials and knowledge locally derived (e.g. from relatives). Instead of knowledge being a product, it is a *process*; indeed, a collective performance of contingency and movement where no singular discourses/interpretative repertoires predominate. So alongside discourses which represent these sources as leading to a product-like knowledge, we also see a collective *process* of picking up, comparing, stringing together without *necessarily* reaching any resolution/product. This implies that while the public can, for some purposes, settle upon a certain knowledge *product* that enables a particular valued activity (in this case, learning/exam-taking, but it could be decision-making or policy formulation), running alongside this is a *process* of on-going negotiation which has value in its own right.

All this again hints at the heterogeneous and relational nature of science–public interactions. In fact, as we shall see in subsequent chapters, for all that (as suggested above) the public melds into other constituencies (not least in what we have tentatively called ethno-epistemic assemblages), it is also emergent – the object of much discourse and practice. At this point, and having completed the first twist of our spiral involving PUS research, scientific governance and social theory, it becomes necessary to take stock of our progress so far. How compatible exactly are these different accounts of the relationship between science and the wider publics? And how might we hope to move on in conceptual, empirical and practical terms? That is the task we address in the following chapter.

5 Reconceptualizing science, society and governance

Taking stock

In the three preceding chapters, we have examined the different ways in which the relationship between science and the public has been interpreted across the domains of public understanding of science, scientific governance and social theory. In this chapter, we draw together some of the themes developed so far. In particular, we consider how each of these domains has formulated key features of the relationship between science and society, and discuss the extent to which these can be said to resonate (or clash) with one another. By the end of the chapter, we will have provided an overview and comparison of the main perspectives and domains. We will also have suggested a more satisfactory basis for future social scientific investigation and practical activity in the broad area of science, social theory and public knowledge.

As we discuss, the conventional distinction between scientific governance, PUS research and social theory should now give way to a richer and better informed view of science–public relations. Certainly, we aim to bring these three domains into greater alignment, but also to extend and reconceptualize each of them. In this chapter, we will do this both by presenting an overview and comparison of the key points from the previous chapters and by exploring one particular example of science–public relations.

The case study of Jarrow (in the North East of England) can be presented as an illustration of the ethnographic PUS tradition – where a long-established community stands in opposition to modernistic forms of progress and the technical systems upon which these depend. Jarrow can also be put forward as a significant challenge to scientific governance and the encouragement of active citizenship. In the midst of apparent apathy and social alienation, what are the best methods of encouraging public engagement with science and technology? At the same time, Jarrow can be portrayed as the manifestation of globalization and shifting forms of self-identity: a world where transnational companies have displaced local industry and traditional working-class employment has given way to the service sector. While each of these accounts has its own validity, we propose instead that new ways of thinking are required which both build upon and cut across this three-way distinction. At this point, concepts of ethno-epistemic assemblage and the blurring of the science–society distinction come to the fore.

Pulling the strands together

When we look back over the three preceding chapters, and overfly the literatures, case studies and examples with which they grapple, many common themes and motifs become apparent. These motifs can now serve as the basis for a comparative discussion of the previous chapters. In bald outline these include:

- the model of the public;
- the figure of the citizen;
- the model of democracy;
- the role of culture, the status of values and the place of knowledge;
- the nature of society;
- the character of science and the 'nature of nature';
- the mode of communication.

Of course, it goes without saying that this list is not exhaustive, and that the items within it are anything but mutually exclusive. Moreover, in homing in on these dimensions, we inevitably have to abstract from the complex domains of public understanding of science, science policy and social theory. That is to say, what we will end up comparing within these domains are those endeavours that seem to us to be particularly interesting, innovative and fecund. Thus, ethnographic public understanding of science is, we believe, potentially more revealing than survey perspectives; social theoretical treatments of globalization strike us as more insightful than those constrained by national and regional boundaries; policy initiatives that lay stress on the public as active citizens seem to us to hold greater promise than those that conceive of the public as necessarily passive and chronically lacking in knowledge. In sum, we have had to be selective. This also means that we have cut the main elements down to the basics, although hopefully without caricaturing any of these complex discussions.

In this section, then, we begin to compare our three domains along a number of key dimensions.

The model of the public

The PUS literature clearly operates with a diversity of models of the public: as passive or active, knowledgeable or ignorant, unitary or divergent, atomized or collective. These models have been contested but, as we have argued, there does seem to be one in particular that is gaining predominance: the public as social actors who can reflexively engage with science, making contingent judgements about the trustworthiness of experts and their knowledge in the context of their own cultural and social investments. We call this the 'citizen scientist' model (Irwin 1995). By comparison, key writers in social theory, while accepting much of this version of the public, increasingly embed it within the dynamics of globalization. The public is thus an altogether more dispersed and emergent entity: coming together in pragmatic alliances (Beck 1992) only to fragment once the perceived need has receded. In contrast, science policy, while increasingly giving expression to a 'citizen scientist' version of the public, nevertheless still has recourse to more traditional models: for example, the public as being chronically deficient in the appropriate knowledge and thus in need of 'education'.

The figure of the citizen

Related to the foregoing is the figure of the citizen. For science policy, it is increasingly (but variably) accepted that the public as citizens should have greater voice in the policy-making process. But this seems primarily to be on the basis of some notion of the public as embodying or holding 'values' that need to be addressed by policy makers. Certainly, this recent invitation to the policy-making forum does suggest a determination on the part of policy and government actors to re-establish legitimacy and authority in the face of expressed public concerns and criticisms. The assumption seems to be that public support and trust can be regained if questions of value are explicitly addressed within the policy process. Meanwhile, residual within policy-making circles is a view of the public as being empowered as citizens only once they have been exposed to, and properly assimilated, 'real scientific facts'. The notion of a 'firewall' between the 'scientific' and 'public' aspects of scientific governance serves also to restrict the influence of public views and assessments.

In contrast, ethnographic public understanding of science draws upon a model of the public as, as it were, a 'de-voiced' citizen. In its dealing with scientific institutions, the public, despite its rich and valuable situated knowledge, is marginalized from the policy-making process. So, here it is assumed that the public is already equipped to act in a citizenly capacity, but is obstructed by current forms of government consultation and the institutional principles upon which these are based. When we come to social theory, the emphases upon consumption and globalization suggest that citizenship itself has a rather fluid status, one that is increasingly manifested in new activities (forms of consumption, political and economic practices, social movements), but also directed towards global actors (the media, the broader public, commercial concerns) as well as nation states.

The model of democracy

Closely allied with these different models of the citizen are models of democracy or, more broadly, of political process. For science policy, it can be argued (Michael and Brown 2000) that there is an assumption that politics takes place within a parliamentary forum, and within the institutional structures that make up a representative democracy. What then comes to be at issue is the actual representativeness of different interests. For a public to be included in policy negotiations, it must be 'representative' of some constituency or else serve as a key 'stakeholder'. In contrast, ethnographic public understanding of science tends to suggest that 'democracy' should take place at (and be responsive to) the local level. It is at these sites where the situated knowledges of lay local publics should interact on, at the very least, an equal footing with scientific expertise in the production of locally contingent decisions and policies (which can eventually feed into broader policy initiatives).

Finally, for social theory, one might say that political process expands 'beyond' the local to encompass the global. By virtue of the new technological and social networks that make up the 'global', citizenly activities at one site (e.g. boycotting the products of a particular multinational or nation state) can have impacts at a distant site. Each of these three perspectives suggests different 'locales of negotiation': respectively, the national parliament and apparatus of government as representative of the interests that make up the nation state; the local as a site where practical decisions are made between 'experts' (whether they be scientific, regulatory or lay); and the global network where distributed, collective lay actors impact at a distance upon particular political and economic agents.

The role of culture, the status of values and the place of knowledge

We have put together these categories of culture, values and knowledge because they all, in one way or another, in one domain or another, are seen to characterize the public and the citizen. Thus, for science policy, the public is particularly important because it embodies certain values (say, concerning the environment or animal rights or animal welfare) that are seen to be necessary for the policy-making process. However, it is also assumed that values sometimes militate against the uptake of 'accurate scientific information' – values in so far as they facilitate 'prejudice' (and thus resistance to the supposed 'facts of the matter') are often attached to a deficit model of the public. But this focus upon values also reflects another set of conditions: values as 'assumptions' that shape cognition and practice are related to ethics, being a less formal version. They are, in principle, 'abstractable' or formalizable and thus can be incorporated into a general discussion *about* values. However difficult this discussion might turn out to be, there is still nevertheless a framework of rational deliberation in which values (and ethics) are expressed and articulated (often with the aid of 'ethics professionals' – by and large, utilitarians of various sorts; cf. Barns 1995).

In contrast, for ethnographic public understanding of science, the emphasis is upon identity and culture which is seen to be 'contextual', and emergent in opposition to the inappropriate body language of scientific institutions. In so far as the culture and identity attached to publics also encompass forms of communication, what counts as negotiation, discussion or debate is up for grabs. As has been pointed out with respect to AIDS activism, new modes of argumentation were brought into play by activists. This issue of modes of communication is addressed in a subsection below. Suffice it to say here that science policy assumes that an overarching framework or forum is attainable within which knowledge, values and culture can be 'negotiated', whereas for ethnographic public understanding of science, such frameworks or fora are themselves the objects of negotiation, contextual analysis and contestation.

Within social theoretical treatments of culture, values and knowledge, we find that, because people in a globalized world are exposed via a multiplicity of media to an enormous array of knowledges, cultures and values, identities are altogether more febrile. There is, at least in principle, a lot more flexibility in the positions one might take on a given scientific issue or, indeed, in relation to science-in-general. In the context of these expanded horizons, politics (sometimes in the form of altered consumption patterns) is conducted through networks that tie together different 'locals' (and thus cultures, values, identities and knowledges). Moreover, given the rise of consumer culture as discussed by many social theorists, knowledge, values and culture are not simply concerned with practical matters. Aesthetic concerns also characterize how science is appropriated by lay publics. If science policy points to the importance of more or less stable values in the public, and ethnographic public understanding highlights more or less stable cultural identities (derived from the traditions of the lay local and emergent in the 'confrontation' with scientific institutions), social theory picks out the potential fluidity of such values, identities and natures (which is not to say that, under certain circumstances, these do not congeal into something stable, cogent and incisive).

The nature of society

The preceding headings are all tied to tacit models of society. For ethnographic public understanding, society is made up of a series of 'local' contexts and social sites. Some of these are exclusively 'lay', others are expert or scientific. Clearly there is some connection between different lay settings and between the lay and the scientific (not least in those confrontations where the lay responds to the antagonistic body language of the scientific). The nature of these connections is somewhat under-theorized in ethnographic public understanding of science, although some attention has been paid to the role of the media in this regard. In contrast, for relevant social theory, such connections are of utmost importance. Indeed, arguably, it is precisely the connective process mediated by the new technological and social conduits that has become a major object of study in social theory. In the process, the 'locals' rather seem to lose the distinctiveness attributed to them by ethnographic public understanding of science. Instead of society being conceptualized in terms of the local, the emphasis in contemporary social theory is upon the new and increasingly extensive connective processes that make society 'global'.

When we turn our attention to science policy, society emerges as a series of interest groups (or 'stakeholders') in possession of interests and values that must be managed to generate policy that, to whatever feasible degree, accommodates those interests and values. Of course, part of this accommodation is ensuring that there exists some common ground for debate. As we have already noted, while this entails some change on the part of scientific institutions (e.g. becoming more responsive to the concerns and expertise of lay groups), there is also an element of 'educating' (or else marginalizing) those interests that remain beyond the common ground (e.g. 'extreme' environmental or animals rights groups).

The character of science and the nature of nature

In reviewing some of these comparisons, we have inevitably made mention, in one way or another, of science. For science policy, despite the rich uncertainties that surround, indeed constitute, what Funtowicz and Ravetz (1993) have called post-normal science, science still continues to be viewed in terms of 'facts'. There is a real nature 'out there' and scientists, while often hampered in their endeavours, can in principle derive a true representation of it. Science in the abstract, in the end, is the locus where the truth about nature resides. In contrast, ethnographic public understanding of science with its lineage to the sociology of scientific knowledge's concern with the concrete doings of scientists (see Chapter 2) focuses much more on the local practices of scientists and laypeople. Knowledges emerge from their peculiar social, technological and institutional contexts. What is to count as nature is thus 'up for grabs'. Sometimes it is the case that the 'nature' constructed by lay local communities is much more useful than that produced by scientists (as Wynne has amply shown). According to this perspective, then, we have multiple knowledges attached to particular groups (expert or lay) vying with each other for supremacy among the appropriate constituencies. Now, of course, within lay groups there may be identifiable experts operating (and vice versa), but the conceptual divide between expert and lay largely still holds.

Within relevant social theory, there is no standard version of science – rather, not altogether unexpectedly, there is some variation. For example, Wynne (1996) has criticized social theorists such as Giddens and Beck for simplifying science by leaving under-interrogated its ability to find facts. At the same time, as we have seen in Chapter 4, other contributors to social theory have focused upon the way that science is now part of a global task-scape to which laypeople have access. Within this new terrain, science is interwoven with other forms of knowledge (lay, legal, commercial) in the production of complex arguments and practices directed towards various economic and political actors. Thus, certain new social movements (e.g. environmental) have available to them local knowledge, scientific knowledge, legal knowledge, economic knowledge and so on, and these are combined in the contingent process of argumentation. So, in keeping with ethnographic public understanding of science and its sociology of scientific knowledge inflection, such social theoretical accounts assume that scientific knowledge is the product of local circumstance (of the laboratory, the field site, the technique or the paradigm). But this scientific knowledge is not regarded as oppositional to, or antagonistic towards, lay knowledge. Rather, it is part of the disparate knowledges that flow globally as components in a huge intellectual resource that can be drawn upon in the process of 'making a case' in some or other process contestation (with GPs, politicians, companies, etc.). Of course, this does not mean that such knowledges are chosen and combined willy nilly: they must still obey whatever warrants characterize the local site of contestation (e.g. in the GP's surgery, in public inquiry, within a social movement). In sum, we have seen science being simultaneously ascribed the status of fount of truth, site of contingent knowledge production and global resource.

The mode of communication

Another somewhat more tacit dimension along which our three domains might be compared concerns what we might call the 'mode of communication'. In the context of the present discussion, this phrase refers to the ways in which science and the public 'speak' to one another. This, of course, means that the term 'communicate' must carry a lot of conceptual baggage, for these interactions between science and the public are, as we have already discussed, rather complicated. First, mode of communication can refer to the sorts of intermediaries that relay 'knowledge' across these two constituencies (for example, teachers, the media, scientists themselves, public relations spokespersons). Secondly, it can refer to the sorts of technologies (in the broad sense) that can serve as the conduit of information flow (various fora, papers, museums, telephones, television, new information and communication technologies). Thirdly, it can refer to the 'stylistic' aspect of information – certain, uncertain, metaphorical, quantitative, textual, graphic and so on.

For science policy, the range of modes of communication seems to be increasing. This is all of a piece with various governmental initiatives to enhance the 'public understanding of science', initiatives which Gregory and Miller (1998) parody as policy makers delivering 'a new commandment from on high: thou shalt communicate' (p. 1). For ethnographic public understanding of science, attention has in the past been focused on rather traditional fora where publics and scientists meet up to discuss face-to-face the issues at stake (e.g. public inquiries, local meetings). However, this is changing, as research into such matters as internet debates begins to grow (Finney 1998).

In contrast, social theory has tended to stress the role of new information and communication technologies in this relation. Thus, the internet is seen as a key medium for the dissemination of information and the (re)production of new social movements. However, this new emphasis might well be at the expense of thinking about the significance of more mundane technologies (such as the telephone or newsletter). We shall return to the way that the mode of communication shapes the relations between, and the 'indistinction' of, science and the public below.

Making connections

The foregoing list is, to reiterate, anything but complete. It should be glaringly obvious that the items are not discrete categories and also that we have dealt with each in rather a blunt fashion. In this section, we further draw out their connections in part to summarize the previous discussions.

We can distil out of the various comparisons three broader dimensions:

- social world;
- knowing;
- governance.

The identification of the 'social world' addresses in particular the way that the divide between expert and lay is rendered in public understanding of science, social theory and the institutional practices of science policy. The notion of 'knowing' is directed at the range of practices – cognitive, emotional, cultural – by which scientific and lay actors interact. As such, knowing encompasses a disparate array of relations that entail, for example, facts, values, culture, identity, trust and opinions. Finally, 'governance' denotes the complex relations of power that pertain between various scientific and lay actors. Such relations include how these scientific and lay actors are represented (e.g. as ignorant or enfranchised), the configurations of agonistic actors (as individuals, local publics, new social movements, or as we have suggested above, 'ethno-epistemic assemblages') and the modes of communication that mediate these relations of 'governance'.

To state the obvious once more, these three dimensions are deeply implicated in one another. Thus the 'social world' is attached to 'knowing' and 'governance'. Expert–lay distinctions reflect the type of 'knowing' practised by each and the relations of power – that is, the process of 'governance' – that mediate these distinctions. Similarly, 'knowing' assumes that knowledge, values and cultural artefacts flow between different social groupings, in the process reflecting and configuring both the character of the 'social world' and the forms of governance that shape how, by and to whom such knowledges, values and cultural artefacts are articulated. Finally, 'governance' is instrumental in the ranking and organization of different forms of knowing, and thus in the categorization of the 'social world' in terms of those constituencies that should or should not have a voice in policy making (and how that voice is heard).

We are now in a position to relate these three dimensions of 'social world', 'knowing' and 'governance' to our three domains of science policy, ethnographic public understanding of science and social theory.

In brief, we can say that science policy tends to articulate the relation between science and lay actors by either still assuming a cognitive 'deficit' among lay actors, or representing the public as the embodiment of 'values' which somehow need to be accommodated within the science policy-making process. As such, the model of the social world here is a more or less sharp distinction drawn, on the basis of different forms of 'knowing', between science and society. In this context, governance – in its most liberal aspect – is geared towards bringing together the relevant scientific and lay actors. In its more elitist manifestation, governance entails the education of publics whose subsequent scientific literacy better qualifies them to contribute to such dialogue. However, the form of this 'bringing together' is still relatively untested, even if institutional discussion and inquiry is now taking place (e.g. the consultation exercise discussed in Chapter 3 or more recent European initiatives over GM food). New fora such as science juries and consensus conferences have yet to be integrated into science policy – their function and status are still somewhat uncertain in the UK but also, for example, in Scandinavian countries, where practical experience is more substantial but doubts over practical significance and political relevance remain.

For ethnographic public understanding of science, the 'social world' is comprised, in crucial part, of local lay communities and scientific actors that are themselves conceptualized as no less local. Thus 'knowing' is fundamentally attached to, and derived within, these locals, which are characterized in terms of complex configurations of situated knowledges and practices, interests, values, identities, local cultures and traditions. Lay actors are thus defined by the specificities of their local characteristics. However, they are also regarded as emergent, especially in relation to their conflicts with relevant scientific actors. Scientific institutions that practise inappropriate forms of governance (for example, by adopting particular sorts of over-confident institutional body language) deny the specificity and contingency of their own 'knowing' and thus are likely to disaffect lay local communities. The appropriate governance model for ethnographic public understanding of science thus rests on a recognition of the value of lay local publics' own knowledges and cultural identities.

When we move on to consider our use of social theory, we have emphasized those variants that draw particular attention to the social world as composed of global and dynamic flows of information, materials, persons, finance. In this version of the social world, what counts as science and lay becomes blurred by the fact that scientific experts contribute to, and are an indispensable part of, particular publics, and particular publics (such as self-help groups, non-governmental organizations) are major players in the production of scientific knowledge. Publics, in this model, are no longer 'local' – they are resourced (intellectually, ethically, culturally) via various media from many different and distant sources, both lay and scientific. Moreover, such global resourcing is now crucially tied up with expressive dimensions of identity which are no longer solely local. Governance, in this dynamic context, is conceptualized as decentred – scientific experts, communications professionals, policy analysts, lay activists and so on form alliances (which we have described as 'ethno-epistemic' in character) that compete with one another for legitimation to impact upon particular targeted actors (which might be governmental, commercial or public). Knowing thus becomes an eclectic, heterogeneous and distributed process. We summarize these patterns in Table 5.1.

Exploring the Jarrow case study

So far in this chapter, we have presented some of the key differences and contrasts between the three core elements of the book. In the previous sections, we have done this in very schematic and abstract terms. In what follows, we will test out some of these points in a more grounded (albeit brief) fashion through the consideration of one empirical example originally conducted within the ethnographic PUS tradition. This will allow us to assess the implications of each of these three perspectives for our interpretation of

Table 5.1 Summary of domains

	Ethnographic PUS	Scientific governance	Social theory
Social world	Publics defined in terms of lay local culture, but also characterized *against* science	Ambivalent divide between science and lay, vestiges of deficit model still in evidence. However, partial shift toward PUS-style sensibilities	The social world composed of global, fluid connections and flows, not least of knowledges and cultural artefacts. Distinction between science and public thus blurred
Knowing	Both lay and scientific knowledge is contingent, situated. Knowing entails cultural identity which affects local knowledge and trust-worthiness of others and their knowledges	Cognitive deficit model of knowing still in evidence: ambiguous status of science as arbiter of true knowledge. However, public increasingly seen to have voice, not least since they embody 'values'	Knowing – both for science and lay constitu-encies – entails contingent processes combining knowledge, culture, ethics, trust. These flow into groupings through multiplicity of media
Governance	Public assumed to have relevant knowledge and citizenly skills. Institutional body language alienates public. Advocates open dialogue at local or national level where lay publics have equal voice	More public participation desirable, but mechanisms still experimental. Assumed that 'action' is coordin-ated at national level. Form and status of public input still unclear or untested	Political actors shifting from nation state to global stage: non-governmental organizations/new social movements *vs* multinationals. Main points of conflict seem to be between *ethno-epistemic alliances* that are international, if not global

science–public relations. Equally, it will serve as a platform upon which to build discussions in the second part of this book over the development of fresh analytical and practical approaches.

Accordingly, we now move from a schematic overview to one very specific locality: the town of Jarrow in the South Tyneside region of North East England. As we will see in this section, although the Jarrow case was originally selected as the basis for a qualitative research project, it is also open to analysis from each of our three contrasting perspectives. Following this, we go on to consider new ways of analysing our chosen example.

Background

Jarrow is a place with a strong sense of its own cultural heritage and local history. Although Jarrow has more recently been associated with industrial development and decline, it has had a longer standing association with the Venerable Bede (A.D. 673–735), one of the greatest Christian scholars. As Ellen Wilkinson began the first chapter of her classic 1939 account, *The Town that was Murdered: The Life-story of Jarrow*: 'Jarrow's first export was not battleships but Christianity' (p. 11). As Wilkinson noted, Bede was based at the monastery of St. Paul in Jarrow from where he helped turn Jarrow into a centre for learning across early medieval Europe. The church of St. Paul still stands today, prompting Wilkinson (1939: 11–12) to write:

> A little way out of the town . . . there stands a squat little church with a curious square tower . . . It is grimy with industrial soot. The churchyard though carefully tended now, is grimy, too. But if you stand by the Saxon doorway, your feet will be on land that for 1225 years has been continuously the site of Christian service.

However, even a succinct summary of the recent history of Jarrow necessitates going back to the late-eighteenth and, especially, nineteenth centuries when the town grew spectacularly through two main industries, shipbuilding and coal mining – with the chemical industry following close behind. On that basis, Jarrow's population grew from 3500 in 1851 to 35,000 in 1921. Following this dramatic growth at the heart of the industrial development of North East England, industrial decline hit the area very hard. Unemployment grew in the 1930s and the closure of the main shipyards was a final blow to the town. In 1936, in a famous moment in British labour history, some 200 people marched the 300 miles from Jarrow to London in protest at the miseries of unemployment and the level of poverty in the area.

Jarrow had become by the middle of the twentieth century an emotive symbol of social deprivation but also of working-class identity. The 'Jarrow March' still represents a powerful image of poverty and social degradation, but also has come to be associated with contemporary nostalgia for a forgotten world of strong social roots and traditional lifestyle (with black and white photographs of the marchers presented to the haunting background of traditional music). This working-class background of poverty, regional dialect and strong local ties has been exploited to the full by one of South Tyneside's better known (and bestselling) authors, Catherine Cookson. Indeed, boundary signs for South Tyneside proudly proclaim the area's identity as 'Catherine Cookson country' (suggesting a merging of industrial history and literary portrayal).

Over the last few decades, Jarrow has continued to be marked by urban deprivation and unemployment (although absolute levels of affluence have certainly improved). Jarrow remains a relatively poor district and one which scores low on most of the conventional indices of wealth and prosperity. While the North East of England has not enjoyed the economic growth and prosperity enjoyed by other parts of England (despite continued efforts to bring large employers to the area), Jarrow has been relatively disadvantaged even within the region.

However, the case study being presented here was not primarily about the general social welfare of the district but instead about the relationship between the community and the local chemical industry. Commissioned by the Health and Safety Executive as part of a wider study of public perceptions of risk associated with major accident hazards (Walker *et al.* 1998), the research project involved a series of focus groups with local residents. These discussions explored the local public's sense of community and way of life, with special attention to nearby industry and the hazards it represented.

At the core of the research project was one chemical works near the centre of the town. The works in question began operation in the mid-1950s. Since the early 1980s, chlorine has been stored and used at the plant. Nearly 2000 people live within 400 metres of the site boundary and these residents became the focus of sociological investigation. Central to the project were concepts of risk and local communication. The research was also designed to consider the relationship between the 'lay local' and various sources of advice and expertise, including, of course, the chemical plant itself.

Jarrow as ethnographic PUS

The very way in which this case study has so far been presented suggests a strong connection with the ethnographic PUS tradition (as indeed might be expected given the research team). The research focus was very much on one defined locality and on the specific cultural setting within which issues of risk, knowledge, citizenship and social change were discussed and generated. As previously identified (Irwin *et al.* 1999), powerful themes to emerge from the project included:

- memory;
- situated expertise;
- morality and social powerlessness.

Memory
The researchers found that discussions of hazard issues and the local environment within Jarrow were strongly coloured by previous events and memories, sometimes going all the way back to the 1936 Jarrow March. New statements from the company in question, local initiatives to 'educate' the public about the local environment (for example, through school visits and talks), minor

incidents and near misses, all would be considered against the backdrop of what had gone before. This meant also that assessments of the safety of the plant were inseparable from the larger backdrop of locally understood cultural and industrial change. Thus, while some would speak nostalgically of the old days when work was plentiful, hard and, predominantly, male, others would dismiss this as a backward-looking view which did little to help the area. In that way also the Jarrow March functioned both as a matter of local pride but also (for some) as an albatross impeding a 'modern' vision of Jarrow.

Either way, Jarrow memories were often associated with a sense of bitterness that this was a place forgotten by wider society. This point was often linked to the North American ownership of the chemical works in question: if it is so safe, why have they chosen to site it in a neglected part of England? More generally, local memories form a central element of the 'sense of place' and, indeed, could be said to constitute the community and its separation from the rest of British society (and even from the rest of South Tyneside). Collective memories both reinforce a self-image of a community under threat from the outside world and, in this case, heighten a sense of powerlessness and alienation. This then provides a significant cultural context for the discussion of risk perceptions and environmental awareness.

Situated expertise

The topic of information and 'informedness' was central to this project. Of course, the conventional wisdom as applied in advance to this case was that the local public is ignorant about the risks of the chemical industry – and specifically about the risks of a major toxic release. Although the research acknowledged that the local public was inclined to complain about bad smells, childhood asthma and river pollution rather than the potential problems of a failure of the containment vessels, this was not presented as ignorance. Instead, the project explored the lay knowledges and contextual understandings developed by residents as a consequence of living and working in the area. Thus, focus groups included lucid accounts of the effects of local pollution on the fish in the nearby river and the connection between routine gas releases and children's respiratory problems.

The point, as one of us has already expressed (Irwin 2001b), is that such 'situated knowledge' represents an important local resource, but one that is very much rooted in the community rather than being provided by official institutions such as government or industry. While science emphasizes generalization, facts and the need for objectivity, 'contextual knowledge' gives weight to local factors, personal views and subjectivities. In this, situated expertise closely reflects the characteristics and culture of the local contexts in which it is generated and maintained.

What also emerged from the project was that this 'knowledge' should not be seen simply as a passive resource from which residents could 'borrow', but also as an active process of sense-making (what the researchers termed 'knowledging'). Thus, statements about, for example, environmental pollution in the locality were open to challenge, retraction and alteration within everyday talk. This was especially important within a culture where any tendency to pomposity or arrogance would be ruthlessly exposed.

Morality and social powerlessness

Prominent in the qualitative analysis of Jarrow residents were statements about right and wrong: usually taking the form of resentment that they were forced to live in such a hazardous and neglected environment. Thus, the widespread perception that the chemical works 'put little back' into the community fuelled outrage that local people should suffer the adverse consequences with none of the benefits. This moral judgement linked very strongly with a sense of social isolation and alienation. In a variety of areas – including housing, education, crime, employment, heath care – there was something morally wrong in the lack of attention and support being given to Jarrow people (a judgement also powerfully expressed in Ellen Wilkinson's 1939 account of Jarrow). In that sense also, criticisms of the environmental performance of local industry formed part of a much wider cultural world-view – suggesting, too, that a similar pattern of responses might have been elucidated to a range of different lines of inquiry.

Troublingly, however, the powerful sense of local alienation both raised public concern and left it frustrated – Jarrow had struggled for decades to be given recognition for its problems, so why should it change now? This contextual analysis, therefore, raises definite problems for governance. The implication from this case is that those who have the starkest views about technical, political and environmental matters are also the least likely to express those views within the conventional processes of representative democracy.

Jarrow and the challenges of scientific governance

The account just offered is both enlightening and challenging to the processes of governance. On the one hand, it brings a whole range of fresh observations and new perspectives to bear on scientific decision making. Among these, we can count the knowledgeability and awareness of local people. Indeed, one product from the larger national research project of which the Jarrow study was one part was a video of residents discussing, in generally intelligent and reflective terms, the issues at hand. This video was received with great interest by Health and Safety Executive officials who had not universally anticipated such a thoughtful response. It should also be noted that knowledgeability extended to include a significant number of people within the Jarrow area with relevant technical skills and understanding – for example, those who had worked in hazardous industries (including the plant in question) or the armed forces.

The context-laden character of Jarrow responses to petrochemical hazards also suggests that (contrary to one extreme version of the deficit model) people are not likely to become hysterical when confronted with new facts and information. Indeed, given the rich local culture of storytelling and robust discussion, it seems only right that industrialists and government officials should also give their version of the situation in an equally candid fashion. Particularly relevant for policy responses also was the finding that all sources of information (including local experts) will be opened up to sceptical treatment. Rather than accepting any single authoritative account, residents are more inclined to balance conditionally a range of views in terms of their trustworthiness, knowledgeability and perceived self-interestedness. This finding suggests the need for a more pluralist approach to public debate (rather than taking the more conventional view that there should be a single 'authoritative' source). To this list of policy-relevant findings we can add the implication from this study that uncertainty is very familiar to local people. Rather than attempting to deny or downplay elements of risk, there seems to be some further scope for industry and government to acknowledge but also justify this.

One final implication from the Jarrow study concerns the need for policy makers and risk communicators to know their audience. As we stressed within the larger research project (which considered various major hazard sites across England and Wales), Jarrow cannot be said to be 'typical' or 'representative'. Instead, and this follows directly from the ethnographic PUS tradition, we must approach local publics on a 'context by context' basis. The larger project identified a range of public responses to similar issues with, it must be said, Jarrow something of an extreme case in terms of negative public attitudes. This is not to deny that common themes can be identified across contexts – for example, the possible connection between social alienation and a suspicion of social institutions such as government and industry. However, it does suggest the difficulty of moving from such a contextual study to wider statements about the UK population as a whole.

On the other hand, and now we move to the challenging part of the equation, this account poses problems for national governance. If the aim is to establish a representative account of the population, then the qualitative methodology causes difficulties. Equally, most of the Jarrow population will hardly qualify as a 'stakeholder' for the very reasons discussed above. In this situation, one response from policy makers has been (as in the biosciences consultation) to apply a mixed methodology of quantitative as well as qualitative approaches. The justification for this is that, while the former can supply the 'black and white', the latter can give 'colour'. Although ethnographers inevitably include some quantitative data in their analyses (e.g. the size of different population groups), this does not suggest that these different methods can so easily be brought together (or 'triangulated'), as the discussion in Chapter 2 indicated. As we have already suggested, questionnaire-based approaches tend to exclude the kinds of contextual factors so successfully identified in the Jarrow study. According to context, therefore, it may not simply be a matter of 'black and white' or 'colour' but instead a *different picture* that emerges from these two methodologies.

Even more problematic for scientific governance is the challenge of drawing such voices into a meaningful national framework. Of course, it is possible to select a person from the Jarrow region as a 'representative' within a regional or national panel but this immediately removes the local context of discussion and interaction. It must also be said that many local people already are involved in various representative roles, from the community–industry liaison committee to councillors in local government. However, there is a characteristic distancing of 'ordinary' Jarrow people from such roles, as if their very selection as representatives automatically rendered them unrepresentative.

There is also (as was again demonstrated by the biosciences case) a question of how opinion is 'framed' within exercises in public 'dialogue'. The whole point of the ethnographic approach is that local people should themselves prioritize and structure issues rather than passively responding to pre-prepared questions which may be totally unfamiliar and unconsidered. Once again, the very framing of local opinion within such exercises can affect the kinds of public assessment that are subsequently offered. Of course, this is a problem for focus groups also, since the external selection of the 'key problem' (in our case, major accident hazards) will inevitably bias the discussion (so that there is a real danger that one is creating as well as reflecting attitudes and concerns). However, contextually sensitive discussions have possibilities that national studies must inevitably neglect.

More fundamentally, the whole basis for current policy is that there exists some 'national interest'. The Jarrow study's emphasis on contextuality suggests instead that there may be a variety of interests and that these can be seen from very different perspectives. From the viewpoint of a national government official who has been asked to inform her minister about 'public opinion' on the biosciences, major accident hazards or nuclear waste, this is a very challenging problem indeed. While the need for better communications and, especially, to 'know one's audience' can be accepted, the implication that national policy should be different in different parts of the country is hard to apply in areas such as these. Qualitative PUS analysis, therefore, leads to classic problems of governance such as the balance between regions and the nation state and the justification for imposing risks on certain sections of the population for the benefit of others. Looked at from the viewpoint of everyday discussions in a Jarrow pub or health centre, the requirements of London-based civil servants appear very remote indeed.

It should be stressed that none of this implies the absence of a practical significance for ethnographic research in this area. However, it does suggest that research such as the Jarrow study poses real challenges to national systems of governance – and the assumptions about the public (for example, as relatively homogeneous and led by certain 'stakeholders') upon which these typically draw.

Jarrow as social theory

When the Jarrow research project was conducted in 1996, the concept of 'searching Jarrow' on the internet was hardly considered. A cursory search today reveals literally thousands of results. The small jeweller's shop in the town centre has its own site. There is a website for the science fiction role-playing group based in Jarrow. A site is devoted to Dame Catherine Cookson and several to the Venerable Bede. Local estate agents advertise their services. One can locate a helpful guide to local (unofficial) skateboarding facilities. Inevitably, the Jarrow March features in several websites, including attempts to recreate the march in protest against unemployment from the 1970s onwards. There is an especially interesting Jarrow March connection to November 2000 when fuel protestors set out on a new 'Jarrow Crusade' down to London. This time, the journey would be made in a convoy of trucks as a rebellion against what were seen as excessive fuel taxes. One trade union chief is reported as condemning this imitation of the 1936 march. He stated that the fuel protest was offensive to the original marchers who were fighting for jobs and decent conditions rather than being 'employers simply seeking their own profits'. Jarrow featured prominently in the 2000 fuel protests before they slowly disappeared from public view.

Meanwhile, at another site, the web surfer is welcomed to 'Bede's World'. This educational facility and tourist attraction – physically located close to the study area discussed above – 'will entrance all members of the family with its unique blend of history, visual and hands-on displays, Christian heritage and farm life'. This attraction has been supported by the European Union as part of a local regeneration scheme. As if to emphasize the inseparability of local life from the nation, at the time of writing (August 2001) the site prominently states that the farm area has been closed as a precautionary measure against the spread of foot and mouth disease. However, there is a job vacancy for a farm assistant to work on the 'Anglo-Saxon demonstration farm'.

Bede's World represents an ambitious attempt at recreating the landscape of A.D. 700. The farm includes full-size reconstructions of buildings from Anglo-Saxon times. Pigs are specially bred to 'simulate the type of animal that was seen in Anglo-Saxon England'. Ancient strains of wheat and vegetable are grown. Hardly surprisingly, the farm assistant post requires 'good customer care skills'. A series of events at the tourist attraction aims to draw in visitors from around the world: including 'Anglo-Saxon Graves! Hands-on activities for all the family' and 'Meet the Anglo-Saxons!'. The centre is close to the 'Bede' railway station (and the 'Bede industrial estate'). The instructions on how to find Bede's World include advice for visitors arriving from the Scandinavian and Amsterdam ferries (which disembark nearby on the Tyne).

The point, of course, is that Jarrow has a national and global presence as well as a local one. The Jarrow March is an emblem of protest against national policy, but also against international capitalism. As Ellen Wilkinson observed, the decline of shipbuilding in Jarrow was a reflection of the growth of international competition. Jarrow could not be separated from wider economic forces and, indeed, the failure of local shipbuilders to keep up with world forces helped bring about their downfall. Attractions such as Bede's World represent an attempt to reach out to a national and international audience and, just like the symbolism of the Jarrow March (albeit in very different ways), they recreate Jarrow as a global centre. Meanwhile, the ethnographic study reported above took little account of the penetration of a place like Jarrow by road networks, television and, today, computer technologies. Even the ubiquitous football shirts proudly worn by local people represent symbols of international companies with a worldwide marketing presence.

As a further example of this national and global connectedness, every year the athletic one of us joins over 30,000 fellow runners from every part of the UK and many overseas countries in a road race (The Great North Run) which travels across parts of the area. Jogging awkwardly through the Jarrow roads with television cameras relaying pictures to a sleepy Sunday morning nation and helicopters tracking (albeit some way ahead) the elite international athletes, it is difficult to imagine Jarrow as an isolated community. Instead, the boundaries disappear in a 13-mile carnival of enthusiastic spectators and lumbering participants. At this moment, Jarrow becomes part of a national and international spectacle, even if this is by its very nature momentary. The run is at the same time a symbol of local culture and a carefully orchestrated manifestation of that culture to the world beyond the Jarrow boundary.

Seen in this light, the identity of Jarrow becomes considerably more fluid than first presented. Of course, it would be easier for us to select a place in the suburbs of London or in the heart of Silicon Valley, California to make this point. Jarrow, with its terraced houses and strong (and strongly self-conscious) regional ties, seems the very symbol of the lay local. However, the area cannot be cut off from global influences, whether these be television, the internet, youth culture or economic factors such as the presence of a North American company in the midst of the town (or the major Japanese car plant just a few miles down the road). Even the very artefacts and symbols which give this area its particular character – including the lingering imagery of the Jarrow March – are not exclusively 'owned' by the local population but have instead become associated with an internationally recognized form of political protest and, especially, the politics of class.

For ethnographic research, this presents something of a challenge. To take one example, ethnographic work has often downplayed the role of the national media, since this can appear very distanced from the specificities of everyday local life. It is not too hard to see how this can come about: national news reports, for instance, are hardly likely to give coverage to hazardous industry in Jarrow or local socio-economic problems (unless there is a particular crisis or newsworthy incident). However, this may downplay the more subtle influences of the media within everyday discussion. Thus, in one particularly evocative Jarrow discussion, the chemical works in question was compared with the US television series, *The X-Files* ('cos you never see anybody going in . . . Or coming out'). This suggests both an awareness of global television culture but also an imaginative link back to local life. At this point, we become very aware that the 'lay local' and the 'fluid global' are in closer interaction than is conventionally suggested by either social theory or contextual research.

New departures

As presented so far, ethnographic PUS, social theory and scientific governance represent three different domains. Certainly, it is not too hard – as we have partially demonstrated with the Jarrow case – to present these as very separate perspectives on the world. However, the previous section has, in making that very point, also begun to move us beyond it. While the perspective on scientific governance held by well-intentioned civil servants may be quite remote from the everyday life of an unemployed welder in Jarrow (or, indeed, from that of a Californian intellectual), this is not to say that there cannot be common ground between them – or that there cannot be mutual education and development. It is for this reason that we favour steps towards greater openness and participation even as we also recognize the inherent difficulties involved in such a move. Equally, and as we have just suggested, the apparent gulf between ethnographic studies of the 'lay local' and theoretical treatments of global culture may not be uncrossable. The challenge instead is to link the contextual specificities of a geographically defined community with a larger sense of national and international forces. In this, we are of course essentially re-stating C. Wright Mills' classic definition of the purpose of sociology (Mills 1959).

Acknowledgement of the existence, and the legitimacy, of these different perspectives represents a first step in the right direction. Going further, a number of observations offer at least the possibility of a more productive approach to the issues at the core of this book. These will be specifically developed in the following chapters. Briefly put, they can be expressed as follows:

1   The recognition of fresh connections between the local and the global or, more precisely, between *localizing* and *globalizing* ways of interpreting and acting upon the world. While certain forms of discourse emphasize the localizing aspects of, for example, Jarrow culture (whether local dialect, memories or sense of a hostile external world), others simultaneously offer a globalizing influence (the internet, television, fashion). The challenge both in theoretical and practical terms is to recognize these elements as being simultaneously at work without suggesting that either the local or the global is fixed or neatly separable.

2   An improved understanding of the dynamics and distribution of knowledge sources, including the recognition of knowledge development as an active process in which more than simply scientists participate. A recognition of *dynamic knowledge relations* also leads to a blurring of the lay/expert division upon which many initiatives in the public understanding of science are still based. Rather than seeking to impose single authoritative sources of knowledge and expertise, it becomes important to recognize the more distributed character of knowledge within society.

3   The possibility of new forms of local–global alliance: what we have already termed *ethno-epistemic assemblages*. Such assemblages in a case such as Jarrow might include particular groups of residents, national environmental organizations, scientists, factory inspectors and local newspapers. The point is, however, that these alliances are not fixed or unchanging but represent more transitory communities that coalesce and then melt. This also allows a more fluid treatment of social groups and citizens than is implied by simply allocating individuals to one camp or another.

4   *Citizenship* also may attract new meaning in this context. As we have discussed, challenges of scientific governance will not necessarily obey national boundaries. It becomes important, therefore, to recognize the transnational character of citizen activity – as demonstrated, for example, in global protests directed at the G8 summits in Seattle and Davos. Equally, and as in the Jarrow case, it is important to recognize the significance of sub-national activities even if these appear remote from the conventional model of representative democracy. In a more complex and heterogeneous world, it is important for national decision makers in particular to respond positively to

local variations and the existence of multiple communities (whether geographically defined or not).

5   Although we have not developed it here, *corporate governance* must also be addressed within this reconsideration of citizenship and assemblages. The fact that an international company is at the centre of the Jarrow case study (and, indeed, the GM case with which this book began) is in itself important and raises many questions about both public responses to industry and the degree to which corporations choose (or choose not) to engage themselves in public 'dialogue'. Once again, the company represents both a localizing and a globalizing mode of operation and can selectively emphasize either of these faces. Equally, the company in this case study participates in different alliances at different moments – for example, as part of the Jarrow community, as one cog in a multinational machine, as a key player within local economic development, as a benevolent employer and charity sponsor. Certainly, the approach developed in this book is very much applicable to corporate governance and the shifting assemblages this reflects and mediates.

6   At this point, and as we will discuss in the next chapter, rather than seeing concepts such as 'public', 'knowledge' and 'science' as separate fixed categories, we present them as the outcome of processes of *co-construction*. Each is made and re-made in differing ways within the conditions of social life, an observation that immediately brings together both the 'contextual' and 'theoretical' traditions discussed in this book. Co-construction also suggests that public responses can be variable and contextually dependent rather than predetermined and available for the researcher (or decision maker) to 'read off' whenever convenient. This is especially the case when dealing with new and unfamiliar issues.

7   More generally, we are living in a world where the distinction between 'science' and 'society' has become blurred – emphasizing both interconnection and mutual dependence. In numerous ways, the activities of science cannot be separated from those of society – with concepts such as 'regulatory science' (discussed in Chapter 3) emphasizing the meshing of technical and research activities with social, economic and regulatory concerns in a global setting. At the same time, 'society' cannot be said to exist independently of the activities of science, whether it be telecommunications, industrial development or our very way of interpreting the world around us. As we will discuss, this has major consequences both for social scientific understanding and for governance.

In the case of Jarrow, what starts as a very restricted manifestation of local and environmental conditions can be seen more promisingly as an example of the interconnectedness of the 'lay local' and the 'fluid global'. The challenge with which we are left is to find new ways of addressing this relationship while also tackling more practical concerns over scientific governance and public policy. It is this challenge which is addressed in the remaining chapters of this book.

6 Ethno-epistemic assemblages: heterogeneity and relationality in scientific citizenship

In the preceding chapters, we have progressively complicated what it means to 'do' public understanding of science. By 'do' we mean two things. On the one hand, there are the activities of members of the public as they come to grips with scientific knowledge. On the other, there are the activities of academics as they come to grips with these lay activities of coming to grips with scientific knowledge. However, as we saw in the Jarrow case, it becomes very difficult to sustain a vision of the public as a 'pure' lay community. For instance:

- These publics are already highly knowledgeable in ways that could fruitfully inform scientific assessment of the risks posed by local scientific institutions – there is a blurring of expert and lay knowledge.
- These publics are also embroiled in networks of alliances with such actors as national environmental organizations, scientists, factory inspectors and local newspapers – there is a blurring of lay and expert actors.
- These publics are at once embedded in a highly distinctive local cultural context, and are able to draw on globally available culture in articulating their relations with local scientific institutions – there is a blurring of the local and the global.

These 'blurrings' raise important issues for how we are to study the public understanding of science. Indeed, it is arguable that the very phrase the 'public understanding of science' becomes misleading given that both 'public' and 'science' no longer stand as distinct entities. In other words, and this addresses the second meaning of 'doing' public understanding of science, as social scientists we must ask ourselves whether we need new categories that better represent these processes and dynamics. Instead of assuming the contrast between science and society, it becomes necessary to explore contrasts between actors or constituencies each comprised of mixtures of both science and society.

Here is another example of this process of mixing things up. In 2000, one of us attended a Helsinki conference on transgenic animals in medicine. At this meeting, gathered from across Europe, were a number of disparate actors – scientists, regulators, politicians, animal welfare activists, patient group spokespersons, social scientists, pharmaceutical company representatives. Over the course of the two-day meeting, two mixed groupings (or what we shall call 'ethno-epistemic assemblages') took shape. These were, unsurprisingly, polarized into pro and anti transgenic animal research blocs. But each bloc was comprised of a range of actors that included the ostensibly 'expert' (e.g. commercially and publicly funded scientists) and 'lay' (regulators, patient and animal spokespersons). In the plenary sessions, the debate ranged over a number of topics, including the scientific, the regulatory, the cultural, the ethical and the experiential. Each of these was given voice and each seemed to form part of a discursive mosaic. Thus, the arguments against the use of transgenic animals were grounded in accounts of personal suffering (despite being a patient, one could still disagree wholeheartedly with the development and use of transgenic animals) that also referred to the possibility of alternative research agendas and health policy options.

Here, we saw admixtures of ethical, experiential, scientific and regulatory discourses that together served to build a case against the use of transgenic animals in medical research. This dynamic, in which so many different forms of knowledge are brought together, related and patterned, might be called a process of *co-construction*, which captures the dual process of the social and the natural being varyingly constructed (Irwin 2001b). In this case, we see many 'natures' and many 'socials' being co-constructed by many co-actors who are themselves co-constructed as both lay and expert.

Thus, actors who are favourable towards transgenic animal experimentation might represent animals as pragmatically and regrettably subservient to the needs of human sufferers. As such, and very crudely formulated, nature and society are co-constructed in a relation where nature is subject to change (is genetically pliable), whereas society is represented as stable (human needs are reified). In contrast, those who are negative towards transgenic animal experimentation provide the opposite co-construction: nature is stable (species integrity is reified) whereas society is pliable (there are many ways of 'socially doing' death and health).

This example hopefully illustrates the processes of blurring or mixing up or hybridization (and there are many more terms we could deploy) that we have come across again and again in the course of this book. For instance, we witnessed this mixing up in Epstein's account of the AIDS movement and in our own analysis of the GM crops debate. We have seen the ways that resources of all sorts (including scientific knowledge) flow across communities, institutions and organizations, serving to make connections between what would usually be thought of as discrete constituencies. These flows enable, and reflect, the emergence of particular blocs or groupings of actors that cut across scientific, commercial, civic, regulatory, media and lay sectors. It is these blocs or groupings that enter into controversy and contest the 'truth' and 'value' of various knowledges (scientific, institutional, ethical, governmental, economic and so on). In the transgenic animal example sketched above, we see these flows conveniently concentrated at a single meeting. Instead of arguments that are 'largely scientific' or 'largely lay', there is a series of statements that weave in and out of expert and lay domains. The crucial point is that such *discursive promiscuity* is totally unremarkable within, and across, such blocs or groupings.

Our various examples seem to point to the emergence of new entities, new hybrids, new *ethno-epistemic assemblages*. This last, rather cumbersome, term has been developed to help us explore these admixtures of science and society. It is a term that we shall unravel in some detail below. Its main function is as a heuristic: it is a tool with which to explore how such heterogeneous groupings might be characterized. Ethno-epistemic assemblages are meant to aid us in examining how such 'odd' mixtures come together, cohere and 'work' as, perhaps, unitary or singular actors.

Furthermore, and as we shall see, ethno-epistemic assemblages represent a possible way of investigating how the blurring of science and society (and the emergence of assemblages) might entail rather surprising new resources and methods. For instance, one example we consider below involves the performance of personal suffering, which is sometimes used to justify certain scientific knowledge-making practices. What ethno-epistemic assemblages can thus do is sensitize us to the ways that, in making knowledge claims, many disparate techniques (both discursive and practical) can be utilized.

Ethno-epistemic assemblages also do something rather interesting. They can serve as a vehicle for examining more difficult issues. One such issue concerns the way that the two versions of 'doing' public understanding of science are, empirically at least, less distinct than at first might appear. That is to say, studying academically the public's understanding of science – articulating, representing and disseminating this in a particular way – serves in shaping *how* the public understands not only science, but also *itself*. Ethno-epistemic assemblages thus sensitize us to the way that academic analysis is part of the production of particular versions of public and science and, therefore, of the hybrid admixtures that make up the assemblages themselves. Another issue that ethno-epistemic assemblages can serve to highlight concerns the role of non-humans (whether 'technological' or 'natural') in the process of knowledge-making and -claiming. To the extent that our 'humanity' cannot be separated from these non-humans, ethno-epistemic assemblages (together with cognate approaches) enable us to raise questions about who or what contributes to a scientific controversy. In identifying these issues and raising these questions, we do not claim to offer definitive answers: ethno-epistemic assemblages are not designed for this. Rather, in the exploration of blurring and mixing, these assemblages are a means of *expanding the range* of entities, actors, processes and relations that get blurred and mixed up. In general, then, ethno-epistemic assemblages are about renewing and refashioning the agenda of public understanding of science.

In what follows, we will revisit and elaborate the concept of ethno-epistemic assemblage. As we draw out particular aspects, we illustrate these with the aid of a number of further examples and analyses taken from recent developments in social and cultural theory. First, we refine the notion of ethno-epistemic assemblage by showing how it is derived and differentiated from a number of other key perspectives in science studies. Secondly, we explicate some key features through a consideration of the main inspiration behind this concept, namely the work of Deleuze and Guattari. Thirdly, we explore several issues raised by the notion of ethno-epistemic assemblages, not least for the figure of the scientific citizen. How, in constituting the scientific citizen, ethno-epistemic assemblages interact, draw upon social scientific discourses and practices, and encompass a variety of non-humans will be discussed with reference to five headings: the tenacious and tenuous dichotomy between science and lay; the 'suffering' scientific citizen; emergent forms of scientific accountability and 'transparency'; enunciation and governmentality; the hybridity of citizenship. In the concluding section, we briefly sketch, on the one hand, the prospects for 'operationalizing' ethno-epistemic assemblages as research tools and, on the other, their potential to generate policy innovation. These dual concerns are taken up and elaborated in Chapter 7.

Blurring and mixing: some theoretical resources

In this section, we unpack the intellectual lineage of the notion of 'ethno-epistemic assemblage' as a means of clarifying the sorts of analytic insights it might furnish. In the process, we connect it to, and differentiate it from, a number of ways of thinking about such heterogeneous connections across constituencies. It has been a key concern of recent science and technology studies to show how scientists and science policy actors in, respectively, construing and entrenching scientific facts, or developing and establishing science policy, necessarily have to draw upon the 'support' of disparate and heterogeneous actors. That is to say, to ensure the 'facticity' of a scientific fact or the 'implementability' of a policy, actors from markedly different constituencies have to be coordinated in some way. The actions of scientists, policy makers, administrators, publics and practitioners have to be patterned in such a way that a scientific 'fact' or science policy becomes ostensibly stable or practicable. Sometimes, as we shall see, this works the other way round: a scientific fact or science policy is so flexible that it enables coordination, or the more or less stable patterning of relations, among disparate constituencies. The general point, however, is that within science and technology studies there are a number of ways of thinking about such heterogeneity that we need to consider in explicating ethno-epistemic assemblages. As such, we consider, in brief, four perspectives (which are largely associated with science and technology studies), each of which has contributed to the development of ethno-epistemic assemblages: epistemic communities, discourse coalitions, actor network theory and social worlds theory. We then go on to discuss the work of Deleuze and Guattari.

Haas's (1992) notion of *epistemic communities*, superficially at least, resembles ethno-epistemic assemblages. Certainly he is concerned with how 'professionals from a variety of disciplines and backgrounds' develop policy, and the sorts of 'shared causal beliefs . . . [or] . . . shared notions of validity' (p. 3) that facilitate this process. However, ethno-epistemic assemblages are also oriented towards how non-professionals contribute to this process. Moreover, the concept of ethno-epistemic assemblage requires no assumptions about whether beliefs and notions need to be shared for collaboration or coordination to proceed. Indeed, the ethno-epistemic assemblage perspective attends to the means by which such beliefs and notions emerge and stabilize in the process of collaboration or coordination.

One approach that does encompass a more heterogeneous set of actors is Hajer's (1997) *discourse coalitions* perspective. Such coalitions of disparate actors are held together by what Hajer calls 'story-lines', narratives on social reality through which understandings, concerns and perceptions from many different domains (scientific, policy, lay) are combined so as to suggest a common understanding (say, a common definition of a problem such as acid rain). In this sense, story-lines reduce complexity and thus facilitate coordination among different actors. At the same time, story-lines enable actors to expand their discursive horizons and see how their particular practices fit into an overall set of practices (a 'jigsaw', as Hajer would have it).

Hajer's approach is very promising, straddling as it does expert and lay understandings. Nevertheless, there are some instructive problems with this perspective. First, a 'coalition' might cohere not because story-lines reduce complexity, but rather because they *increase* it. In other words, plural – even contradictory – story-lines might afford a discursive flexibility that facilitates coordination among disparate actors. Such coordination might, for example, be realized through discourses that entail expert knowledge, policy strategy, funding possibilities, experiential 'styles' and modes of consumption. Secondly, a *variety* of practices, not simply narrative ones, can enable, at least for a time, coordination among and coherence between actors. These practices might entail, for example, the display of social identity through particular forms of consumption, or the ways actors warrant their right to be heard within a coalition (say, through the performance of certain forms of suffering –

see below). Thirdly, we would want to take into account the fact that story-lines need to travel materially from actor to actor. The sorts of routes taken (conferences, the internet, newspapers) by such story-lines also serve in binding together actors into a coalition. Finally, we would need to ask whether such coalitions are made up only of humans – arguably, various technologies and various natures can be said to be crucial in the coordination of actors. In sum, our notion of ethno-epistemic assemblages is designed to accommodate these four concerns about how coordination among disparate actors is accomplished: the role of *discursive complexity*; the *variety of practices*; the impact of the *media* through which discourses and practices circulate; the *heterogeneity* of actors involved.

On these issues and concerns, it is perhaps *actor network theory* that has provided most insight. Actor network theory has been wedded to a key problematic of science and technology studies, namely, the production and dissemination of scientific and, more generally, accredited knowledge. It has also explored this in a distinctive way. The core concern of actor network theory has been with how scientists enrol, marshal and arrange various heterogeneous resources – texts, humans, technologies, funds, nature – to form a network that ensures that their findings are what come to be seen as 'the facts'.

As Michael (1996b) has suggested, when it comes to the relations between science and the public, it is science, or rather technoscience (science as related to, and emergent from, political, economic, commercial, social concerns; cf. Latour 1987), that is seen to be the prime mover. Scientists problematize and redefine the interests of members of the public such that it becomes apparent that it is the scientists' own offerings (skills, techniques, facts, remedies, policies, etc.) that answer those interests (e.g. Callon 1986). In other words, science proceeds through a process of *enrolling* its publics – redefining their interests and allotting them new roles. This it accomplishes through its capacity to produce particular 'intermediaries' (e.g. texts, persons, technologies, natures) that are resistant to alternative interpretations and thus can shape the understandings of relevant publics. What this approach offers is an account of how, to make the public 'understand', technoscience must simultaneously shape the interests and identities of that public. In doing so, 'target' actors become bound to technoscientific actors in such a way as to produce an expanded network which acts as a new unitary entity. For example, as we shall see below, advocates of an innovation such as xenotransplantation try to redefine the interests of the public. Very crudely, the redefinition of interests might proceed as follows: if we are all interested in combating organ failure, and if we all agree that there is a dearth of human donors, then we must all accept that animal organs are the obvious solution. Of course, the rhetorical move from 'combating organ failure' to using animal organs is couched primarily in scientific (but also ethical and cultural) terms.

Clearly, this is a very top-down, managerialist view of (techno)scientists and knowledge production (e.g. Law 1991; Star 1991). Actor network theory exemplifies what Martin (1998) has called the 'citadel model', which assumes that knowledge is produced within the 'citadel' of science, and then proceeds to seep out into the world, among the ' "untutored" public' (p. 30). In contrast, Martin suggests that both 'science' and 'society' are 'categories . . . produced inside the heterogeneous matrix of culture' (p. 30). As such, science is itself shot through with the cultural (e.g. Martin 1987, 1994; Haraway 1991). To get at this, and to get away from the structuring motif of the citadel, Martin draws on the imagery of Deleuze and Guattari's (1988) 'rhizome'. This is a system whose various protrusions can join at any point with one another, can become concretized as bulbs or tubers, can be cut up and fragmented only to regenerate. She deploys this image as a way of capturing 'the kind of discontinuous, fractured and nonlinear relationships between science and the rest of culture' (Martin 1998: 33). This contrasts with the 'root-ish' citadel metaphor of linearity and bifurcation (technoscience either succeeds or fails in enrolling publics) that is characteristic of actor network theory. We shall have reason to return to this rhizomic model below when we consider ethno-epistemic assemblages in more detail. Suffice it to note for the moment that it is important to reify neither 'root' nor 'rhizome'.

The core contribution of the rhizome metaphor is that it highlights fluidity and complexity in the relations between science and public (also see Mol and Law 1994). Importantly, such fluidity suggests not enrolment but collaboration and coordination. *Social worlds theory* (e.g. Clarke and Fujimura 1992; Clarke and Montini 1993) has been particularly concerned with such processes. If social worlds are interactive units of regularized mutual communication or discourse (for example, certain scientific or lay communities), then society as a whole comprises a 'mosaic of social worlds that both touch and interpenetrate' (Clarke 1990: 18–19). Given the differences in knowledge, discourse and routines that characterize different social worlds, a key analytic issue is how these interact. One means is through 'boundary objects' (artefacts such as a questionnaire or a map) that are sufficiently flexible to allow members of different social worlds to interpret them according to the character of their own respective social world, but in a way that nevertheless facilitates coordination across social worlds (cf. Star and Griesemer 1989; Bowker and Star 1999). Here, then, rather than any one social world (or network) enrolling another by sending out intermediaries to shape the other's identity, coordination proceeds by mutual use of objects that allow each world to retain its typical character.

The notion of boundary object clearly has echoes of the story-lines that hold together discourse coalitions. However, whereas story-lines are linguistic, boundary objects include a variety of entities. Of course, these boundary objects are also suffused with discourse – they can be interpreted by different social worlds in ways that reflect the character of those social worlds. For example, Michael (1992, 1996b) shows how radon detectors placed in people's homes by a local environmental authority in the North West of England were interpreted in variable ways that differed, sometimes spectacularly, from the way that the authority perceived their role and function. Nevertheless, these boundary objects served in coordinating the social worlds of the public (concerned with civic responsibility) and the authority (concerned with technical measurement of household radon levels and the surveying of radon levels both locally and nationally). A potentially similar example of this mediating role of technical objects can be found in air quality measurement devices (cf. Barry 2001; Bush *et al.* 2001). However, in this latter case, the coordination between publics and experts is far looser and in some ways quite problematic (laypeople had a grasp of both the usefulness and shortcomings of these devices). This suggests that 'coordination' and 'collaboration' should actually be thought of in terms of a spectrum ranging from more or less peaceful co-existence to near-integration (as in the AIDS case described in Chapter 2).

It is also possible to see these two social worlds – of lay householders and expert environmental health officers – as much more intertwined than a social worlds account would usually suggest: they can be seen as coalitions or networks or assemblages because together they could be said to function as a unit. Certainly, members of the public who volunteered to have the radon detectors in their homes were not averse to representing their relations with the authority in these (unifying) terms (Michael 1992). Moreover, the sorts of intermediaries (whether boundary objects or story-lines) that mediate these relations do not need to be scientific or technical – as noted above, they can be ethical or economic or experiential.

At this point, it is useful briefly to draw together some of the themes that have emerged in the preceding discussion. These themes relate directly to how we will come to characterize ethno-epistemic assemblages. In the relations between various actors (publics, scientists, regulators, etc.), there can be a spectrum of levels of coordination or interpenetration. Sometimes these are loose collections of actors, at others they form a more or less coherent new unit (or singularity). These relations are mediated by a variety of intermediaries such as story-lines and boundary objects which allow for coordination. These do not have to be coherent – they can be interpreted in many disparate ways. This plurality can actually facilitate coordination. Moreover, in addition to this flexibility of interpretation, involved in the production of coordination there is a *range* (perhaps even a pattern) of intermediaries that might include the scientific and the technical but also the ethical, the economic, the experiential and so on (as was detected in the Helsinki colloquium on transgenic animals in medical research). Our notion of ethno-epistemic assemblage is designed to encompass this *variety* of relations (and blurrings) between science and lay. In the next and subsequent sections, we consider in detail how ethno-epistemic assemblages accomplish this.

Ethno-epistemic assemblages revisited

To reiterate, the ethno-epistemic assemblage is a conceptual tool that allows us to explore the interrelations between, and blurrings of, science and society. In this section, we will consider the relevant work of Deleuze and Guattari so as to characterize what we mean by assemblage. However, before doing this, and for the sake of further clarification, we want to unpack the term 'ethno-epistemic' a little more carefully. 'Epistemic' is meant to invoke the production of truth or, more accurately, truth claims. It thus draws attention to the fact that the sorts of assemblages in which we are interested are fundamentally oriented towards the production and distribution of claims about what is real. This knowledge about the real can be classed as scientific but, as preceding discussions have made clear, there are other knowledges (more or less articulated) that sustain and support the scientificity of such truth claims: knowledges about politics and democratic process, about ethics and moral responsibility, about economics and commercial implications, about human experience and identity.

The term 'ethno' connotes a complex of themes. First, 'ethno' echoes the idea of locality (in the way that ethnobotany suggests ethnographically local classifications of plants). Thus, all knowledge, however far it has travelled (however 'global' it is), is always produced and taken up in the context of local cultural conditions. In other words, we take it that all knowledge is, following Donna Haraway (1991), *situated*. Secondly, 'ethno' is meant to evoke the sociological tradition of ethnomethodology (Garfinkel 1967) with its emphasis on 'indexicality' – that is, the view that all social activity can only be understood by reference to where and when it occurs – and 'reflexivity' – that is, the view that the meaning of social activity can, in principle, be redefined moment to moment. In the present context, 'reflexivity' translates into the assumption that the meanings of scientific (but also ethical, political, etc.) knowledges are always *contestable*. People continuously reproduce those meanings. The implication is that, within an assemblage, the stability of story-lines or boundary objects can always be compromised – actors must work to keep these intermediaries circulating and thus to keep an assemblage intact.

We now turn to 'assemblage'. This term has been drawn from the work of Deleuze and Guattari (1988). Inevitably, we can do full justice neither to the richness of this concept nor to the related terms which comprise Deleuze and Guattari's complex metaphysics. However, we can draw out some of the key aspects of their concept as a way of helping us better grasp the interweavings of lay and expert, science and society. For Deleuze and Guattari, an assemblage entails a 'territory' made up of various heterogeneous fragments. This territory is a 'territorialization' in the sense that it embodies patterns and routines. There are two aspects to assemblages – their content and their expression. By 'content' Deleuze and Guattari want to address an assemblage as 'machinic', as an assemblage 'of bodies, actions and passions, an intermingling of bodies reacting to one another' (p. 88). By 'expression', they point to the way that an assemblage is 'a *collective assemblage of enunciation*, of acts and statements, of incorporeal transformations attributed to bodies' (p. 88, emphasis in original). To gloss these two aspects, albeit crudely: 'machinic' refers to the causal relations between objects that make up an assemblage; 'enunciation' refers to the statements and signs that allow the elements of an assemblage to communicate with one another. In both cases, these causes and communications serve in the territorialization of the assemblage – that is, the stabilization of its peculiar configuration of elements.

This notion of territorialization can be related to the metaphor of a root system. The 'citadel' version of science–society relations identified by Martin (1998) possessed just this rootish character: on one side there was science, on the other society, and these related to one another in a linear fashion (scientific knowledge and technical objects going from science to society). This can be contrasted, as we saw, to the rhizome where science and society were far more interwoven: science itself can incorporate all manner of knowledges and objects drawn from society and vice versa. Thus, an assemblage of science and society can become deterritorialized – existing relations can be scrambled so that novel relations emerge. In the process, the distinction between science and society becomes thoroughly problematic.

Having made this point, there is a danger of over-stressing the difference between root and rhizome, territorialization and deterritorialization. For Deleuze and Guattari (1988), the contrast between root and rhizome, territorialization and deterritorialization is not absolute (after all, that would be to practise exclusively territorializing rootish thought). Deleuze and Guattari pose the rhetorical question: 'How could movements of deterritorialization and processes of reterritorialization not be relative, always connected, caught up in one another?' (p. 10). For them, 'there are knots of arborescence (rootishness) in rhizomes, and rhizomic offshoots in roots . . . The important point is that the root-tree and the canal rhizome are not two opposed models' (p. 20). In other words, where there appears to be stability in the arrangements that make up an assemblage, there can intervene moments of destabilization that lead to a major reconfiguration of arrangements, which might then themselves stabilize (reterritorialize).

This account of assemblages, overly abstract though it is, does allow us to address several important questions about the complex and changeable relations between science and society. These can be listed as follows:

- What is the extent of the heterogeneity of elements that make up an ethno-epistemic assemblage?
- What is the relation between the content (the 'machinic' aspect) and the expression (the 'enunciatory' aspect) of an ethno-epistemic assemblage?
- What are the relations between different ethno-epistemic assemblages?

Buried within these three questions is a rather broad range of further issues to explore. Already, however, we can apply this perspective to one example of science–society relations as a means of illustrating its potential analytic value.

Novas and Rose's (2000) study of a webforum discussion group concerned with Huntington's disease (HD) traces the ways in which people face decisions to undergo genetic testing and how, in the process, they address the ethical and social ramifications of such decisions. Novas and Rose suggest that such discussions reflect what they call a 'somaticization of personhood' and the emergence of 'somatic identity'. These entail 'an array of practices and styles of thought, from techniques of bodily modification to the rise of corporealism in social and feminist theory and philosophy' that are associated with 'recent developments in the life sciences, biomedicine and biotechnology' (p. 491). What becomes apparent is that people are developing life strategies that cut across genetic identities and other sorts of identities concerned with health, expertise, relatives, friends, fellow 'sufferers'. This somaticization suggests a particular sort of assemblage in which there is testimony (that is, enunciation) in terms of the state of the body and the benefits and disbenefits of knowing about the state of one's body (e.g. whether one is a carrier of the HD gene). This has been partly enabled by the recent (machinic) developments in bio-technology and genetics, that have allowed for the identification of the HD gene, but also a sense of the potential both of a greater knowledge of the body and a greater intervention in its workings [and in the workings of nature more generally, what Rabinow (1996) has called 'biosociality']. 'Somaticization' also works back upon science, not least in that it encourages people to seek particular sorts of corporeal solutions, and thus to support and fund particular sorts of research programmes. As such, this assemblage comprises a pattern of heterogeneous elements patterned, that is territorialized, in a particular way.

However, it is possible to imagine changes in this assemblage, not least with the apparent promise of prospective treatments for Huntington's disease. One line of research has concerned the possibility of implanting fetal brain cells, whether human or animal, into HD sufferers to ameliorate symptoms. Each of these options (human or animal 'donors'; cf. Cooper and Lanza 2000) generates a series of technical and social problems. For example, in the case of animal fetal cell implants there are issues to do with animal welfare, species integrity, hyperacute rejection and transpecies disease. Ironically, it is conceivable that these concerns begin to move the assemblage away from enunciation in terms of 'somaticization' and towards more collective and relational discourses that address, say, the material and symbolic relations to animals (cf. Franklin 1999; Michael 2001). Again, this development – this deterritorialization – is not simply an upshot of technical innovations and trajectories. These have been, and are being, subjected to considerable (and contrasting) political and ethical scrutiny in various countries. Society has been at the heart of these technoscientific dynamics. The point is that it is readily possible to see how this assemblage, territorialized in one configuration, can in some portion or at some point become deterritorialized and reterritorialized to form another assemblage. It is also possible to imagine how such an assemblage might well splinter to generate oppositional assemblages.

This example has touched upon all three of our questions outlined above:

- What is the extent of the heterogeneity of elements that make up an ethno-epistemic assemblage? Within this assemblage are such heterogeneous elements as HD sufferers and families, doctors, scientists, regulators, funding bodies, computers, internet connections, animals, laboratory technologies and techniques, and so on.
- What is the relation between the content (the 'machinic' aspect) and the expression (the 'enunciatory' aspect) of an ethno-epistemic assemblage? Enunciations which reflect the somaticization of personhood proceed partly through machinic production of particular sorts of laboratory animal bodies. These machinic productions are enabled by enunciations which support the research programmes of which they are a product. Conversely, these enunciations (about particular sorts of condition, cure or treatment) have also been partly enabled by certain machinic developments, such as a technical innovation like polymerase chain reaction which underpins much 'genetic medicine'. It will be apparent that the machinic and enunciatory dimensions are by no means distinct.
- What are the relations between ethno-epistemic assemblages? What resources much of the configuration of our assemblage is the production of certain enunciations among the webforum users: enunciations in the form of *testimony*, which, as Novas and Rose point out, has roots in other assemblages concerned with psychology, psychiatry, education and work management (cf. Rose 1996).

However, these questions have only scratched the surface of the sorts of issues that arise through the heuristic use of ethno-epistemic assemblages. In the next section, we explore ethno-epistemic assemblages in more detail. In doing so, the implications of this perspective for what it means for a public to 'do politics' in relation to science – that is, to be a *scientific citizen* – are drawn out.

Assembling scientific citizenship

In the next sections, we will examine ethno-epistemic assemblages with special attention to the emergence of the 'scientific citizen'. In brief, what the
ethno-epistemic assemblage brings to the analysis of the 'scientific citizen' is
an awareness of the complex and heterogeneous actors and relations that constitute the 'scientific citizen'. This awareness translates, as we shall see, into a
range of concerns, by no means exhausted here, that touch both the internal
workings of science–lay ethno-epistemic assemblages and their external relations. For example, science–lay ethno-epistemic assemblages might be simultaneously rigid and fluid (territorialized and deterritorialized); they might be
partly constituted by the commentaries provided by social scientists; they
might be shaped by the impact of techniques that belong to other seemingly
distant ethno-epistemic assemblages; they might be populated not simply by
human scientific citizens, but by hybrid mixtures of humans, technologies
and natures. In what follows, these (and other topics) will be addressed under
the following headings: the tenacious and tenuous dichotomy between science and lay; the 'suffering' scientific citizen; emergent forms of scientific
accountability and 'transparency'; enunciation and governmentality; the
hybridity of citizenship.

The tenacious and tenuous dichotomy between science and lay

While several of our preceding discussions have emphasized the ways in which
science and the public blur and stressed the means by which to theorize the
interconnections between science and lay, there is nothing to say that under
certain circumstances the dichotomy between science and society does not re-
establish itself. These processes of differentiation and de-differentiation do not
map so readily onto, respectively, the root and rhizome metaphors as might
first appear. Contrary to Martin's account (see above), sometimes the extrica-
tion of science from society entails deterritorialization (a loosening up of
established or putative connections). Thus, to deny the relevance of science to
particular issues as in what Michael (1996a) has called the 'I don't *want* to
know about science' variant of discourses of ignorance (see Chapter 2) is a
means of 'co-constructing' (Irwin 2001b) science and society as distinctly different. So, for example, to argue that scientific knowledge about the technical
nature of the risks of nuclear power installations is irrelevant, and to insist that
it is the economic viability of these industrial plants that is important, is at
once to reify, isolate and demote science. The traditional status of science thus
becomes deterritorialized (although there might be reterritorialization
through the ascendant authority of another specialism such as economics).

The point is that forms of differentiation and de-differentiation can co-exist and emerge in different sorts of context: connections between different actors can be brought into or out of focus depending upon conditions. The science–lay dichotomy is both highly tenuous and highly tenacious. The notion of assemblage (and the complex dynamics this concept denotes) suggests that we must be wary of over-emphasizing the role of science in the emergence of political or citizenly practices. To think in terms of assemblages is to be sensitive to the contingent status of science and scientific knowledge, and to the fact that these can operate both as part of, and as distinct from, lay constituencies.

The 'suffering' scientific citizen

We have already drawn particular attention to the ways in which 'understanding' is co-constructed across disparate constituencies. In doing so, we noted the fact that the connections drawing together different actors into an assemblage are grounded not only in technical knowledge *per se* but also in aesthetics, ethics, politics and culture. Furthermore, we have explored the role played by trust in the rendering of connections and relations that constitute an assemblage. However, unsurprisingly, 'trust' is, in this context, a compound concept that touches upon notions such as credibility, authority, legitimacy, status and power to name but a few. But it also relates, as we have emphasized, to *identification* between lay and scientific actors (see Chapters 2, 4 and 5). Where scientists and laypersons are attached to a particular new social movement, a mutual identification can be interwoven with mutual trust which enables the operations of that social movement as a unit (or assemblage). Such forms of identification can entail certain common 'understandings' (or, rather, co-constructions) of the natural, the social and, indeed, the political worlds (of course, as we argued above, this is not necessarily the case).

Interestingly, such common 'understandings' also draw upon other somewhat 'alien' resources in the production of relations within an assemblage. For example, a pressure group such as 'Seriously Ill for Medical Research' (SIMR) in promoting biotechnology (and animal experiments) stresses that, while this has to be conducted with due ethical regard for animals, it is 'unethical and immoral not to use powerful modern (biotechnological) techniques to research the 5,000 single gene disorders which affect 2.5 million people or the major diseases which have a genetic factor' (taken from SIMR's 1998 pamphlet *Biotechnology and You*, p. 2). Arguably, it is the personal suffering of members of SIMR that warrants this research programme, that is, that partly establishes the credibility of its statements. The 'performance' of personal suffering (in the sense of display, and of having a social impact or *performative* effect – this term is certainly *not* meant to derogate the experience of personal suffering) thus serves in grounding certain claims (about the best directions for biomedical research) in conventions surrounding the authenticity of suffering.

However, personal suffering can also be used to warrant the opposite argument. In the Helsinki conference on 'Transgenic Animals in Medicine' held in 2000, and at the 2001 launch of the UK Xenotransplantation Interim Regulatory Authority's annual report, a number of animal rights activists argued against the use of animals in transgenic and xenotransplantation research. What made the arguments of these spokespersons' particularly compelling was their testimony that they were also patients. They introduced their animal rights arguments by talking about their own medical conditions and suffering: despite being patients, they still felt unable to endorse transgenic animal research. What now warrants such a view, of course, is the suffering of the patients – it is an 'authentic' view because they are faced with suffering, and not an 'inauthentic' one as voiced by non-patient animal rights advocates. In sum, the performance of personal suffering seems to be a generally available 'rhetoric' that can be used in an effort to 'argue for' (diametrically opposing) research agendas.

Let us reflect on this form of social action. In contrast to the work of Novas and Rose and others, testimony is not being deployed to expound on practical experience and thus to reinforce or challenge relevant scientific knowledge and biomedical advice. This is not a case of articulating the experience of particular symptoms (e.g. of repetitive strain injury, RSI), the efficacy of certain treatments (e.g. recombinant human insulin) or the dilemmas faced by the availability of given diagnostic techniques (e.g. genetic screening) to establish some fact or other (respectively, the actuality of RSI, the genuine dangers that arise for some diabetics on human insulin, or the bona fide social risks of genetic screening). Rather, this 'performance of personal suffering' draws on broader conventions of authenticity – an ethos of testimony, we might say – in order to warrant ethical stances and particular research agendas and programmes. Here, there is an attempted crafting of connections on the basis of conventions of empathy that make for a different sort of assemblage – there has been a deterritorialization and reterritorialization in which associations based on 'cultural' identification and trust have been replaced by 'bodily' identification and empathy. In other words, associations are based not on identifying with others on the basis of factional social qualities ('you're on my side'), but on putatively universal (corporeal) circumstance ('this suffering is part of the human condition'). Arguably, such an assemblage draws on another assemblage, what Nikolas Rose (1996) has called the 'psy complex' (comprising the knowledges and practices of such disciplines as psychology, psychiatry and psychotherapy), with its conventions, discourses and techniques of self-revelation and self-governance.

A number of points can be drawn from the preceding discussion. First, assemblages draw on other assemblages in de- and re-territorializing. In the above example, as we have seen, a contributing assemblage might be the psy complex. But this is an assemblage that spans many 'institutions', ranging from psychiatric hospitals to self-help groups. Characteristic of such an assemblage seems to be what might be called an 'ethos of testimony', a necessary process of reflection upon self and personal experience. The 'performance of personal suffering' might be interpreted as an adaptation of this ethos to the circumstances of biomedical transgenic research. Secondly, the display of, and claims about, the body of the citizen can be used in arguments about science policy matters: it is not simply a question of sound argumentation or trust based on identification. In other words, the connections that bind the actors in an assemblage are multiple and can, on the surface at least, appear quite alien to the ostensible character of that assemblage. Having noted this, there is also the matter of matter, as it were. Bodies of persons do not (as representations) serve rhetorical ends alone; they are also implicated in material relations with natures and technologies that shape, albeit in complex ways, what it means to be a scientific citizen. We shall return to this issue below. Thirdly, this process of display can be seen as a mode of transparency. What these spokespersons seem to be doing is tacitly claiming to make transparent their reasoning (over the decision to support one research strategy rather than another). It is just that it is their suffering which is made transparent (performed) and which, so to speak, in the final instance, 'authenticates' their reasoning. We shall explore this argument in the next section where we consider an example of such personal suffering performed by a scientist.

Emergent forms of scientific accountability and 'transparency'

It has been a feature of our account of science–society relations that these constituencies are blurring into one another for a number of reasons. We have noted the concern in ethnographic PUS to alter scientific institutions' 'body language' so that it does not alienate various publics. And we have also commented on the seeming fact that this concern is beginning to have some impact, not least in programmatic statements by various governmental expert bodies of their wish to enter into a 'dialogue' with the public.

Such 'dialogues' take various forms. For example, it might take the form of scientists attempting to identify in some way with the audience – that is, to claim that they have already incorporated the voice of the public in their deliberations. Brown and Michael (2001a) have shown how scientists can justify, at least in part, their choice of the pig as a 'donor' of organs for xenotransplantation by arguing that they, *just like the public*, see no ethical difference between using pigs for food and using pigs as organ 'donors'. This rhetorical move also chides those parts of the public which persist in seeing a difference. The upshot is that the scientists represent themselves not only as members of the public, but also as members of its best (most 'logical') fraction. Of course, the public might well have good reason not to see the equivalence. After all, there is a prima facie difference between incorporating pigs molecularly through digestion and incorporating whole pig organs through transplantation (cf. Brown and Michael 2001b). Our point, then, is that scientists can lay claim to commonsense modes of reasoning to warrant their decisions (for similar examples in relation to animal experimentation, see Michael and Birke 1994a,b), but also to draw lay constituencies into their ethno-epistemic assemblage.

However, this form of 'dialogue' can also be seen in a different way. Such commentaries by scientific institutions are a means of making their reasoning 'transparent' to external audiences. In addition to the arguments for more dialogic or participative mechanisms of science–society interactions, part of the ethnographic PUS message has been that the knowledge-producing and decision-making processes of scientific institutions need to become more transparent. It is therefore possible to see the ethical arguments for the choice of pig as 'donor' as part of making the process of scientific decision making transparent. Rendering such processes transparent becomes yet another means of persuading publics and binding them into an ethno-epistemic assemblage.

Now, this apparent aspiration to transparency is highly problematic. As sociologists of scientific knowledge (and others) have long documented, both within the laboratory and in other venues such as the courts, trying to render transparent the process of scientific practice (and that includes decision making even over such mundane matters as the choice of one technique, or piece of equipment, over another) very quickly runs into trouble (e.g. Collins 1985; Smith and Wynne 1988; Bowker and Star 1999). This is because the criteria by which a decision was reached can always be problematized. For example, lawyers can readily show that the decision to use one piece of equipment over another (e.g. a test tube) in the detection of illegal drug residues rests on a whole series of assumptions – for instance, that the test tube is uncontaminated. How is it possible to know this? By using a test. But how is this test known to be accurate? By using another test. And so on in an infinite regress. The point is that such contingencies will always, as it were, subvert any attempt at being transparent: in the end, the only transparency that is possible is one which invokes the contingency of all scientific knowledge processes. The only logical (but practically impossible) basis of transparency is omniscience.

However, there might be ways in which it is possible to evoke *a sense of transparency* on the part of scientific spokespersons. Let us consider an example. In a recent television UK documentary on xenotransplantation, the cameras were given what seemed to be unprecedented access to the laboratories, operating theatres and animal facilities in which transgenic pigs were produced, housed and used. As a key scientist-spokesperson made clear, this access was meant to show viewers what goes on so that they could make up their own minds. In other words, such transparency was a way of enabling viewers to draw informed conclusions and make informed decisions.

Yet, as argued above, transparency is a practical impossibility. One cannot possibly reveal *everything* – certain decisions have had to be made about what is filmed and what is not. So, the question that follows is 'what is being rendered transparent?' Let us make a few tentative remarks. The transparency being offered is attached to the ethos of testimony – what is actually being 'opened up' is the researcher/spokesperson who testifies to (that is, performs) her personal suffering in having to conduct discomfiting animal experimental work for our benefit. More importantly, she performs for us her personal suffering at dealing with impossibly difficult cost–benefit calculations in regard of animal suffering and sacrifice, and human suffering and potential benefit. The viewers' trust in the scientist is to be grounded not so much in her willingness to make her institution transparent (it is easy enough to raise criticisms about this). Rather, it is her apparent personal transparency – her testimony about, and performance of, her personal suffering – that makes her authentic and credible. Of course, it is also possible that such attempts at authenticity can fail or be considered inappropriate: hospital patients may not wish to hear the 'suffering' of their surgeon, consumers and voters can react negatively to the personal testimony of business leaders and politicians.

If this interpretation holds any water, then we might say that in making scientific decision making transparent, there is recourse to the 'ethos of testimony' mentioned above. In the process, the scientist-spokesperson becomes more like the public – there is, once again, another instantiation of de-differentiation, and refashioning of an ethno-epistemic assemblage, as the techniques of testimony are appropriated by science. Clearly, all these points need to be properly elaborated. For example, this process of opening-up decision making may be associated with another assemblage, namely what Michael Power (1999) has called the Audit Society, in which there is an increasing drive to have institutions articulate their rationale, account for their procedures, formalize their practices and so on. In the meantime, we can style the following hypothesis: the process of de-differentiation between experts and non-experts is partly based on an emergent, possibly globalizing, ethos of testimony linked to the performance of personal suffering. This links up to claims of transparency, not least in policy making and even democratic participative forms. In sum, an ethno-epistemic assemblage perspective raises the issue of how a decision-making process is rendered *credibly* transparent. Equally, ethno-epistemic assemblages direct us to explore the possibly disparate resources that are brought to bear in 'doing' transparency.

Enunciation and governmentality

The above discussion has attempted to get at some of the 'odd' ways in which science and society de-differentiate. Of course, as we have already seen in our discussion of de- and re-territorialization, these processes can also serve in the retrenchment of certain divides. Thus, to evoke transparency through the performance of personal suffering is at once to identify with the public and make the public part of science, and also to stake a tacit claim to science's autonomy.

However, so far we have treated ethno-epistemic assemblages largely as if they are composed of pre-existing constituents: minimally, members of the public, regulators, scientists. And yet, implicit in much of our argument about the blurring of the boundaries between these various actors is the view that such actors are not fixed or discrete. At the same time, there are many actors (academic, policy, lay) who promote particular views of science–society relation which re-assert distinctions between science and society. Note that in making this point we have levelled the discursive playing field, as it were. Our analytic accounts are permitted neither more nor less epistemic privilege than those of the other actors who comprise an assemblage. In other words, we too are members of such assemblages – enunciating particular views, co-constructing science, society and nature just as everyone else does. There is a difference, however. Certain actors have more leverage within an assemblage – they can draw upon, marshal and put into circulation greater and more potent resources with the result that their enunciations tend to predominate.

The important point here is that such enunciations *have effects*. They can shape other actors in an assemblage; indeed, it is out of these assemblages (and the complex relations between assemblages) that there emerge human agents of various sorts. Drawing on the literature on 'governmentality', we shall see that certain enunciations that are put into circulation under a number of guises – from newspaper reports about the public's lack of scientific literacy, through government initiatives on consultative policy making, to qualitative social scientific investigation of the relations between cultural identity and local knowledge – have a major impact on what it means to be a 'scientific citizen'.

In Mitchell Dean's (1999) excellent introduction to this topic, there is a very useful definition of 'governmentality', not least in relation to that of 'government'. Government is

> any more or less calculated or rational activity, undertaken by a multiplicity of authorities and agencies, employing a variety of techniques and forms of knowledge, that seeks to shape our conduct by working through our desires, aspirations, interests and beliefs, for definite but shifting ends and with a diverse set of relatively unpredictable consequences, effects and outcomes. Agencies of government,

in this sense, can be local, regional, national, international or global; they can be philanthropic, for profit or public.

(Dean 1999: 207)

By contrast, Dean defines 'governmentality' in the following way:

How we think about governing others and ourselves in a wide variety of contexts. In a more limited sense, the different ways governing is thought about in the contemporary world and which can in large part be traced to Western Europe from the sixteenth century. Such forms of thought have been exported to large parts of the globe owing to colonial expansion and the post-colonial set of international arrangement of a system of sovereign states.

(Dean 1999: 209–10)

Crucially, governmentality is concerned with how 'the way we think about exercising authority draws upon the theories, ideas, philosophies and forms of knowledge that are part of our social and cultural products' (p. 16). Expert knowledges such as psychology, economics or medicine thus need to be studied in terms of how they operate 'within our organized ways of doing things, our regimes of practice' and are 'embedded within programmes for the direction and reform of conduct' (p. 18).

To study governance in relation to the 'scientific citizen' from the perspective of governmentality is thus to ask a number of questions about how such a citizen has been formulated. Indeed, it is to ask what such a scientific citizenly self *is* such that it *can* be governed. In Dean's account, this exercise would involve four questions:

- *What* substance is it that is being governed? (e.g. the flesh in Christianity; the cognitive underpinnings of scientific literacy of the scientific citizen).
- *How* is this substance governed? (e.g. spiritual exercises in Christianity; education of the scientific citizen).
- *Who* are we when we are governed in this way? (e.g. prey to carnal weakness in Christianity; ignorant but concerned citizens).
- *Why* govern in this way? What is the end or goal that is sought? (e.g. other-worldly salvation; empowerment of scientific-citizenly capacities).

It will not have escaped attention that the version of the scientific citizen used as an example in the preceding discussion is derived from traditional public understanding of science, and the more 'top-down' model of scientific governance. However, the same mode of analysis can be applied to ethnographic PUS with its focus upon, and valorization of, the lay local community. As Rose (1999) has put it in relation to 'technologies of community':

> Over the second half of the twentieth century, a whole array of little devices and techniques have been invented to make communities real. Surveys of attitudes and values, market research, opinion polls, focus groups, citizens' juries and much more have mapped out these new spaces of culture, brought these values and virtues into visibility and injected them into the deliberations of authorities.
>
> (Rose 1999: 189)

The techniques of ethnographic public understanding of science are thus not simply a 'recovery' of the real 'units' of the public that have been obscured by traditional PUS: ethnographic PUS has also been instrumental in the production of such collectivities. Moreover, there has been a parallel account (a co-construction) of the scientific institutions with which these communities have come into contact. In the context of the knowledges and practices of ethnographic PUS, Dean's four questions could be answered in the following way:

- *What* substance is it that is being governed? The 'voice' of the scientific citizen via the 'body language' of scientific institutions.
- *How* is this substance governed? The democratic reform of scientific institutions, the rendering transparent of scientific decision making, thus the entry of citizenly voices.
- *Who* are we when we are governed in this way? The disempowered but highly knowledgeable lay local public, and over-confident scientific institutions.
- *Why* govern in this way? What is the end or goal that is sought? To ensure recognition of the value of the lay local public: to democratize scientific decision making.

At minimum, what all this implies is, of course, that these 'perspectives on' science–lay relations are, actually, partly constitutive of those relations. They feed upon, and contribute to, those distributed governmental processes and procedures out of which emerge particular (and contradictory) scientific citizens. Needless to say, this problematic of governmentality applies equally to the present analysis (not least as developed in Chapter 4). By stressing the dynamics of globalization, the centrality of consumption, the disembedding from communities and so on, we too have drawn upon, and contributed to, those knowledges and practices that comprise contemporary governmentality.

The reflexive point is, to repeat, that we are a part of these ethno-epistemic assemblages. Our role within them is to 'loosen them up', to make them more rhizomic. But as we have already argued above, this is a hazardous process not least because one person's rhizome can be another's root. For example, to problematize the ethnographic PUS model might, under certain circumstances, be tactically naive – not least when faced with powerful or influential practitioners of traditional top-down scientific governance.

Be that as it may, there is one additional ramification of the ethno-epistemic assemblage approach that we need to unpack, one that also has highly ambiguous political implications. This is the role of non-humans in the production of human actors.

The hybridity of citizenship

Another way of considering governmentality in relation to the production of the scientific citizen is in terms of the pervasive discourses of humanism. Here, humanism refers to the common theme shared by traditional and ethno-graphic PUS, namely the model of the member of the public as a 'pure human'. As Michael (2002) notes, for traditional PUS this takes the individualistic form of people as 'assimilators of knowledge', that is cognitive repositories or deposit boxes in which can be stored the requisite information. In contrast, the humanism of ethnographic PUS rests on a model of the member of the public as a socialized, culturalized human. It is an entity that is emergent from its cultural setting and which has investments in this setting. As we have noted, this is often couched in the terms of 'cultural identity'. In the case of science policy and governance, the scientific citizen is a human who must either be educated or consulted (or some mixture of the two) for decision making to proceed in a 'democratic way'.

Now, this humanistic view of the public, the scientific citizen, and more generally, the person, has been subjected to much critical thought in recent social theory. For example, this version of the citizen is a strangely dis-embodied one. Many scholars are currently attempting to think through how the body and its many and heterogeneous embroilments with the social and material world affect such everyday phenomena as 'understanding' and 'knowing' (e.g. Burkitt 1999), social interaction (e.g. Turner 1996) or relations with nature and technology (e.g. Michael 2000; Macnaghten and Urry 2001).

This list – knowledge, society, nature, technology – is heterogeneous indeed. It reflects a concern to look at how these elements are implicated in one another. In other words, there is an interest in exploring how what counts as nature, society, technology and knowledge (among many other things) emerges out of the complex relations between nature, society, technology and knowledge. In the present context of a concern with the scientific citizen, we can reframe this problematic as the following question: how is it that the heterogeneous relations between people, technologies, texts, bodies, natures, architectures and so on yield a particular model of the person and particular types of human conduct? Here, then, we draw attention to the profound heterogeneity of ethno-epistemic assemblages – the fact that they comprise technologies and natures as well as signs and persons.

There are, not unexpectedly, many ways in which this sort of question has been taken up in social thought. We will limit ourselves to treatments that derive, at least in part, from sociology of scientific knowledge. According to such writers as Bruno Latour and John Law (in the tradition of actor network theory), humans and technological non-humans are thoroughly interwoven. As Law (1994) notes, take away the technologies – telephone, fax machine, computer, but also desk, chair, light – from a manager and she can no longer function in that role. At a more general level, there are many everyday technologies which serve in rendering us 'pure humans' or 'sovereign individuals' (Abercrombie *et al.* 1986) able to act as (scientific) citizens. Technologies such as surveillance machines (e.g. CCTV), person ordering machines (e.g. revolving doors), information-processing machines (e.g. automatic cash dispensers) are all instrumental in the reproduction of sovereign individualism (Michael 2000).

This centrality of technologies to human conduct suggests that we should think of humans as 'hybrid'. According to Latour (1993), hybrids are everywhere. Imbroglios of humans and non-humans have always been, and are increasingly becoming, part of our everyday life. In this sort of 'hybridic' account, the human is emergent from heterogeneous relations – what is to count as human and non-human is a complex, heterogeneous accomplishment.

One implication of this perspective for our discussion of ethno-epistemic assemblages and scientific citizenship is that any analysis of the process of engagement with expert knowledge should also take into account the impact of various media through which this, and related, knowledge circulates. These media (TV, IT, newspapers, telephones), which are simultaneously cultural and material, might well play a part in 'shaping' the ways knowledges – scientific, personal, experiential, ethical, economic, political – interact, come together, combine or polarize. Let us return to the example of Novas and Rose's (2000) study of a webforum discussion group concerned with Huntington's disease. Through the sociotechnical medium that makes up the webforum, people are developing life strategies that cut across genetic identities and other sorts of identities concerned with health, expertise, relatives, friends, fellow 'sufferers'. Through these mediated discussions, expert knowledges about Huntington's disease and genetic diagnostics become embedded within various discourses and practices concerning bodies, conditions, relations, the future and so on. The more general point is that, with the aid of such technologies of communication, negotiations are conducted which facilitate both the emergence of new relations and identities *and* the retrenchment of existing ones. So, on the one hand, we can detect with Novas and Rose the development of a 'somaticization of personhood'. On the other, we see established identities such as parents, friends or consumers reinforced. Of course, we must be wary of over-emphasizing the importance of such innovations as the webforum – more established technologies such as telephones retain their function and influence. Nevertheless, the webforum does seem to 'speed up' the movement and mixing of different knowledges. For a while at least, the 'Huntington's disease assemblage' becomes a little more 'rhizomic' and deterritorialized. The ethno-epistemic assemblage perspective would seek to explore how these media – old and new – have impacted upon the ways in which lay and expert knowledges interact.

Now, there is another way in which non-humans can contribute to the workings of an ethno-epistemic assemblage. This is altogether more controversial in so far as scientific citizenship is seen to involve non-humans: that is, citizens are *comprised of mixtures of humans and non-humans*. To think about people in terms of hybrids (or cyborgs; Haraway 1991) is to ask how scientific citizenship includes technologies, environments and animals. As such, these hybrids (or cyborgs) can, at first sight, be seen as strange collectives. Thus, when Haraway (1992) analyses a photograph in *Discover* magazine of a Kayapo Indian, in indigenous dress, using a video camera, she does not see this as an ironic contrast between the modern and the primitive. Rather, it can be thought of as a 'forging [of] a recent collective of humans and unhumans, in this case made up of the Kayapo, videocams, land, plants, animals, near and distant audiences, and other constituents' (p. 314). Indigenous people, in fighting to protect their ways of life and their ecosystems (which are not necessarily differentiated from one another), appear readily able to draw on these new technologies. Indeed, we can say that for certain purposes it becomes unwise to differentiate between humans and non-humans – they form a strange collective that is itself a multifarious political actor – a new, heterogeneous sort of scientific citizen.

Concepts such as Latour's hybrid and Haraway's cyborg point towards a 'relational' politics. Here, what is politically acted upon, and politically active, is not an individualized or singularized human. Now, certainly it is possible to attribute rights and citizenship to non-humans, not least by pointing to reciprocal duties performed by these non-humans (see Urry 2000). But, the work of Haraway, Latour and others stresses the *relationality* between the human and the non-human: humans would not be the singularized, agential citizens with which 'we' are familiar were it not for the heterogeneous networks in which they are immersed. In light of this relationality, distributed-ness and heterogeneity, what might become the unit bearer of rights, or the cogent practitioner of citizenship, becomes altogether more diffuse.

In sum, what the notion of ethno-epistemic assemblage is also meant to evoke is this sense of a relational citizenship (and ethics; cf. Birke and Michael

1997; Whatmore 1997). Obviously, this is controversial, for it assumes that 'nature' can have some voice in human political affairs. The argument against this is that it is people who always speak for nature. The counter-argument is that we need to get away from the deeply anthropocentric way of looking at human–non-human relations (cf. Latour 1999). Having noted all this, there is no *a priori* superiority that attaches to this relational version of citizenship: as we have stressed throughout our unpacking of the concerns that arise from the perspective of ethno-epistemic assemblages, the value of relational versus singularized scientific citizenship is always contingent, not least upon the concrete circumstances that pertain within an assemblage.

Conclusion

In this chapter, we have attempted to delineate what we mean by ethno-epistemic assemblages, first by comparing and contrasting this concept against other perspectives, then by illustrating it with regard to scientific citizenship. We have stressed from the outset that the concept is heuristic and that its value lies in its usefulness in shedding light on the complex blurrings between science and public. By thinking about scientific citizenship with the aid of ethno-epistemic assemblages, we have raised what seem to us to be important and intriguing issues which are often neglected. For example, we have begun to explore the possible ways in which scientific accountability and the transparency of scientific policy making might draw on discourses and practices of emotionality that are, at least ostensibly, alien to them. We have also developed an awareness of the fact that we as analysts cannot maintain a separation from the ethno-epistemic assemblages we study, since we provide some of the discourses through which these assemblages articulate themselves. The most we can claim to have accomplished in this chapter is to open up some avenues of thought by pointing to a few surprising connections that seem to blur further the dichotomies of science and public, expert and lay. We cannot claim that our analysis is exhaustive – it is merely indicative. Our aim is to generate a theoretical and conceptual space where these issues of blurring and dynamism can be fruitfully explored.

The sceptic, with whom we are not altogether unfamiliar, while ironically applauding these fine sentiments will sport the keenest of smirks. Behind the smirk will lie a simple query: This is all well and good, but what can we *do* with ethno-epistemic assemblages? Can this perspective inform policy making in some way? Can it be operationalized as a research tool? Our answer to both these questions is 'yes'. Ethno-epistemic assemblages, at once suggest new ways of situating scientific policy making in the context of complex social and political dynamics, and open up what it *means* to engage in policy making. In the process of enabling the *redefinition* of such terms as policy making, alternative options for the interaction of scientific and public constituencies become conceivable. Furthermore, ethno-epistemic assemblages, while suggesting no new research methodologies as such, do point to the use of *novel arrays of methods* that can gather data on those points of mixing and blurring. It is in the next chapter that we begin to delineate the practical – in terms of policy and research – implications of ethno-epistemic assemblages.

7 Governing the assemblage, unearthing the rhizome

The previous chapter's presentation of ethno-epistemic assemblages has apparently taken us a long way beyond the three main frameworks (of PUS, of governance and social theory) with which the opening half of this book was concerned (and which we summarized in Chapter 5). To relate this back to our Jarrow case study, where previously we had three perspectives sitting side by side, we now move to a more complex world where human and non-human action are no longer readily distinguishable and nature, society, science and technology blur into one another. Assemblages are dynamic rather than static and can both embody and transcend locality. Equally, assemblages suggest the more shifting and heterogeneous character of contemporary life. To state what should now be obvious, issues of the public understanding of science become transformed and new analytical possibilities emerge.

In such a situation, rather than seeking to answer in a once and for all fashion the question of 'what is really going on in Jarrow?' (whether in terms of the lay local, scientific citizens or local–global relations), we instead begin to recognize that these different forms of citizenship, identity and technical understanding are occurring simultaneously. The citizens of Jarrow cannot be squeezed into one category or another (for instance, as local or global, active or passive, ignorant or expert), but instead offer different self-representations at different points. Rhizome-like, just as one categorization has been completed, new categories start to pop up in the most unexpected places.

As one example of this, focus groups often commence with a vehement denial of any expert knowledge about the locality only to be followed by strong assertions that 'the only people who really understand this area are those who live here'. Equally, questions about the health of people in the locality may be met with learned discussions about the state of salmon in the nearby River Tyne. What this also suggests is that the context within which questions are asked (a focus group, a questionnaire, a ballot slip) can be extremely important for the answers that are given. Once again, it is not a question of which is the 'real' form of citizenship but rather of which forms of public and individual expression emerge in which settings. The Saturday afternoon animal rights activist is a Monday morning filing clerk, the politically active citizen is also a couch potato, the avid viewer of television wildlife programmes is uninterested in the local chemical works (and, of course, vice versa). Old essentialist notions of citizenship and of scientific awareness give way to more flexible, partial and, at times, contradictory forms (the committed environmentalist who drives to work, the company director who is proud of her Greenpeace membership). While this can frustrate those who wish to encourage their own preferred, and usually one-dimensional, form of citizenship (whether of the active or passive, local or global, lay or scientific variety), we see this cross-cutting, fragmented and shifting character of contemporary citizenship as suggestive of new possibilities and opportunities.

To focus on the industrial operation at the centre of the Jarrow case, rather than seeing the local and the global (or industry and the public) as simply separate – or in opposition to – one another, rhizomic connections run through the locality and indeed interlink the North East of England to a corporate headquarters in Pennsylvania, USA, and to the research and manufacturing activities of the company in twenty-seven different countries. As an excellent illustration of the governance theme of this book, the corporate website stresses a commitment to 'community dialogue' and to a 'Responsible Neighbor' programme, which has at its core the promotion of science, technology and mathematics education. The website suggests that for 'more than 50 years' the company

> has operated under the philosophy that maintaining an open line of communication with neighboring residents about all aspects of manufacturing processes and community issues is the responsible way to do business. One-way communication, however, is not adequate to assure that residents' concerns are appropriately addressed.
> (http://www.rohmhaas.com/community/dialogue/dia_overv.htm)

Here, then, we have a global commitment to the local (and vice versa) via an assemblage which is not simply 'corporate' in character (which would suggest a unitary and discrete entity) but which 'blurs' local–global, lay–expert, industry–public relations. The English of the website may be American in construction, but it is also spoken in many regional dialects (and, indeed, languages) and given its embodiment in very specific contexts. Although the examples in this book have often related to *public* rather than industrial policy, we would suggest that the assemblage concept is very appropriate to corporations (and, indeed, to other non-governmental organizations such as campaigning groups).

Having presented this framework for understanding the relationship between *Science, Social Theory and Public Knowledge*, the obvious questions now concern the significance for academic understanding and for scientific governance. If we begin with matters of governance, what possible application has such an approach to the world of practical policy and everyday decision making? Certainly, one obvious objection to our account is that we have disassembled the conventional conceptions of scientific government and public understanding of science only to replace them with a looser and more slippery series of assemblages and fleeting alliances. How can any constructive path be plotted across such shifting and treacherous territory?

It must be acknowledged from the outset that translating the ethno-epistemic assemblage perspective into a practicable policy/governance (and also research) agenda is by no means a straightforward task. This is because the ethno-epistemic assemblage approach advocated in Chapter 6 is crucially geared to uncovering the complexity, heterogeneity and dynamism of science–lay relations. Indeed, as the structure of Chapter 6 amply attests, the ethno-epistemic assemblage perspective cannot by any stretch of the imagination be considered 'linear'. That is to say, such a perspective is not about articulating a coherent set of predicates from which can be derived a series of practical implications or research strategies. Rather, the ethno-epistemic assemblage approach consists of a range of heterogeneous analytic concerns (as indicated in the latter half of Chapter 6). These disparate concerns reflect the heterogeneity of the actors, relations and processes that make up ethno-epistemic assemblages. The performance of transparency, the partial role of technology in the production of 'identity', the enunciatory techniques of governmentality, these can be shown to be connected together and, as an assemblage, to shape the 'public understanding of science'. However, there is nothing *a priori* 'coherent' or 'cohesive' in their connections or relations. As the metaphor of the rhizome suggests, these connections or relations are *ad hoc* (and, indeed, sometimes surprising), extending out like a mishapen, knotted web rather than fitting together to form readily discernible patterns.

It is decidedly problematic, then, to assume that these heterogeneous analyses can be directly converted into discrete political or policy recommendations or focused research programmes. Certainly, it is considerably easier to derive from the ethno-epistemic assemblage perspective a series of rather loose pronouncements on the need for an analytic reorientation in the study of science–lay relations or for renewed political sensibilities. This has certainly been a temptation. However, we believe it important, despite these difficulties, to offer an, albeit circumspect and contingent, attempt at articulating a series of what we hope to be implementable measures in relation to both governance and research. What ties these measures together is an acknowledgement of the changing circumstances of science–public–governance relations at the beginning of the twenty-first century. As we will also suggest, perhaps the major implication of our analysis is that we need to reconsider the very notion of governance itself. Before this, however, we will consider some of the further conceptual implications of this new framework for interpreting science–public relations.

Researching the ethno-epistemic assemblage

In the most general terms, rather than discarding the analytical perspectives with which this book began, our suggestion is that we are now in a position to re-evaluate current academic approaches – but also re-orient them so as to take account of emerging possibilities. Instead of seeking to downplay the significance of ethnographic studies, we have sought to give them new significance. Instead of endlessly recreating the argument for context, we can begin to assess the relevance of such studies within a broader framework. This alerts us also to some of the in-built limitations of the lay local, especially the tendency to romanticize and homogenize the communities under study.

At the same time, we have attempted to move beyond the more sterile abstractions of social theory. In particular, and as we have emphasized, there has been a considerable tendency to ignore local and ethnographic research, to treat it as a mere illustration of wider theoretical concerns. We have endeavoured to point out the complex and contradictory constitution of communities, groups, movements caught up in scientific controversy, stressing the ways in which they reflect and, crucially, mediate some of the processes and dynamics articulated by social theorists. In other words, we have treated the local as both distinct and general – a site through which putatively global processes (such as consumption or ambivalence) must pass and find local, sometimes peculiar, expression on their way to 'becoming global'.

For us, much of the stimulation and excitement in this field comes at the meeting point of intellectual approaches. Rather than sticking to one analytic category, conceptual framework or problematique, we have preferred to explore how disparate issues cross-cut and variably interweave, and, thus, to develop new insights, shed light on relevancies that would routinely remain obscure and lend new significance to what might otherwise be taken for granted.

These points can be made succinctly if we return to the Jarrow case. This is not a 'single' community and not all citizens wish to engage with risk and environmental problems. This suggests distinct limits to over-enthusiastic attempts at promoting active citizenship. Meanwhile, simply viewing Jarrow as an island of modernity (or even pre-modernity) in a postmodern world misses the point. Local people are not slavishly following some grand trend of history but are instead making their own lives as they see fit (and within social structures that both constrain and enable).

What we find in the Jarrow case, then, is not simply a public's (mis)-understanding of science, or a community's assertion of social identity in the face of a monolithic scientific institution. Rather, we would wish to trace in Jarrow the contingent and subtle ethno-epistemic assemblages that embody several disparate cultural artefacts (for example, formal scientific knowledge *and* folk expertise, ferocious localist *and* globalized identities) and incorporate many heterogeneous actors (local people, university scientists, company employees, civic bodies, non-goverment organizations, localizing and globalizing media, commercial and industrial concerns, fish – in and out of water).

These different actors do not necessarily 'cohere' as an assemblage – their interrelations are contingent upon a whole series of conditions and circumstances. Indeed, such interrelations are 'in process' in so far as they need ongoing maintenance. This 'processuality' would apply even to ostensibly cohesive actors such as 'the community of local Jarrow folk'. Let us imagine a scenario in Jarrow through which to explore this point. In particular, we could readily envision attempts made by relevant scientific institutions to engage in a process of transparent consultation. If such an attempt at transparency were to draw upon the performance of individual suffering (as, for example, by a company engineer expressing the personal stress caused by constantly balancing economic practicability against the highest levels of environmental protection), then one would expect a complex response from 'the community of local Jarrow folk'. On the one hand, one might expect 'local Jarrow folk' to respond with a sceptical dismissal of such performance, since it may be perceived as 'false', a crass attempt at manipulation. On the other hand, not least among those 'local Jarrow folk' exposed to confessional TV programmes, one can envisage an acceptance of such a performance because it is seen as holding to modern norms of authenticity. In those terms, 'being human' becomes a good thing.

Sketchy and speculative though this illustration undoubtedly is, it does have the merit of throwing into relief the way that changes or developments in an assemblage can fragment even the most ostensibly stable of actors such as 'the community of local Jarrow folk'. In our scenario, the consultative procedure has, as it were, interrupted – even interfered with – the process of reproducing an ostensibly unitary community. Ethno-epistemic alliances have emerged between fragments of that community and aspects of scientific institutions that counterpose alliances between other fragments of that community and a different set of political actors. In other words, new ethno-epistemic assemblages have taken shape.

This brief and imaginary return excursion to the Jarrow case has raised a range of issues that, obviously enough, require substantive empirical study. In what follows, we formalize the ways in which we might go about empirically investigating the various strands that make up ethno-epistemic assemblages. We present five interrelated methodological orientations: the emergence of actors and assemblages; the heterogeneity of assemblages; the promiscuous mediation of assemblages; the enunciation of assemblages; the constitution of assemblages.

The emergence of actors and assemblages

In studying lay–science relations, it is important to recognize the possible dynamism of these relations. In particular, as we have seen several times, for example in the AIDS movement, alliances form between fragments of the public and factions within scientific institutions such that new science–lay hybrid assemblages can be said to emerge and to act as the core antagonistic actors in a particular controversy. Thus, we should be sensitive to the possibility that it is not the 'obvious' or 'unitary' constituencies of public, or scientific, or governmental actors that are key to understanding a given case, but admixtures of these.

Methodologically, the main implication of this is the need to seek and collect data (e.g. documentation of meetings, collaborations, joint statements, or statements that while coming from seemingly disparate actors bear a close resemblance to one another – for example, share 'story lines') that indicate such hybrid alliances. Part and parcel of this would be a longitudinal study of shifts in the sorts of discourses that various actors evince, tracing the ways that these de-differentiate or polarize. Moreover, discursive data from scientific, lay or governmental participants that either celebrate or denounce new or emergent alliances can also serve as valuable pointers (see below for elaborations of this).

The heterogeneity of assemblages

In Chapter 6, we stressed that ethno-epistemic assemblages were composed not only of humans (in whatever strange or hybrid admixtures), but also of non-humans. Included among these non-humans were both technologies and natures. Our aim was to get away from seeing technologies and natures as 'mere' social constructions, and to acknowledge their role in the constitution of humans. In other words, we see humans, technologies and natures as relational, emerging by virtue of their relations to one another.

In the context of ethno-epistemic assemblages, non-humans play a number of roles. As technologies of communication (in the broadest sense that includes computers, cars, telephones), these non-humans enable contacts to be made among different actors and thus the possibility of new alliances being forged and new assemblages emerging. In investigating the role of such communications technologies, we can focus more directly upon them by, for example, examining the ways that new technologies such as the internet have enabled the emergence or consolidation of such assemblages as self-help groups, non-government organizations, website discussion groups. Moreover, we can take a counterfactual analytic strategy and ask: what sort of assemblage would have been possible in the absence of particular technologies?

Rather than treating aspects of nature as separate from humans (that is acted upon by humans – protected, constructed, exploited, modified, deified and so on), we would rather see such natures as constitutive components of assemblages. We are acutely aware that this is a knotty issue to be sure – we do not have unmediated access to these natures. We know them through culture. If we wish to treat seriously people's sense of belonging to particular places, and their lived mutualistic relationships with particular bodies, animals and environments, then we will need to consider carefully how such bodies, animals and environments might act within assemblages.

Methodologically, accessing these sorts of constitutive associations requires longitudinal ethnographical study to establish the nature of these relations with nature. In the context of specific scientific policy controversies, it means treating seriously – that is, unironically – people's attempts to articulate such relations with nature. For example, we would need to chart in greater detail than was possible for Wynne the relation between the Cumbrian farmers and their sheep and fells. We would need to begin to think about lay local people's folk knowledge of their local natures (and such knowledge comes in many forms, including stories, pictures, poetry) as an expression *of and by* an assemblage that includes those natures. [While we have stressed lay people's connection to natures, the same logic of analysis applies to scientific actors whose own expert stories no less incorporate their own peculiar nature as it is manifested – or 'mangled' (Pickering 1995) – in, say, the laboratory.] However, we would, of course, also need to embed these folk knowledges in more widely available, even globalized knowledges about, for example, ecology or animal welfare or health.

In the end, to map out these 'hybrid communities' will be a fraught exercise, not least because it is intrinsically difficult to grasp what natures are relevant to an assemblage. Nevertheless, the pay-off of such an approach is not only a broader apprehension of what comprises an assemblage (and a community), but also, as mentioned in Chapter 6, an initial movement towards a wider, perhaps more fruitful, relational form of ethics and citizenship.

The promiscuous mediation of assemblages

Assemblages contain, as constitutive components, discourses, techniques, methods and practices that are, as it were, 'alien' to them. In Chapter 6, we saw how attempts to perform transparency in the scientific decision-making process could draw upon a rather different institutional and popular area, specifically the 'psy-complex'. In tracing what makes an assemblage cohere, it is important to be alert to norms, values and assumptions that have been imported, or have been incorporated, from other assemblages. Another example: ethno-epistemic assemblages consisting of scientific institutions, public understanding of science academics and governmental bodies that have stressed the value of scientific knowledge for citizenship, have gradually taken on discourses in which citizens are increasingly regarded as consumers. Accordingly, to know or understand the relevant science is to be, it is assumed, accepting of its products (e.g. biotechnological goods). As has been argued (cf. Hill and Michael 1998), surveys that were once designed to measure understanding (and cognitive deficit) begin to gauge 'product recognition'.

Methodologically, it is important to have a grasp of developments over time within assemblages. Through longitudinal study, the aim would be to detect changes in forms of discourse or technique, such as innovations in social scientific methodology concerned with understanding the public understanding of science, or new modes of consultative or participatory scientific governance, or novel criteria by which lay trust is invested. The complementary aim would be to explore the extent to which it is possible to 'align' these innovations with similar changes occurring in other prominent assemblages – that is, to trace historically how such innovations have 'migrated' across assemblages.

For instance, we might ask why it is that focus group methodology has become increasingly common in public understanding of science research. Certainly, we would situate this development in the context of the popularity of focus group methodology in market research and governmental measures of public opinion. The supplementary question that can be asked is: does the importation of this technique signal tacit modification of the object of study – no longer a scientific citizen but an informed consumer? More subtly, it might be the case that we can detect the importation of discourses and practices from other assemblages in the most mundane, even trivial, activities. As we have seen, assurances of transparency and performances of personal suffering are not, on the surface, necessarily noteworthy. They have become 'normal', almost invisible. The methodological implication is that it is important to attend to seemingly trivial details of assemblages for it might well be in among these that we detect significant importations from other assemblages.

The enunciation of assemblages

Who is seen as a bona fide contributor to a scientific or policy controversy, who is regarded as worthy of consultation, who is trusted and valued – in sum, who is incorporated into this or that ethno-epistemic assemblage – is the subject of constant enunciation, or discursive activity. That is to say, ethno-epistemic assemblages do not just exist as 'objective' arrangements of various actors and relations. Part and parcel of their very existence are the on-going attempts to enunciate and articulate who is and is not a genuine part of a community, public, alliance, group or movement out of which ethno-epistemic assemblages are formed.

In other words, actors, in attempting to fashion particular ethno-epistemic alliances, are constantly trying to argue for the inclusion or exclusion of particular actors and particular relations. For example, to consult a particular constituency involves prioritizing what the pertinent constituency is, and what *aspect* of that constituency is directly relevant to the issue at hand. Thus, to develop a policy-making strategy on animal experimentation (that is, to put together institutional bodies that can address the issues around animal experimentation in order to develop policy), is to choose which portion of the public to consult and/or to invite into the process of discussion and argumentation (i.e. to select who becomes a part of the ethno-epistemic assemblage). It is also to decide on what the criteria should be for drafting such public actors. As Michael and Birke (1994b) have shown, sometimes this public is tightly delineated (must be ethics professionals such as members of the clergy), sometimes loosely delineated (must be 'rational' or unemotional). As with any scientific controversy, who has 'voice' within – that is, the right to contribute to – the process of argumentation is always a point of contention and contestation (see Collins 1985).

In essence, our point here is that we need to document the sorts of discourses that demarcate who can and cannot be included within a particular alliance or assemblage. The broader methodological imperative, therefore, concerns the need to collect and analyse what might be called meta-discourses or meta-commentaries. These are discourses deployed by actors which do not so much argue for this or that point within a controversy, but argue for this or that *form of controversy*: who has rights to contribute arguments and who does not; the 'proper' and improper content and conduct of those arguments; the appropriate and inappropriate manner of consultation or participation. Here, then, we are effectively aiming to map actors' discourses and commentaries on the *conduct of politics* and political process, and how these discourses and commentaries actually impact upon the conduct of politics and political process. To put this another way, our method focuses upon the ways in which actors, in enacting politics, citizenship and democracy, simultaneously draw discursively upon such notions as politics, citizenship, democracy and so on *as resources*.

There is a reflexive twist to this dimension of our method. Researchers in the public understanding of science are no more or less prone than other actors to making these sorts of meta-commentaries about the proper conduct of, especially, science–lay relations (see Chapter 2; Michael and Brown 2000). It is therefore important to take into account the ways that such academic commentaries contribute to the production of particular sorts of science–lay relations and, therefore, particular sorts of ethno-epistemic assemblage. This point applies to our own analysis and raises the ethical issue of how our meta-commentaries serve in the shaping of ethno-epistemic assemblages. In particular, it seems wise to reflect upon the ways in which our own analytic stance should be engaged in the advocacy of a particular form of politics (and, thus, a particular version of democracy and citizenship), or whether our task as academics is to keep open and fluid the range of such forms of politics.

The constitution of assemblages

The preceding discussion of how the enunciation of ethno-epistemic assemblages is part and parcel of what these assemblages are has highlighted the fact that such enunciations are in competition. In other words, various actors argue against one another for this or that constitution of assemblages. The issue we want to address here is: who wins in the process of discursive contestation over the form of discursive contestation? That is to say, we want to trace how particular discourses about the composition of, and the process of composing, an ethno-epistemic assemblage become privileged. As was the case for our first methodological orientation, to address this concern requires longitudinal ethnographic study. By tracking the sorts of processes by which these discourses were disseminated (meetings, venues, media which are themselves the objects of such discourses), by examining the rhetorical means by which such discourses were rendered persuasive or ridiculous (why have this meeting? why invite these speakers?), by charting the changes in actors' behaviour and self-definition (as committed to this or that form of political process), it is possible to sketch in richer detail the trajectory by which ethno-epistemic assemblages emerge and evolve.

To summarize this section on researching the ethno-epistemic assemblage, we can make three points. First, we must underline that the ethno-epistemic assemblage is a heuristic concept that serves the primary purpose of helping us focus on, and excavate, the empirical complexity and heterogeneity of relations between lay publics, scientific institutions and forms of governance. Secondly, the ethno-epistemic assemblage perspective is designed to enable the nuanced and mutual embedding of 'public understanding of science' in the context of broader social theoretical concerns and governance initiatives. Thirdly, it offers an, albeit limited, potential mechanism by which to review the role of academic analysis in the reproduction or production of existing or emergent forms of governance.

Governing the assemblage

In what ways does the treatment here suggest a new perspective on scientific governance? What in particular occurs when the scientific citizen becomes a more complex and heterogeneous character and the issues refuse to be constrained by traditional categories of science, citizenship and public policy? In the following, we will explore some of the immediate implications of the approach sketched out in this book. All of these observations take as their starting point the need for a new approach to science, social theory and public knowledge which does not simply trade in the language of a clear division between the 'lay' and the 'scientific' and of citizenship as a fixed (and decidedly idealized) categorization. Accordingly, we will be mindful both of the need to respond to wider criticisms of current forms of governance but also to embrace the new possibilities being generated by the changing conditions of scientific citizenship and sociotechnical change.

The starting point for this fresh treatment of public policy concerns the expanded notion of *scientific governance* that now emerges. Seen from the ethno-epistemic assemblage perspective, 'scientific governance' takes on a much broader form than its traditional definition as a predominantly technical process of policy making. Where government could once at least offer the illusion of retaining control over scientific innovation and the direction of societal change, the new social circumstances allow no such easy comfort. This is especially clear in a case like GM food where individual nations confront an international life science industry and where the issues themselves are under constant review in the face of new public concerns and technical amendments. Of course, it is also the case that international rather than national controls have become increasingly important. As we saw in the GM issue, what Canada, Australia or Britain has to say at governmental level may be less relevant than the strategic direction chosen by cross-national industries.

In making this point, however, we must also be careful about homogenizing the food biotechnology (or any other) industry – and also of overplaying its political influence and control. The whole point of the ethno-epistemic assemblage concept is to indicate the new alliances that can potentially be formed in this area. Accordingly, we should avoid the notion that 'industry', 'government' and 'non-governmental organizations' necessarily operate as separate monolithic blocs. In the case of the biosciences, for example, governments and industries characteristically interconnect and feed off one another. Government helps provide the scientists upon which industry depends, industry is essential to the economic prosperity of the nation, regulation depends upon trust and mutual understanding across industry and government. Equally, and as in the British consumer reaction to the BSE crisis, neither industry nor government can simply take for granted the supremacy of their own power and authority. Instead, they succeed or fail in gaining influence due to the 'ethno-epistemic alliances' in which they participate. In an age of growing scepticism in all institutions, such alliances become essential to political survival and economic success.

This point about the changing character of scientific governance relates closely to the emergent character of national decision making. Government in the past has often been geared up to consultation with the 'usual suspects': the established stakeholders, representing clearly defined issues, who can speak the language of government (often a mix of scientific and economic argumentation, as US public hearings seem to demonstrate). The ethno-epistemic assemblage perspective suggests the need for more flexible forms of encounter with differing perspectives and with groups who may not necessarily participate in the same forms of discourse. As we saw in the case of the Public Consultation on Developments in the Biosciences, this presents new challenges. There is no single pathway for public engagement and even the level of response may be variable (since there are other calls on our time and other problems to tackle). This also suggests that there may be, from a governmental perspective, a troubling lack of consistency in public responses: even the most comprehensive series of advanced consultations does not guarantee a passive public response to actual implementation and innovation. However, and as we will suggest, this inconsistent and heterogeneous character does not imply that consultation is without value or importance. On the contrary, in such dynamic situations it is important to maximize the level of social awareness and intelligence.

There is certainly a major challenge involved in the recognition of potentially multiple and co-existing forms of scientific citizenship: active/passive, single issue/generic, local/global, consumer/political. In this situation, it is no longer sufficient to construct only one form of citizenship: to assume that 'one size fits all' in citizen terms. Instead, government and industry may be faced with a multiplicity of 'scientific citizenships' in simultaneous operation. For enthusiastic proponents of active citizenship, this suggests an acknowledgement that not all citizens will be drawn to an intensive (or over-energetic) form of engagement – and that citizens active on one issue will not wish (or, indeed, be able) to engage across every issue.

This broad point about the emerging character of scientific governance links closely to the characteristic assumptions upon which conventional approaches to scientific governance are based. In the traditional approach to science policy, the assumption is that technical issues are paramount and that matters of public discussion then follow. In the case of GM foods, considerable emphasis has been given to 'getting the science right' as a precursor to informed public discussion. Of course, this 'science-led' model of scientific governance relies heavily on enlightenment notions that science is at the heart of rational policy with democratic discussion taking place within the framework provided by these 'facts'. Thus, there is a strong tendency within current debate over the biosciences to assume that the core issues are scientific and that everything then fits around these. With specific regard to GM crops, the implication is that wider public discussion is somehow of less importance than scientific testing. Equally, and while the merits of a complex and nuanced treatment of the scientific issues are generally lauded, public consultation is often presented as an exercise strictly constrained by time and money. A 'quick and dirty' approach to consultation is unlikely to meet the demands suggested by the previous analysis.

The 'science-led' perspective presents a very loaded – and also misleading – picture. Social, ethical and political concerns are inevitably downgraded and those raising such issues are presented as either premature in their concerns (why raise such problems when the basic evidence is unclear?) or else obstructive (why allow a social minority with ideologically motivated concerns to hold up technical progress?). The challenge ahead is to recognize the importance of both technical and cultural factors and, of course, the close interrelationship between these. Rather than beginning with 'the facts' and fitting 'politics and values' around these, it becomes important to place scientific issues in their full cultural context from the beginning.

At this point, we move directly to the linked question of how to *enhance public, scientific and political discussion over technological futures*. It follows from the discussion here that the current 'thin' culture of scientific governance needs to give way to a richer interpretation of contemporary social debates. Rather than assuming that the issues are 'really' scientific, the challenge is to operate with a broader notion of scientific governance. To take one issue that has run through this book, who says that the real issues concerning the biosciences are scientific? Why should the possible scientific approval of GM food mean that public discussion can now end? We can only put into practice the notion that cultural expression and public engagement are an integral element within scientific governance when we abandon the 'scientific core/social periphery' model of technical change. At the same time, and as we have noted, enhanced discussion over these issues is not a panacea for the difficulties of governance – not least because of the inevitably patchy and changing character of public responses. Rather than presenting 'the public' as a fixed and homogeneous entity, it becomes necessary to view the possibly diverse and dynamic character of public responses as a resource within the decision-making process.

This argument for the enhancement of the currently 'thin' culture of scientific governance also needs to take account of the practical and political obstacles facing more active citizen participation. As Brown and Mikkelsen relate, fighting toxic waste pollution can be

> extremely difficult and full of contradictions . . . The victims and their families, already suffering physical and emotional pain, must relive painful memories as they delve into the causes of their trouble. Indeed, the more ammunition they find for their case, the more reasons they have to be angry and afraid. To become activists, citizens must overcome an ingrained reluctance to challenge authority: they must shed their preconceptions about the role and function of

government and about democratic participation. They must also develop a new outlook on the nature of scientific inquiry and the participation of the public in scientific controversy.

(Brown and Mikkelsen 1990/1997: 43)

In presenting ethno-epistemic assemblages, therefore, we certainly do not wish to imply that these simply (or necessarily) fall effortlessly into place. It is here again that looser theoretical talk of globalization needs to be tempered by a more ethnographic awareness of the energies, struggles and commitments that may be necessary before active citizenship emerges. This is clearly a significant challenge for national and international processes of scientific governance. Some of the immediate implications of this challenge can be summarized as follows.

First, it becomes necessary to re-assess the nature of *scientific communication* to take account of these more complex social patterns of representation and expression. Previously, science communication has conventionally been defined as a matter of either 'disseminating the facts' (the old deficit model) or else as deliberate manipulation of the wider publics (the 'public relations' model). Of course, neither of these approaches can practically be avoided in the future. However, they need to be supplemented with the acknowledgement of more diverse connections between different social groups – and between issues (ethics and science, risk and quality of life) which are often kept apart. Central to this wider operation of science communication will be the ability of government to listen and respond to messages which are not expressed according to the discourse – or agenda – of government.

Secondly, and rather than viewing these as separate headings, it is important to recognize the *indivisibility of science, society and citizenship*. Here, there is a particular need to connect scientific citizenship to wider forms of expression (whether concerned with quality of life, health or perceived alienation). This suggests that scientific governance should be explicitly linked to questions of public welfare and societal development rather than being placed in a scientific and technical ghetto. At this point, it becomes especially important that scientific governance should not be ring-fenced as a specialist or technicized sub-field but instead is explicitly tied in with economic, political and ethical discussion over our social futures.

Thirdly, one particular consequence of this broader approach is that we begin to recognize – and mobilize – different understandings of *risk, uncertainty and ignorance*. Risk, as was suggested above, can take on different forms beyond its conventional construction as a technical matter of probabilities and consequences. As we have emphasized in previous chapters, risk can appear very different from a lay local (or social theoretical) perspective. The challenge for new approaches to scientific governance is that they value such different conceptions rather than forcing them into a narrow and technocratic framework.

Fourthly, one significant obstacle within the governance of science is the strong tendency to maintain a *firewall between 'public engagement' and 'technological innovation'*. This leaves public discussion permanently on the defensive, since such engagement only takes place after the technological momentum has been firmly established by industry. The challenge here is to establish forward-looking forms of critical scrutiny which at least set the broad societal framework within which innovation can occur.

Fifthly, and since there is clearly no single pathway forward from here, it is necessary to encourage *deliberate experimentation and critical reflection*. This is especially important when the doing of governance is also part of the process of producing citizens of particular kinds. The multiplicity of governmental engagement with the public thus needs to be facilitated, but also scrutinized. There is a need also to examine how claims to transparency, inclusion and so on are made and warranted, and to consider which resources that ostensibly lie outside of governance and science can be drawn upon. This strongly suggests the need for close independent monitoring of attempts at inclusion and other new initiatives.

Sixthly, it is worth re-emphasizing the importance of *industrial activities* within this wider framework. As we have seen especially in the Jarrow and GM cases, corporate governance and scientific citizenship are inseparable. It follows that practical intervention in this area needs to incorporate industrial strategies and corporate policies, without suggesting that 'corporations' should be ring-fenced or seen as any more homogeneous or neatly defined than either government or the public.

Finally, this perspective opens up further questions concerning the nature of *power and politics* within scientific governance. As Brown and Mikkelsen (1990/1997) argue, 'the only reason government and corporations pay attention to environmental and occupational safety issues is that the affected persons have recognized and acted on the problem' (p. 197). This suggests that the successful creation and maintenance of ethno-epistemic assemblages represent a powerful means of enabling social change. In that sense, and rather than offering a diversion *from* politics, ethno-epistemic assemblages become a crucial route *to* political influence. Of course, this point in turn raises questions of differential access to the necessary cultural and technical resources for the construction of a successful ethno-epistemic assemblage, although such resources may involve far more than money and 'sound science'.

Taking these points together, it is clear that 'governing the assemblage' requires fresh thinking about the relationship between society, science and the wider publics but also about the *nature of governance* itself. Assemblages by their very character entail the proliferation of connections and effects (both intended and unintended). This suggests that governance needs to be seen as an iterative process with no 'once and for all' solution available. Government is also itself a part of various assemblages – as it were, not only overseeing but also embodying epistemic alliances. Crucially, government is internally fractured with the different fragments being part of different coalitions and different ethno-epistemic assemblages.

At the most general level, therefore, one very practical implication of this book is that governance does not represent the application of higher rationality or the imposition of unchanging order. Instead, the call is for more fluid and contingent forms of leadership. Government in particular must acknowledge the need for open and explicit partnerships with a variety of ethno-epistemic alliances. This means that the modernistic illusion of national control should give way to an acknowledgement of the limitations – but also the potential significance – of public policy. In the end, there is no single answer. Instead, the call is for the open and reflective exploration of options.

Ultimately, this form of governance entails moving beyond the adoption of particular bureaucratic 'fixes' (whether public consultation exercises or new advisory structures) important as these can be in themselves. Instead, the governance of complex societies across a range of multiply-constructed issues necessitates a new form of *leadership*: concerned with social legitimation but not seeking an artificial social consensus; aware of the special character of scientific issues but also of their interconnection with broader social, political and economic concerns; conscious of the limitations of central authority but willing to establish new alliances and allegiances.

To return one last time to the Jarrow case discussed in Chapter 5, the approach advocated here suggests that governance entails a diffuse and dynamic series of networks and alliances: from local clubs and societies through to the formalized structures of local government and industry-community liaison. Such alliances rarely relate to one issue alone but will cut across local concerns and issues. As discussed in Chapter 5, these networks typically combine the local and the global, the specific and the generic. Rather than viewing the contrast between these overlapping networks and the specific aims of government and industry as a source of frustration and concern, the challenge is to view such assemblages as a resource and a stimulus to action. In giving up a rigid and one-dimensional notion of governance, we may gain a richer and multifaceted conception of the possibilities ahead. Of course, this represents considerably less than a blueprint for action. However, our most practical suggestion is that new policy approaches can only emerge when the wider constellation of scientific governance is fully acknowledged.

We recognize that the presentation of governance issues in this way represents a considerable shift from current government thinking. While official recognition of the legitimacy and importance of public engagement and openness still remains a distant prospect in many countries, our approach suggests the limitations of the emergent approaches to 'engagement' with their 'science first' ethos, characteristic separation of innovation and public debate, and failure to grasp the heterogeneity and dynamism of contemporary citizenship expressions. Thus, the new litany of 'transparency', 'rebuilding public trust and confidence' and 'democratic engagement' appears decidedly weak and one-dimensional when placed in the wider context of heterogeneous alliances and cross-cutting expressions of citizenship.

To take the example of 'transparency', we have suggested that complete transparency is utterly unobtainable, depending as it does upon shared assumptions about what should be revealed and the processes by which decisions are taken. A similar point can be made about the operationalization of 'public trust' which again assumes a simplified set of social relations (typically between two key parties: 'government' and 'the public') rather than multiple and heterogeneous identities. 'Engagement' also, as we have seen, is typically framed within the requirements of official institutions rather than acknowledging more diverse forms of expression and shifting levels of concern.

Far from advocating some utopian state of complete and active democracy (tempting though this always is), we are proposing a more measured and reflective approach to scientific governance. Crucial to this will be a spirit of experimentation and critical scrutiny, but also a willingness to accept that all interventions will inevitably be partial, diverse and surprising in their impacts. Such an approach follows directly from the framework for the public understanding of science presented in this book. While this presents a considerably more complex picture of the process of scientific governance than has previously been presented, we argue that it is a prerequisite for more considered action.

Conclusion

Inevitably, such a sprawling conceptual framework (or rather ragged network) as ethno-epistemic assemblage could do with some refining, not least through the continued testing of its utility. Drawing upon the ethno-epistemic assemblage perspective in researching new case studies of public scientific controversy, or in the re-examination of old case studies, would be a rather obvious step. However, within this simple move is the rather more challenging task of unravelling such cases in their complexity and heterogeneity. As we have seen, this necessitates a multiplicity of techniques addressing a variety of distinct but interrelated issues. Of course, it is not envisaged that such a broad approach is in any way comprehensive. This would, in any case, be an impossibility not least because the very analysis of an ethno-epistemic assemblage contributes to its enunciation and thus its 'being' and 'becoming'. The upshot is that ethno-epistemic assemblage analyses are always contingent, situated and reflexive.

Chapter 6 outlined the range of actors and relations that we should pursue in describing an ethno-epistemic assemblage that addresses science, social theory and public knowledge, and that engages with the concerns of processes of governance. Chapter 7 has looked at the sorts of political and practical ramifications that the ethno-epistemic assemblage perspective would have for scientific governance, and has disaggregated a series of analytic concerns and their methodological implications. However, our efforts to derive pragmatic inputs into forms of governance and our attempts to develop do-able analytic and methodological strategies are not as separable as the organization of this chapter might suggest. The problems that any form of governance must deal with in the face of the fluidity and complexity of relations between science and the public – indeed, in the face of the indivisibility of science, society and citizenship – echo the difficulties that researchers face in articulating new combinations and configurations of science, society and citizenship. Just as the ethno-epistemic assemblage approach must do, scientific governance needs to become oriented to emergent, hybrid actors that incorporate elements that would once have been seen to be alien or irrelevant. Both would benefit from a willingness to innovate and experiment, methodologically, intellectually and politically. But, over and above this parallel, the academic study and scientific governance of 'the public understanding of science' are not distinct endeavours. They feed off each other. Thus, part and parcel of scientific governance is the sponsorship of academic research: academic research impacts upon what governmental actors see as 'important issues in scientific governance'. What we hope to see emerging is a new ethno-epistemic assemblage in which these mutual relations continue to be enacted, but, this time around, embody the very insights of the ethno-epistemic assemblage perspective.

8 Conclusion

In this final chapter, we intend, on the one hand, to underline what we see as our main contributions to the various fields with which we have engaged, and, on the other, to address where our ethno-epistemic assemblage perspective leads us politically, empirically and theoretically. The book has dealt with three broad areas – public understanding of science, scientific governance and social theory. In reviewing these, we have been particularly attuned to the ways that these literatures have, by and large, constructed a dichotomy between science and lay. Having made that point, we have also emphasized that, within these areas, there have been significant attempts to get beyond, if not transcend, the dichotomy:

- In the case of PUS, both traditional and ethnographic approaches assumed this distinction, albeit drawn in rather different ways: the former stressing lay cognitive deficit and scientific truth, the latter emphasizing lay social identity and scientific contingency. Nevertheless, recent work in the field has begun to challenge these dichotomies and to pay closer empirical attention to the ways in which the border between science and lay is being breached in particular instances, notably the AIDS movement in the USA.
- In the case of scientific governance, the predominant model for engagement with public constituencies remains one in which the public is regarded as a separate entity that requires 'education' so that it might engage 'appropriately' in issues of scientific controversy or decision making. However, we detected a partial shift away from this model and pointed to several examples where public groups were seemingly afforded a far more prominent role in the process of negotiation and discussion. Despite this, closer inspection suggested that, even in those instances where the public were invited to 'participate' or were 'consulted', the notion of the public as deficient was still very much in evidence.

• In the case of social theory, we noted that earlier conceptualizations of science and lay as distinct spheres have been overhauled in light of perceived changes – the dynamics of globalization, the rise of consumer culture, the emergence of risk society. Modern social theory has (sometimes indirectly) addressed the ways in which relations between public and science are in transition. The current aim of many theoretical studies is to account for the (late modern or post-modern) processes by which the border between science and lay is becoming more fluid (a fluidity that is attached to the erosion of a series of other related dichotomies such as local/global and citizen/consumer). However, with all this emphasis on fluidity, there is the danger of neglecting ethnographic observations that these modernist dichotomies can be re-asserted and re-enacted within specific contexts.

Chapters 2, 3 and 4 reviewed the three areas of public understanding of science, governance and social theory. In each case, we traced the ways in which the distinction between science and lay was upheld and challenged. This was summarized in Chapter 5. More importantly, that chapter linked the preceding three chapters by articulating how each area engaged with a number of motifs (such as the models of the public, the citizen, democracy, the role of culture and processes of communication). In drawing out the commonalities and differences between the three areas, we made use of a specific case study to illustrate the ways in which, even in an apparently resolutely 'lay local' setting, science and society were blurred. Thus, we traced how science, public and knowledge were co-constructed, and how as part and parcel of this dynamic relations were being forged between local and global, relations that complicated the meaning and status of 'citizenship'.

Chapter 5 set the scene for the next layer of complication – the next twist in the narrative spiral that has structured this book. It laid out a series of issues and concerns that are partially addressed across the three areas and which are exemplified in the Jarrow case. However, this was not theorized as such. This is what Chapter 6 aimed to accomplish, albeit circumspectly and heuristically. Here, through the elaboration of the notion of ethno-epistemic assemblages, we tried to crystallize one way of thinking about the de-differentiation between science and lay. Moreover, we raised a series of additional issues that have exercised theorists in a number of fields, issues such as heterogeneity and governmentality. These were elaborated in relation to the figure of the 'scientific citizen'. In other words, in Chapter 6 we presented our theoretical 'punchline'. In Chapter 7, some of the 'practical' ramifications of ethno-epistemic assemblages – both in terms of research and governance – were explored.

In reviewing and rethinking the relations between science, social theory and public knowledge, we have drawn out a number of linked reorientations to public scientific controversy. We have stressed the importance of new fissures and alliances along which controversy, debate and negotiation are played out. No longer are these struggles conducted between experts and public, but between assemblages made up of different combinations of expert and public (as well as other actors such as industry and government). However, we have also emphasized that these more or less agonistic assemblages should not be reified. They are dynamic and processual. To this end we have considered how various non-humans are instrumental in their production and reproduction. Moreover, we have advocated the need for sensitivity to the constructedness of these assemblages for they are the subjects of a whole range of discourses and practices that, so to speak, make them what they are. These practices and discourses are deployed by a variety of actors: those who are most 'involved' – laypeople and scientific experts – certainly, but also more diffuse governmental and social scientific actors as they go about measuring, characterizing, studying, surveying, enabling and mediating the interactions between these assemblages. To put this another way, we blurred not only the boundaries between scientific and lay, but also between social science and scientific governance.

Given our long-standing interest in the public understanding of science, a question we feel obliged to pursue is 'what are the implications of our arguments and approach for the multidiscipline of public understanding of science'? At one level, the proper response is that this should be disbanded (if that is possible for a multidiscipline). Our approach has so problematized the categories of public and science (not to say understanding), that it seems that a rather different intellectual and political project is called for (and we have made suggestions regarding this in Chapter 7). Having said that, PUS is still prominent in the 'making' of different assemblages, assemblages that might be predominantly public or predominantly scientific. Indeed, there are instances where it is perfectly possible for the old dichotomies between science and lay to be analytically, as well as politically, useful. However, our argument in this book suggests that the number of such instances is progressively diminishing.

Our revisioning of PUS also suggests an interim tack. We have, in one way or another, throughout this volume, juxtaposed the public understanding of science to what we might call the 'public understanding of society'. We have stressed that the public's 'understanding' of science is nested in its 'apprehension' of the social world and the way this expresses itself in identities performed and relations forged. Of course, these two understandings – these two PUSes – are not separate. They are iterative, feeding off one another in complex circuits (as we hope to have shown in examples like GM food and Jarrow). What we would propose, partly in keeping with recent political concerns with 'science and society', is a programme of research whose object of study is the 'public understanding' of both 'science in society' and 'society in science' – both can be labelled as PUSS.

Inevitably, as is our wont, we are tempted to complicate matters further. For all PUSS's feline allure, it is also a pantomime character that still overly simplifies the relation between science and public. As such, we would not wish to obscure the fact that the public is itself 'understood' and thus 'made' by and in the activities of science and society. The pronouncements of scientific institutions, the innovations in participatory mechanisms for science policy, the studies generated by social scientific research and so on, all these construct particular publics. If we were to give all this a name, we might call it the *public 'understanding' of science and society and science and society's 'understanding' of the public*. This has the pleasingly palindromic, if unpleasantly sibilant, acronym of PUSSSSUP that evokes the sort of symmetry we have been striving for in this volume – a symmetry in which science and society co-construct one another. In the end, that is our central message, and all we have done is expound one heuristic – that of ethno-epistemic assemblages – towards unravelling this process of co-construction, a heuristic which, in our more optimistic moments, we would like to think contributes to that very process of co-construction.

At the most basic level, the study of science, social theory and public knowledge takes us to the heart of a series of changes occurring not just within often-obscure theoretical texts or within the very practical worlds of science communication and scientific protest. Instead, the previous chapters have raised widely relevant questions of the character of social action, of local–global and human–non-human relations, and of the nature of citizenship and governance in the contemporary world. To stress this final point, issues of scientific governance and scientific citizenship have the potential both to challenge prevailing, rather passive models of democracy and to suggest new possibilities for democratic regeneration and revival. This book has been written in the belief that an open, self-confident and self-critical society is a prerequisite for the successful management of scientific and social change.

References

Abercrombie, N., Hill, S. and Turner, B. (1986) *The Sovereign Individual*. London: Allen & Unwin.

Aldhous, P., Coghlan, A. and Copley, J. (1999) Let the people speak, *New Scientist*, 22 May, pp. 12–14.

Arksey, H. (1998) *RSI and the Experts: The Construction of Medical Knowledge*. London: UCL Press.

Barnes, B. (1977) *Interests and the Growth of Knowledge*. London: RKP.

Barns, I. (1995) Manufacturing consensus: reflection on the UK National Consensus Conference on Plant Biotechnology, *Science as Culture*, 5: 199–216.

Barr, J. and Birke, L. (1998) *Common Science?: Women, Science, and Knowledge*. Bloomington, IN: Indiana University Press.

Barry, A. (2001) *Political Machines*. London: Athlone.

Bauman, Z. (1989) *Modernity and the Holocaust*. Cambridge: Polity.

Bauman, Z. (1991) *Modernity and Ambivalence*. Cambridge: Polity.

Beck, U. (1992) *The Risk Society*. London: Sage.

Beck, U. (2000) Risk society revisited: theory, politics and research programmes, in B. Adam, U. Beck and J. Van Loon (eds) *The Risk Society and Beyond*, pp. 211–29. London: Sage.

Beck, U. and Beck-Gersheim, E. (1995) *The Normal Chaos of Love*. Cambridge: Polity.

Beilharz, P. (2000) *Zygmunt Bauman: Dialectic of Modernity*. London: Sage.

Beveridge, A.A. and Rudell, F. (1988) An evaluation of 'public attitudes toward science and technology' in science indicators: the 1985 Report, *Public Opinion Quarterly*, 52: 374–85.

Bijker, W.E. (1995) *Of Bicycles, Bakelite and Bulbs: Toward a Theory of Sociotechnical Change*. Cambridge, MA: MIT Press.

Bijker, W.E. and Law, J. (eds) (1992) *Shaping Technology/Building Society*. Cambridge, MA: MIT Press.

Birke, L. and Michael, M. (1997) Rights, hybrids and their proliferation, *Animal Issues*, 1: 1–19.

Bloor, D. (1976) *Knowledge and Social Imagery*. London: RKP.

Bourdieu, P. (1984) *Distinction: A Social Critique of the Judgement of Taste*. London: Routledge & Kegan Paul.

Bowker, G.C. and Star, S.L. (1999) *Sorting Things Out: Classification and Its Consequences*. Cambridge, MA: MIT Press.

Brickman, R., Jasanoff, S. and Ilgen, T. (1985) *Controlling Chemicals: The Politics of Regulation in Europe and the United States*. Ithaca, NY: Cornell University Press.

Brown, N. and Michael, M. (2001a) Switching between science and culture in transpecies transplantation, *Science, Technology and Human Values*, 26(1): 3–22.

Brown, N. and Michael, M. (2001b) Transgenics, uncertainty and public credibility, *Transgenic Research*, 10(4): 279–93.

Brown, P. and Mikkelsen, E.J. (1990/1997) *No Safe Place: Toxic Waste, Leukemia and Community Action*. Berkeley, CA: University of California Press.

Burkitt, I. (1999) *Bodies of Thought: Embodiment, Identity and Modernity*. London: Sage.

Bush, J., Moffatt, S. and Dunn, C.E. (2001) Keeping the public informed? Public negotiations of air quality information, *Public Understanding of Science*, 10: 213–29.

Callon, M. (1986) The sociology of an actor-network: the case of the electric vehicle, in M. Callon, J. Law and A. Rip (eds) *Mapping the Dynamics of Science and Technology*, pp. 19–34. London: Macmillan.

Clarke, A.E. (1990) A social worlds research adventure: the case of reproductive science, in S.E. Cozzens and T.F. Gieryn (eds) *Theories of Science in Society*, pp. 15–42. Bloomington, IN: Indiana University Press.

Clarke, A.E. and Fujimura, J.H. (eds) (1992) *The Right Tools for the Job: At Work in Twentieth-century Life Science*. Princeton, NJ: Princeton University Press.

Clarke, A.E. and Montini, T. (1993) The many faces of RU486: tales of situated knowledges and technological contestation, *Science, Technology and Human Values*, 18: 42–78.

Cohen, A.P. (1985) *The Symbolic Construction of Community*. Chichester: Ellis Harwood.

Collins, H.M. (1985) *Changing Order*. London: Sage.

Collins, H. and Pinch, T. (1993) *The Golem: What Everyone Should Know About Science*. Cambridge: Cambridge University Press.

Cooper, D.K.C. and Lanza, R.P. (2000) *Xeno: The Promise of Transplanting Animal Organs into Humans*. Oxford: Oxford University Press.

Couch, S. and Kroll-Smith, J.S. (eds) (1991) *Communities at Risk: Collective Responses to Technological Hazards*. New York: Peter Lang.

Croll, E. and Parkin, D. (eds) (1992) *Bush Base: Forest Farm – Culture, Environment and Development*. London: Routledge.

Crook, S., Pakulski, J. and Walters, M. (1992) *Postmodernization*. London: Sage.

Dean, M. (1999) *Governmentality: Power and Rule in Modern Society*. London: Sage.

Deleuze, G. and Guattari, F. (1988) *A Thousand Plateaus: Capitalism and Schizophrenia*. London: Athlone Press.

Della Porta, D. and Diani, M. (1998) *Social Movements*. Oxford: Blackwell.

Department of Trade and Industry (July 2000) *Excellence and Opportunity: A Science and Innovation Policy for the 21st Century*. London: The Stationery Office.

Department of Trade and Industry (undated) *The Government Response to the House of Lords Select Committee on Science and Technology Third Report* (http://www.dti.gov.uk/scienceind/report3response.htm).

Durant, J.R. (1992) Test your own scientific literacy, *The Observer*, 2 February.

Durant, J.R. (1993) What is scientific literacy?, in J.R. Durant and J. Gregory (eds) *Science and Culture in Europe*, pp. 129–37. London: Science Museum.

Durant, J.R., Evans, G.A. and Thomas, G.P. (1989) The public understanding of science, *Nature*, 340 (6 July): 11–14.

Durant, J.R., Bauer, M. and Gaskell, G. (eds) (1997) *Biotechnology in the Public Sphere: A European Sourcebook*. London: Science Museum.

Epstein, S. (1996) *Impure Science: AIDS Activism and the Politics of Science*. Berkeley, CA: University of California Press.

Epstein, S. (2000) Democracy, expertise and AIDS treatment activism, in D.L. Kleinman (ed.) *Science, Technology and Democracy*, pp. 15–32. Albany, NY: State University of New York Press.

ESRC Global Environmental Change Programme (2000) *Risky Choices, Soft Disasters: Environmental Decision-making Under Uncertainty*. Brighton: University of Sussex.

European Commission (2000) *Governance in the EU: A White Paper* (http://europa. eu.int/comm/governance/areas/group2/index_en.htm).

European Commission (2002) *Science and Society Action Plan*. Luxembourg: Office for Official Publications of the European Communities.

Evans, G. and Durant, J. (1995) The relationship between knowledge and attitudes in the public understanding of science in Britain, *Public Understanding of Science*, 4: 57–74.

Eyerman, R. and Jamison, A. (1991) *Social Movement: A Cognitive Approach*. Cambridge: Polity.

Featherstone, M. (1991) *Consumer Culture and Postmodernism*. London: Sage.

Finney, C. (1998) Scientific citizenship: extending public participation in scientific decision-making. Unpublished doctoral dissertation, University of London.

Franklin, A. (1999) *Animals and Modern Cultures: A Sociology of Human–Animal Relations in Modernity*. London: Sage.

Franklin, S. (1998) *Embodied Progess*. London: Routledge.

Funtowicz, S.O. and Ravetz, J. (1993) Science for the post-normal age, *Futures*, 25(7): 735–55.

Gabriel, Y. and Lang, T. (1995) *The Unmanageable Consumer: Contemporary Consumption and its Fragmentation*. London: Sage.

Garfinkel, H. (1967) *Studies in Ethnomethodology*. Cambridge: Polity Press.

Gergen, K.J. (1982) *Toward Transformation in Social Knowledge*. New York: Springer-Verlag.

Gergen, K.J. (1991) *The Saturated Self*. New York: Basic Books.

Giddens, A. (1990) *Consequences of Modernity*. Cambridge: Polity.

Giddens, A. (1991) *Modernity and Self-identity*. Cambridge: Polity.

Giddens, A. (1992) *The Transformation of Intimacy*. Cambridge: Polity.

Gieryn, T.F. (1999) *Cultural Boundaries of Science: Credibility on the Line*. Chicago, IL: University of Chicago Press.

Gilbert, G.N. and Mulkay, M. (1984) *Opening Pandora's Box: A Sociological Analysis of Scientists' Discourse*. Cambridge: Cambridge University Press.

Goffman, E. (1959) *The Presentation of Self in Everyday Life*. Harmondsworth: Penguin.

Gregory, J. and Miller, S. (1998) *Science in Public: Communication, Culture and Credibility*. New York: Plenum.

Grove-White, R., Macnaghten, P., Mayer, S. and Wynne, B. (1997) *Uncertain World: Genetically Modified Organisms, Food and Public Attitudes in Britain*. Lancaster: Lancaster University.

Haas, P.M. (ed.) (1992) Epistemic communities and international policy coordination (Special Issue), *International Organization*, 46(1).

Hacking, I. (1986) Making up people, in T.C. Heller, M. Sosna and D.E. Wellberg (eds) *Reconstructing Individualism*, pp. 222–36. Stanford, CA: Stanford University Press.

Hajer, M. (1997) *The Politics of Environmental Discourse*. Oxford: Oxford University Press.

Haraway, D. (1991) *Simians, Cyborgs and Nature*. London: Free Association Books.

Haraway, D. (1992) Other worldly conversations; terran topics; local terms. *Science as Culture*, 3: 64–99.

Haraway, D. (1997) *Modest_Witness@Second_Millenium.Female Man.Meets Onco-Mouse: Feminism and Technoscience*. London: Routledge.

Harre, R. and Secord, P.F. (1972) *The Explanation of Social Behaviour*. Oxford: Blackwell.

Harvey, D. (1989) *The Condition of Postmodernity*. Oxford: Blackwell.

Hawking, S.W. (1988) *A Brief History of Time: From the Big Bang to Black Holes*. London: Bantam.

Heritage, J. (1984) *Garfinkel and Ethnomethodology*. Cambridge: Polity.

Hilgartner, S. (2000) *Science on Stage: Expert Advice as Public Drama*. Stanford, CA: Stanford University Press.

Hill, A. and Michael, M. (1998) Engineering acceptance: representations of 'the public' in debates on biotechnologies, in P. Wheale, R. von Schomberg and P. Glasner (eds) *The Social Management of Genetic Engineering*, pp. 201–17. Aldershot: Ashgate.

Hobart, M. (ed.) (1993) *An Anthropological Critique of Development: The Growth of Ignorance*. London: Routledge.

House of Lords Select Committee on Science and Technology (February 2000) *Third Report: Science and Society*. HL Paper 38. London: The Stationery Office.

Ingold, T. (1993) The temporality of the landscape, *World Archeology*, 25: 152–74.

Irwin, A. (1985) *Risk and the Control of Technology: Public Policies for Road Traffic Safety in Britain and the United States*. Manchester: Manchester University Press.

Irwin, A. (1995) *Citizen Science: A Study of People, Expertise and Sustainable Development*. London: Routledge.

Irwin, A. (2001a) Constructing the scientific citizen: science and democracy in the biosciences, *Public Understanding of Science*, 10(1): 1–18.

Irwin, A. (2001b) *Sociology and the Environment: A Critical Introduction to Society, Nature and Knowledge*. Cambridge: Polity.

Irwin, A. and Green, K. (1983) The control of chemical carcinogens in Britain, *Policy and Politics*, 11(4): 439–59.

Irwin, A. and Rothstein, H. (2003) Regulatory science in a global regime, in F. den Hond, P. Groenewegen and N. van Straalen (eds) *Pesticides: Problems, Improvements, Alternatives*, pp. 77–86. Oxford: Blackwell.

Irwin, A. and Wynne, B. (eds) (1996) *Misunderstanding Science? The Public Reconstruction of Science and Technology*. Cambridge: Cambridge University Press.

Irwin, A., Simmons, P. and Walker, G. (1999) Faulty environments and risk reasoning: the local understanding of industrial hazards, *Environment and Planning A*, 31: 1311–26.

Jasanoff, S. (1990) *The Fifth Branch: Science Advisers as Policymakers*. Cambridge, MA: Harvard University Press.

Keat, R., Whiteley, N. and Abercrombie, N. (1994) Introduction, in R. Keat, N. Whiteley and N. Abercrombie (eds) *The Authority of the Consumer*, pp. 1–19. London: Routledge.

Kerr, A. and Cunningham-Burley, S. (2000) On ambivalence and risk: reflexive modernity and the new human genetics, *Sociology*, 32: 283–304.

Kleinman, D.L. (2000) Introduction, in D.L. Kleinman (ed.) *Science, Technology and Democracy*, pp. 1–12. Albany, NY: State University of New York Press.

Knorr-Cetina, K.D. (1981) *The Manufacture of Knowledge: An Essay on the Constructivist and Contextual Nature of Science*. Oxford: Pergamon.

Lash, S. and Urry, J. (1987) *The End of Organized Capitalism*. Cambridge: Polity.

Lash, S. and Urry, J. (1994) *Economies of Signs and Space*. London: Sage.

Latour, B. (1987) *Science in Action: How to Follow Engineers in Society*. Milton Keynes: Open University Press.

Latour, B. (1993) *We Have Never Been Modern*. Hemel Hempstead: Harvester Wheatsheaf.

Latour, B. (1999) *Pandora's Hope: Essays on the Reality of Science Studies*. Cambridge, MA: Harvard University Press.

Latour, B. and Woolgar, S. (1979) *Laboratory Life: The Social Construction of Scientific Facts*. London: Sage.

Law, J. (1991) Introduction: monsters, machines and sociotechnical relations, in J. Law (ed.) *A Sociology of Monsters*, pp. 1–23. London: Routledge.

Law, J. (1994) *Organizing Modernity*. Oxford: Blackwell.

Layton, D., Jenkins, E., MacGill, S. and Davey, A. (1993) *Inarticulate Science?* Driffield: Studies in Education Ltd.

London Centre for Governance, Innovation and Science, and The Genetics Forum (March 1998) *Citizen Foresight: A Tool to Enhance Democratic Policy-making. 1:*

The Future of Food and Agriculture. Available from The Genetics Forum, 94 White Lion Street, London N1 9PF.

Lundin, S. (1999) The boundless body: cultural perspectives on xenotransplantation, *Ethnos*, 64: 5–31.

Lury, C. (1996) *Consumer Culture*. Cambridge: Polity.

Lyotard, J.-F. (1984) *The Postmodern Condition: A Report on Knowledge*. Manchester: Manchester University Press.

Macnaghten, P. and Urry, J. (1998) *Contested Natures*. London: Sage.

Macnaghten, P. and Urry, J. (eds) (2001) *Bodies of Nature*. London: Sage.

Marlier, E. (1992) Eurobarometer 35.1: opinions of Europeans on biotechnology in 1991, in J. Durant (ed.) *Biotechnology in Public: A Review of Recent Research*, pp. 52–108. London: Science Museum.

Martin, E. (1987) *The Woman in the Body*. Milton Keynes: Open University Press.

Martin, E. (1994) *Flexible Bodies*. Boston, MA: Beacon Press.

Martin, E. (1998) Anthropology and cultural study of science, *Science, Technology and Human Values*, 23: 24–44.

Melucci, A. (1989a) *Nomads of the Present*. London: Hutchinson Radius.

Melucci, A. (1989b) The symbolic challenge of contemporary movements, *Social Research*, 52: 789–816.

Michael, M. (1991) Discourses of danger and dangerous discourses: patrolling the borders of nature, society and science, *Discourse and Society*, 2(1): 5–28.

Michael, M. (1992) Lay discourses of science: science-in-general, science-in-particular and self, *Science, Technology and Human Values*, 17(3): 313–33.

Michael, M. (1996a) Ignoring science: discourses of ignorance in the public understanding of science, in A. Irwin and B. Wynne (eds) *Misunderstanding Science? The Public Reconstruction of Science and Technology*, pp. 105–25. Cambridge: Cambridge University Press.

Michael, M. (1996b) *Constructing Identities: The Social, the Nonhuman and Change*. London: Sage.

Michael, M. (1998) Between citizen and consumer: multiplying the meanings of the public understanding of science, *Public Understanding of Science*, 7: 313–27.

Michael, M. (2000) *Reconnecting Culture, Technology and Nature: From Society to Heterogeneity*. London: Routledge.

Michael, M. (2001) Technoscientific bespoking: animals, publics and the new genetics, *New Genetics and Society*, 20(3): 205–24.

Michael, M. (2002) Comprehension, apprehension, and prehension: heterogeneity and the public understanding of science, *Science, Technology and Human Values*, 27(3): 357–70.

Michael, M. and Birke, L. (1994a) Accounting for animal experiments: credibility and disreputable 'others', *Science, Technology and Human Values*, 19(2): 189–204.

Michael, M. and Birke, L. (1994b) Animal experimentation: enrolling the core set, *Social Studies of Science*, 24: 81–95.

Michael, M. and Brown, N. (2000) From the representation of publics to the performance of 'lay political science', *Social Epistemology*, 14(1): 3–19.

Michael, M. and Carter, S. (2001) The facts about fictions and vice versa: public understanding of human genetics, *Science as Culture*, 10(1): 5–32.

Miller, J.D. (1991) *The Public Understanding of Science and Technology in the US*. Report to the US National Science Foundation. DeKalb, IL: National Opinion Research Venture.

Miller, D. (1995) Consumption as the vanguard of history, in D. Miller (ed.) *Acknowledging Consumption*, pp. 1–57. London: Routledge.

Mills, C.W. (1959) *The Sociological Imagination*. New York: Oxford University Press.

Millstone, E. (1986) *Food Additives: Taking the Lid Off What We Really Eat*. Harmondsworth: Penguin.

Mol, A. and Law, J. (1994) Regions, networks and fluids: anaemia and social topology, *Social Studies of Science*, 24: 641–71.

MORI (1999) *The Public Consultation on Developments in the Biosciences. December 1998–April 1999 Vol. 1*. London: Department of Trade and Industry.

Mulkay, M. (1979) *Science and the Sociology of Knowledge*. London: Allen & Unwin.

Nelkin, D. (1975) The political impact of technical expertise, *Social Studies of Science*, 5: 35–54.

Novas, C. and Rose, N. (2000) Genetic risk and the birth of the somatic individual, *Economy and Society*, 29(4): 485–513.

Nowotny, H., Scott, P. and Gibbons, M. (2001) *Re-Thinking Science: Knowledge and the Public in an Age of Uncertainty*. Cambridge: Polity.

Office of Science and Technology (July 2000) *Guidelines 2000: Scientific Advice and Policymaking* (www.dti.gov.uk/ost/aboutost/guidelines.htm).

Office of Science and Technology (March 2001) *Code of Practice for Scientific Advisory Committees: Draft for Second Round Consultation*. London: Department of Trade and Industry.

Phillips Report (October 2000) *The BSE Inquiry: Vol. 1*. London: The Stationery Office.

Pickering, A. (1995) *The Mangle of Practice: Time, Agency and Science*. Chicago, IL: University of Chicago Press.

Potter, J. and Wetherell, M. (1987) *Discourse and Social Psychology*. London: Sage.

Power, M. (1999) *The Audit Society*. Oxford: Oxford University Press.

Price, D.K. (1967) *The Scientific Estate*. Cambridge, MA: Belknap Press of Harvard University Press.

Rabinow, P. (1996) *Essays on the Anthropology of Reason*. Princeton, NJ: Princeton University Press.

Rampton, S. and Stauber, J. (2002) *Trust Us, We're Experts! How Industry Manipulates Science and Gambles with Your Future*. New York: Jeremy P.Tarcher/Putnam.

Rose, N. (1996) *Inventing Our Selves: Psychology, Power and Personhood*. Cambridge: Cambridge University Press.

Rose, N. (1999) *Powers of Freedom*. Cambridge: Cambridge University Press.

Ross, A. (1991) *Strange Weather*. London: Verso.

Rothstein, H., Irwin, A., Yearley, S. and Mc Carthy, E. (1999) Regulatory science, Europeanisation and the control of agrochemicals, *Science, Technology and Human Values*, 24(2): 241–64.

Royal Commission on Environmental Pollution (RCEP) (1998) *21st Report: Setting Environmental Standards*. London: The Stationery Office.

Royal Society of London (1985) *The Public Understanding of Science*. London: The Royal Society.

Sampson, E.E. (1981) Cognitive psychology as ideology, *American Psychologist*, 36: 730–43.

Sampson, E.E. (1983) Deconstructing psychology's subject, *Journal of Mind and Behaviour*, 4: 135–64.

Saunders, P. (1993) Citizenship in a liberal society, in B.S. Turner (ed.) *Citizenship and Social Theory*, pp. 57–90. London: Sage.

Seriously Ill for Medical Research (1998) *Biotechnology and You: What Patients Need to Know*. Dunstable: SIMR.

Shapin, S. (1991) Science and the public, in R.C. Olby, G.N. Cantor, J.R.R. Christie and M.J.S. Hodge (eds) *Companion to the History of Modern Science*, pp. 990–1007. London: Routledge & Kegan Paul.

Shotter, J. (1975) *Images of Man in Psychological Research*. London: Methuen.

Slater, D. (1997) *Consumer Culture and Modernity*. Cambridge: Polity.

Smith, R. and Wynne, B. (eds) (1988) *Expert Evidence*. London: Routledge.

Star, S.L. (1991) Power, technologies and the phenomenology of conventions: on being allergic to onions, in J. Law (ed.) *A Sociology of Monsters*, pp. 26–56. London: Routledge.

Star, S.L. and Griesemer, J.R. (1989) Institutional ecology, 'translations' and boundary objects: amateurs and professionals in Berkeley's Museum of Vertebrate Zoology, 1907–39, *Social Studies of Science*, 19: 387–430.

Sztompka, P. (2000) *Trust: A Sociological Theory*. Cambridge: Cambridge University Press.

Turnbull, D. (2000) *Masons, Tricksters and Cartographers: Comparative Studies in the Sociology of Scientific and Indigenous Knowledge*. Amsterdam: Harwood.

Turner, B. (1996) *The Body and Society, 2nd edn*. London: Sage.

Turner, J. and Michael, M. (1996) What do we know about don't knows? Or, contexts of 'Ignorance', *Social Science Information*, 35(1): 15–37.

Urry, J. (2000) *Sociology Beyond Societies*. London: Routledge.

Vogel, D. (1986) *National Styles of Regulation: Environmental Policy in Great Britain and the United States*. Ithaca, NY: Cornell University Press.

Walker, G., Simmons, P., Wynne, B. and Irwin, A. (1998) *Public Perceptions of Risk Associated with Major Accident Hazards*. London: HSE Books.

Wallis, R. (ed.) (1979) *On the Margins of Science*. Keele: Keele University Press.

Walters, M. (1995) *Globalization*. London: Routledge.

Wexler, P. (1983) *Critical Social Psychology*. Boston, MA: Routledge & Kegan Paul.

Whatmore, S. (1997) Dissecting the autonomous self: hybrid cartographies for a relational ethics, *Environment and Planning D: Society and Space*, 15: 37–53.

Whitley, R. (1984) *The Intellectual and Social Organization of the Sciences*. Oxford: Clarendon.

Wilkinson, E. (1939) *The Town that was Murdered: The Life-story of Jarrow*. London: Victor Gollancz.

Wynne, B.E. (1991) Knowledges in context, *Science, Technology and Human Values*, 16: 111–21.

Wynne, B.E. (1992) Misunderstood misunderstanding: social identities and public uptake of science, *Public Understanding of Science*, 1: 281–304.

Wynne, B.E. (1995) The public understanding of science, in S. Jasanoff, G.E. Markle, J.C. Peterson and T. Pinch (eds) *Handbook of Science and Technology Studies*, pp. 361–88. Thousand Oaks, CA: Sage.

Wynne, B.E. (1996) May the sheep safely graze? A reflexive view of the expert–lay divide, in S. Lash, B. Szerszynski and B. Wynne (eds) *Risk, Environment and Modernity*, pp. 44–83. London: Sage.

Yearley, S. (1993) *Biotechnology, For or Against? Public Beliefs, Attitudes and Understanding*. London: Biotechnology Joint Advisory Board/ESRC.

Ziman, J.M. (1968) *Public Knowledge: An Essay Concerning the Social Dimension of Science*. Cambridge: Cambridge University Press.

Zonabend, F. (1993) *The Nuclear Peninsula*. Cambridge: Cambridge University Press.

Index

Abercrombie, N., 133
accountability, 72, 126–8
activism, AIDS, 14, 31, 34–8, 92, 112
actor network theory, 116–17
actors, 142
    heterogeneity of, 115–16
agriculture, 3, 5
Agriculture and Environment Biotechnology
    Commission, 53, 66
AIDS activism, 14, 31, 34–8, 92, 112
air quality measurement devices, 118
Aldhous, P., 23
alliances, networks of, 85, 97, 98, 108, 111,
    152
    see also ethno-epistemic assemblages
ambivalence, 72–5, 84
animal experimentation, 23
animal fetal cell implants, 121–2
Arksey, H., 37
assemblages, 85, 119–20
    see also ethno-epistemic assemblages
attitudes towards science, 23
audit society, 128
automobile industry, 45

Bauman, Z., 15
BBC website, 2–6, 77
Beck, U., 15, 39, 67, 74, 75, 76–7, 90
Beck-Gersheim, E., 75
Bede, the Venerable, 99, 105
Bede's World, 105–6
Beveridge, A.A., 23
biosciences, 147, 148
    public consultation, 58–62, 148
biotechnology, 3, 25–6
    see also genetically modified (GM)
    foods
Birke, L., 145
boundary objects, 117–18
Bourdieu, P., 78–9
British Council, 52
Brown, N., 91, 126, 127
Brown, P., 39, 149–50, 151
BSE (mad cow disease), 47, 53–4

Carter, S., 86
certainty, 14–15
chemical carcinogens, 44
chemical corporation (Jarrow case study),
    100, 100–1, 102, 102–3, 107, 138
Chernobyl nuclear accident, 32
Chief Scientific Adviser, 53
choice, ignorance as, 29–30
citadel model, 117, 120
citizen, figure of, 89, 90–1
Citizen Foresight consultation, 58–9
citizen scientist model, 38, 90
citizen's jury, 11
citizenship, 56, 63
    consumption and, 77–80
    figure of citizen, 89, 90–1
    local and global, 18, 91, 108
    science, governance and, 10–12
    scientific see scientific citizenship
Clarke, A.E., 117
clinical trials, 36
closed regulatory systems, 43–5
coalitions, 85
    discourse coalitions, 115–16
    networks of alliances, 85, 97, 98, 108,
        111, 152
    see also ethno-epistemic assemblages
co-construction, 109, 112
code of practice, 53
co-evolution, 71–2
cognitive container model, 26–7
Cohen, A.P., 35
collaboration, 117–18
Collins, H.M., 145
communication, 150
    mode of, 89, 94–5
community, 31, 38–40
    AIDS movement and, 34–8
    Cumbrian sheepfarmers, 32–4
    epistemic communities, 115
    nuclear, 38–9
    toxic waste contamination, 39
consultation exercises, 50, 58–62,
    148–9

Theorizing Society

Series Editor: Larry Ray